A Guide to Shaping Up
Your Finances for the
Rest of Your Life

FISCAL FITNESS

A Guide to Shaping Up Your Finances for the Rest of Your Life

by Christine Dugas

NEWSDAY

ANDREWS AND McMEEL
A Universal Press Syndicate Company
Kansas City

Additional copies of this book may be ordered by
calling (800) 642-6480.

Library of Congress Cataloging-in-Publication Data

Dugas, Christine.
    Fiscal fitness : a guide to shaping up your finances for the
rest of your life / by Christine Dugas.
        p.   cm.
    Newsday.
    ISBN 0-8362-7046-0 : $9.95
    1. Finance, Personal. I. Newsday (Melville, N.Y.) II. Title.
HG179.D83 1995
332.024—dc20   95-1058
                                                          CIP

To Robbie

Acknowledgments

Fiscal Fitness was the brainchild of Debra Whitefield, former *Newsday* business editor. She recognized the need for a simple, direct approach to helping readers make informed decisions about managing their money. *Newsday* was committed to making *Fiscal Fitness* a regular feature. And now the first year of columns are being published here in book form.

I would like to thank all the financial experts I interviewed, many of whom are quoted in the book. In addition, I appreciate all the research assistance I received from *Newsday*'s librarians. Thanks also to *Newsday*'s copy editors and graphic artists. And I am most thankful for the skillful editing of Rick Green and the creative input on graphics from Kathy Sizemore.

Finally, I am indebted to my parents who taught me at an early age the value of saving money. And to my husband, for his encouragement and support.

Contents

Introduction

ARE YOU FINANCIALLY fit or flabby?

Most Americans worry that they are not in good shape. Sixty-three percent told pollsters they often worry about money. More than half don't have time to work out a budget. Forty-six percent of Americans say they won't be able to live comfortably when they retire, and nearly 40 percent wish they were better at managing their money.

In fact, money is on the minds of Americans so much that nearly half—43 percent—say it now preoccupies them even more than sex.

If the worries found in these polls by *Money* magazine and Computer Associates sound familiar, join the crowd. You and your family, your friends and your neighbors live in a much more difficult financial world today. You're required to make increasingly complicated decisions that will affect the rest of your life—often with little or no help.

With that in mind, *Fiscal Fitness* began as a yearlong series of weekly newspaper articles aimed at helping you firm up your financial plans and build up your wealth. *Fiscal Fitness* will provide basic knowledge of money management, including many of the financial concepts that are commonly used, but frequently misunderstood.

Fiscal Fitness is not just about investing. The exercises will cover everything from how to read a prospectus to how to pick a mortgage. They will offer guidelines on such things as what questions to ask before selecting a bank, and how to evaluate a financial consultant.

This book is not just for beginners, nor is it only for sophisticated investors. Because financial planning is a lifelong pursuit, *Fiscal Fitness* provides money-making and money-saving advice for people of all ages and experience. Topics include the tax consequences of getting married, saving for college and advice about caring for a terminally ill parent.

Yes, we're going to pump up your bottom line, but first, you have to get up off the couch and want to control your fiscal future. We'll help you get active, building those goals and options. There will be checklists and worksheets, quizzes and interesting facts to help simplify the task of managing your finances.

All the investment choices today can be intimidating and confusing. But if you're like most people, you have less time, not more, to sort out these things. As Paul Sheldon, first vice president at Prudential Securities who teaches a seminar on investing at Baruch College, puts it: "People just want to be able to make sense of it all."

That's what *Fiscal Fitness* is all about.

Are You Out of Control?

Test yourself to see if any of these seem familiar:

I impulsively spend money on myself and
   on other people just to make myself happy.   ☐ TRUE   ☐ FALSE

I don't like to be hemmed in by a written budget.   ☐ TRUE   ☐ FALSE

I've bounced checks in more than one month
   in the past year.   ☐ TRUE   ☐ FALSE

I have some financial records, but I'm not sure
   where and they're a bit disorganized.   ☐ TRUE   ☐ FALSE

I have trouble saving money, and sometimes
   this bothers me.   ☐ TRUE   ☐ FALSE

I switch credit card debts from one card to another.   ☐ TRUE   ☐ FALSE

I tend to spend all the money I have at any
   given moment.   ☐ TRUE   ☐ FALSE

I want the highest yield I can get from my
   investments. Safety isn't my main concern.   ☐ TRUE   ☐ FALSE

I invest in things I can get out of quickly so I can
   have money immediately if I need it.   ☐ TRUE   ☐ FALSE

I owe money to someone who has hired a
   debt collector to get me to pay.   ☐ TRUE   ☐ FALSE

Score yourself. Give yourself 10 points for every "True" answer.
At 20 or less, your sins are probably no worse than anyone else.
For 50 or less, you may want to read this series closely.
And for 60 and up, you might want to hire a financial adviser now.

Record Keeping

Or How to Get a Grip on
Your Finances and Sleep Better

SOME PEOPLE STOW old receipts and records in plastic grocery bags that pile up in the dusty corners of their closets.

Others keep documents and tax returns meticulously organized in fireproof file cabinets.

And then there are those who don't have a clue where they have stashed important papers because they are scattered throughout desk drawers, closets and kitchen cabinets, in tattered file folders and unlabeled envelopes.

There are, perhaps, as many styles of record keeping as there are types of people. And they don't matter very much—until you need to find an important document.

Say, for example, a creditor claims you haven't paid a bill. Or you get audited, sell a home, or decide to travel abroad on the spur of the moment. Then it suddenly matters very much whether or not you've saved the necessary documents—and whether or not you can find them.

As Lewis Altfest, a financial planner, puts it: "If you don't have a system, it can cost you money—as in taxes. It can cost you lost opportunities—for example, a client of mine had a 20-year guarantee on a rug and couldn't find it when he needed it. And it can cause a great deal of aggravation if you're constantly hunting for something."

Nonetheless, Altfest says that he has found that most people are basically disorganized. "Financial planning has made me more organized than I would have been, but I'm not as good in practice as I preach," he confesses.

So how should you begin to put your life in order?

Start by drawing up a list of important documents, such as birth certificates, deeds, passports, insurance policies, etc. Then, ask yourself if you know where all the items on the list are located.

If that question alone gives you heartburn, Ann Diamond, a financial consultant, has a solution: Take the list and pretend that you're on a scavenger hunt, but target only one item each week.

You can go mad looking for everything at once, she says. Look for the easiest things first. Check them off as you locate them. And if it comes down to one or two things that you can't find, it's better to know that now.

At the same time you're gathering important documents, clean out a drawer in a file cabinet or desk, where you can keep bills, receipts and bank records for the current year.

Do You Have These?

A checklist of important documents you need to have on file.

Certain originals belong in a safe deposit box—but remember that the box is typically sealed on the death of the owner for tax purposes, so certain things should stay out. Divide them up like this:

In Your Home

Rental agreement
Bank loan records
Diplomas
Social Security card
Retirement and pension-plan documents
Passport
Health and disability insurance policies
Living will and last wish file
Will (or keep on file with your attorney)
Life insurance policies
Power of attorney
Cemetery records
Master list of bank accounts, credit cards, insurance policies
A key to your safe-deposit box and list of what's inside. (Include serial numbers and dates of stock or bond certificates and appraisals of any jewelry stored there.)

In the Box

Hard-to-replace personal papers, such as birth certificates, adoption papers, marriage certificate, veteran's papers
Automobile titles (or in fireproof safe at home)
Homeowners, tenants and auto insurance policies
Employment contract
Ownership papers, such as bond certificates and deeds
IOUs
Proof that you have paid off debts
Estate planning documents, such as trusts, and a copy of will—not the original.
Seldom-worn jewelry (but be sure it is covered by your household insurance)
An inventory of valuable items in your home, including photos, serial numbers and receipts of expensive items

If you don't itemize deductions on your tax return, you can put most of one year's records into one file.

Whatever you do, says Altfest, make it as simple as possible.

Here are a few record-keeping tips from financial experts:

• Set up a general file for bank statements, household bills, canceled checks, records of credit card purchases, and other relevant receipts for the current tax year.

• If you have big medical bills, you should keep a separate file for those records.

• If you own a home or apartment, you should maintain an ongoing file for all home improvement expenses. Later on, if you sell the property at a profit, the money you spent to upgrade it will lessen your taxable gain. But you must be able to document the expenditures.

• If you invest in mutual funds, stocks or bonds, you should keep a file with a list of all the securities you own and any accompanying account number or identification number. Keep the original purchase record so you have the date and price you paid. Keep brokerage house agreements, confirmations of all trades, prospectuses, and dividend reinvestment statements.

• Set up a file for product warranties. Attach the original proof of purchase to the warranty.

• Create a file for all personal documents, such as birth certificates, and any other items that are difficult to replace. These should be stored in a fireproof safe in your home or in a safe deposit box. Include in this file your will, all insurance policies, deeds, receipts for big-ticket purchases, and an inventory of your household possessions. (The easiest way to make an inventory is to photograph all the rooms in your home; or better yet, make a videotape of your home that you update periodically.)

• Each April, after you complete your taxes, put your copy of the return and all the related records and canceled checks into a large envelope or expandable file folder. Diamond recommends clearing an out-of-the-way space on a closet shelf where you can store the past seven years' worth of tax records.

You aren't required to keep all your records and receipts for seven years (three years from the filing date is long enough for many things), but the IRS has six years to audit you for underreported income, and there is no statute of limitation for fraud. Diamond believes it's just easier to keep everything for seven years. After that, she says you should keep the return but ditch the supporting data (except, of course, any documents relating to home improvement).

An exception: If you've contributed money to an Individual Retirement Account, but weren't entitled to deduct it from your taxes, hang on to those records forever. Otherwise, you won't be able to prove you already paid taxes on that money, and you'll have to pay again when you withdraw it during retirement.

Just one more thing: After you've done all of the above, make a master list of your bank and investment accounts, insurance policies and agents' names, credit cards and account numbers, names and phone numbers of accountant, lawyer and brokers. Mention where your will is located, the name of your executor and where your records are stored. Then tell someone in your family where you've put the master list.

Now you're organized, and you can sleep better at night.

Budget Planning

How to Cut Spending without Skimping on a Good Time

Saving money is a lot like losing weight.

Most people would like to do more of both. Yet the idea of living on a budget is about as appealing as going on a diet.

A budget simply requires you to keep track of your daily expenditures, and as dull as that may sound, it's an important step toward getting a handle on your finances. "My campaign is to get people to be aware of where they're spending their money," says Ann Diamond, a New York City financial consultant. "People know they are going to the cash machine, but they don't know what happens to the money between visits."

So, start by carrying a small notebook with you for a month. Write down every expense—from your morning coffee to the occasional late-night stop at the convenience store for milk or ice cream.

At the end of a month, compare your spending with your income. When people do this exercise, they're amazed by how much they spend, Diamond says. Yet if they make one or two adjustments—say they bring their lunch one or two days a week and get their coffee from the office machine—they often find they can come up with an extra $25 a week. Over a year that alone adds up to an extra $1,300.

Many financial planning books include budget worksheets, which are helpful for keeping track of spending month in and month out. Once you see where your money is going, pick one or two areas where you can save money without making yourself miserable.

Rosella Bannister, the director of the National Institute for Consumer Education at Eastern Michigan University, says a budget should be a tool, not a straitjacket.

"If I know how much I want to spend, I feel good," she says. "It gives me a feeling of financial independence or power over my own resources."

Frank McCrea, a budget and loan counselor for ACORN, a national advocacy group for low and moderate-income families, says that most of the people he counsels don't believe they can afford to save any money; yet after they draw up a budget, they always find they can save something without depriving themselves.

The first thing you should do with your newfound savings is start paying off any credit card balances and other debts you've accumulated. Otherwise, your debts will continue to mount at double-digit rates at a time when many banks are giving relatively low interest rates on savings accounts and CDs.

After you get a handle on your debts, you should set up a fund for emergencies. Experts say it should total between three months' and six months' worth of salary and should be held in a liquid account, such as a money market account, so you won't be penalized if you make a withdrawal.

Few people can resist the temptation to spend money impulsively. So, financial planners agree that the best way to save is pay yourself first. Arrange to have a set amount of money automatically taken from your salary and put into a company retirement plan, a mutual fund or savings account. Diamond suggests that you start with a modest amount, say 3 percent of your salary, and increase it by 1 percent every six months or whenever you get a raise.

But how can you be sure you're saving enough for your long-term goals, such as retirement? Joel Isaacson, a New York City financial planner, says there is a general rule of thumb, depending on your stage in life. Couples who are just starting their careers and have big expenses of setting up a home and having children should be putting away about 5 percent of their earnings, he says. As they move toward middle age, and start to reach their peak earning years, that proportion should rise to about 10 percent. And finally, he says, in the 10 years before retirement they should be saving 15 to 20 percent.

Diamond advises everyone to try to save 10 percent of their salary. She says young people should start saving as much as possible when they're still single and have no financial obligations. Through what she calls the miracle of compounding, their savings will grow into a sizable nest egg by the time they retire.

In reality, however, many college graduates these days start out their careers in low-paying jobs, burdened by big student loan bills. In that case, one of the best gifts they can receive from parents and grandparents is a $2,000 contribution toward an Individual Retirement Account. The idea is to help them get into the habit of saving for the future. It's very difficult to start planning for retirement when you're 50, Diamond says.

A Big Fix

How Much of a Problem Would an Unexpected Bill of $1,000 Be?

A very big problem — 20%

A fairly big problem — 31%

Not a problem at all — 32%

Not too big a problem — 17%

SOURCE:
Americans & Their Money

Money Savers

Thriftiness Will Give You the Last Laugh at Scoffers

TOM AND LORRI LEMKE, a young San Diego couple, appeared on the "Oprah Winfrey" show to discuss their thrifty lifestyle. As Tom enthusiastically described clipping coupons, making pasta at home, and hunting for early bird restaurant specials, the audience snickered.

But the group wasn't laughing when the Lemkes, parents of two small children, said they have managed to save $50,000 in the past four years.

"Some people think we're nickel-and-diming it, but those nickels and dimes are going to add up and going to help put our kids through college," Tom Lemke said.

The Lemkes, who work in grocery stores and together earn about $40,000 a year, plan to save enough in the next 10 years to retire early.

Some people just enjoy being frugal, no matter how much money they have. Sam Walton, the founder of Wal-Mart and one of the richest men in the country, was known for his frugal tastes. For many years before he died, Walton drove a beat-up pickup truck. Jack Stephens, a Little Rock millionaire, once said, "My shoes cost more than everything Sam Walton is wearing today."

But most people learn to economize out of necessity. And it doesn't always come easily.

Mary Hunt became a self-described cheapskate only after she ran up $100,000 in credit card bills over a 12-year period. She estimates that she had 36 different cards during that time and she felt entitled to charge them up to their limit. When the resulting financial crisis nearly ruined her life, Hunt began to change her ways. Today she has no credit cards.

Hunt, who lives in Orange County, Calif., decided to use her experience to help others learn to live within their means. In January 1992, she began publishing a newsletter, *Cheapskate Monthly.*

At the same time, across the country in Smithtown, N.Y., Jackie Iglehart had

---

Coupons' Value

• **47 percent** of 333 shoppers polled by the *Shopper Report,* a monthly newsletter of shopper views, said they believe store brands are equal to national brands.

• **69 percent** of the shoppers said they save a great deal of money using coupons, without ever buying things they don't need or use.

SOURCE: *The Shopper Report,* May 1993

a similar idea. Only she called her newsletter the *Penny Pincher.* The two newsletters joined a growing field of about 20 other publications that are dedicated to frugal living.

Some people are disdainful of such unabashed thriftiness. They assume the economizing means recycling scraps of aluminum foil and finding new ways to use leftovers. Others believe that most money-saving tips are too time-consuming. After all, how many two-income couples have time to make their own clothes, raise their own vegetables, and bake their own bread?

But as the various newsletters show, there are plenty of inventive ways to save money to suit everyone. Hunt is not a big fan of coupons, calling them gimmicks to get people to buy things they wouldn't ordinarily purchase. She prefers to shop at warehouses, which don't accept coupons, but sell food in bulk. Hunt says she shops less often and saves about 25 to 40 percent on her food bill by buying in bulk.

Inglehart, who has four children, knows that even busy people can economize. People may not have time to make their own bread, she says, but they can put ingredients into an automatic bread maker. She tried it and discovered that the machine paid for itself in six months. Now she estimates she saves $500 a year by using the bread maker.

Even simpler than that, Inglehart replaced half of her incandescent light bulbs with fluorescent bulbs. She spent three hours researching the bulbs and shopping for them. She estimates that her utility bill has gone down $480 a year.

Amy Dacyczyn admits that she is a compulsive tightwad. She also is publisher of the *Tightwad Gazette,* one of the first newsletters of its kind. After she got married, Dacyczyn decided she wanted to have a large family and live in a large New England farmhouse. Today she has six children and lives in the home of her dreams. And in her newsletter she dispenses advice on everything from how to reuse old blue jeans to how to save on funerals.

People are more receptive than ever to money-saving tips because they realize they must be self-reliant, Inglehart says. They don't feel they have job security any more. They feel they can't depend on Social Security. And some people who have gotten to retirement age have seen their interest income drop dramatically as bank rates have plummeted.

Buying Guidelines

Smart shopping tips from the Consumer Federation of America:

1. Only purchase products you really want; avoid impulse buying.

2. Don't rely on a salesperson when selecting a particular product to purchase. Read consumer guides and comparison shop.

3. Consider buying private label and store brands.

4. Never purchase a product directly over the telephone unless you request the solicitation. If you are called by a telephone salesperson, request information be sent to you in writing so you can comparison shop.

5. If you have problems that you can't resolve, seek assistance from state and local consumer protection agencies and the Better Business Bureau.

Where Did That Dollar Go?

A breakdown of family expeditures for goods and services:

Housing* .... 31.2¢

Transportation .... 17.4¢

Personal insurance and pensions .... 9.4¢

Food at home .... 9.0¢

Other expenditures .... 8.9¢

Apparel and services* .... 5.9¢

Food away from home .... 5.5¢

Health care .... 5.2¢

Entertainment .... 5.0¢

Education .... 1.5¢

Alcoholic beverages .... 1.0¢

*Housing includes utilities, housekeeping supplies and furnishings. Apparel and services include dry cleaning, clothing and shoe repair.

SOURCE: Bureau of Labor Statistics Consumer Expenditure Survey, 1991.

The key to becoming more frugal, the experts say, is to find ways to economize that fit your personality and lifestyle. For example, Hunt says she personally can't bear the thought of buying clothes in thrift stores, so she finds other ways to cut costs.

Some people may be put off by Iglehart's idea of calling funeral homes to get free flowers before they are discarded. But others may be intrigued by her tip about receiving discounts on shoes by becoming a footwear tester.

After you figure out what works for you, experts say, don't go overboard. It's important to splurge now and then, Iglehart says. She and her husband make a point to go out on a date once a week.

Inflation Fighters

How to Keep Your Savings
Safe from Spiraling Consumer Prices

JOSEPH CIZAUSKAS was a recluse who spurned banks until he died in 1988. When excavators bulldozed his house and yard north of Grand Rapids, Mich., in 1993, they unearthed $11,395 in soggy cash buried in jars, salt shakers, medicine bottles—even a teapot. Some of the bills were just a messy glob that could not even be counted, says Kent County Deputy Treasurer Ken Scott.

Cizauskas, who was in his 80s when he died, was said to have mistrusted banks. But by keeping his cash stuffed in jars in his yard, he was actually penalizing himself. It wasn't just the elements that were gradually eating away at his currency; over time, the value of his money was eroding because of inflation.

Say the money sat in jars for the past 10 years, a decade in which inflation averaged about 4 percent a year. In that case, the $11,395 would now be worth nearly 50 percent less than it was in 1984. Or put another way: Something that cost Cizauskas $1 a decade ago would cost $1.48 today.

While it's unlikely that many people are burying their money in their backyards, this case illustrates how over time, even a relatively low level of inflation can take a dramatic toll on the buying power of money.

Inflation is the average increase in prices across the country as measured by the consumer price index. Two factors usually cause inflation: an increase in demand or a reduction in supply. In the 1970s, for example, the OPEC oil embargo went hand in hand with long lines at the gas pump and prices that spiraled out of control. It wiped out the buying power of savings built up over the years and left a financial scar on people planning for college costs or retirement.

Now the name of the game in saving for the future is to try to beat inflation, or at least to keep up with it. After all, if your money is just going to lose buying power, you might as well spend it now. But the quest to beat inflation has its risks. You can bet on the stock market, for instance, and lose everything.

That's why many people still stick with safe, insured bank accounts. They'd rather have their money earning a modest return than take a chance on having no money at all.

The question is whether you're really earning anything. When you deposit money in a bank, you should at least be protected from inflation, says Maureen Allyn, chief economist at Scudder Stevens & Clark. And if you tie up your money in a long-term CD, you should receive an even better return.

Chipping Away at Inflation

It's much harder to fight inflation during times of rapidly rising prices. But even now with relatively low inflation, experts say you have to keep it in mind. Specifically:

- Review your homeowner insurance coverage periodically and adjust it to account for inflation so it still covers the cost of replacing your home and belongings.

- Be sure your budget accounts for your rising cost of living. If prices start to rise rapidly, buy basic items in bulk.

- If you are planning to buy a home or to pay for college several years from now, factor in the impact of inflation when deciding how much to save.

- If you have an adjustable mortgage, and interest rates start to decline, you might want to switch to a regular, conventional mortgage. Inflation will help push your wages higher, even if you don't work any harder. That means it takes less time to earn your payment each month, leaving a bigger hunk of income to devote to yourself.

But in the early 1990s, bank rates barely kept pace with inflation and sometimes even fell behind. One reason for the low rates, Allyn says, is that banks were not making many loans. That means they didn't need to compete for your deposits by offering higher rates.

Consider this: The average one-year certificate of deposit yielded 3.15 percent in mid-1993, according to *Bank Rate Monitor,* a service that tracks deposit rates. But inflation ran at about 3.20 percent. As a result, those who invested in an average one-year CD effectively lost money. Figure in taxes on the interest income and you might have done just as well burying the money in the backyard.

This came as quite a shock to depositors who had grown accustomed to double-digit interest rates in the 1980s, especially retirees who live on interest income.

Andrew Pontrandolfi, a retired fire department captain, says his pension covers his basic expenses, but he relies on interest income for the extras. "Now I can't travel as much as I'd like to," he said in 1983. "With CD rates so low, it's a no-win situation."

Not surprisingly, as CDs matured, depositors shifted money into mutual funds in record numbers. This prompted experts to worry that in the pursuit of higher yielding investments, which are not federally insured, some people were not considering the additional risk they were taking. And in fact, many investors were unprepared for the negative returns most mutual funds posted in 1994.

One option, industry experts say, is to shop around for bank rates before plunging into uninsured investments. Many magazines and newspapers rou-

The One-Minute Workout

Let's say that you want your 8-year-old scholar to go to Ivy League University. It costs $20,000 this year to send someone to those hallowed halls, so you figure you have to come up with $80,000. But tuition and fees are rising 5 percent a year at the school (rather modest compared with some schools). So in 10 years, when junior is ready to go, approximately how much must you pony up?

☐ **A.** $ 95,000

☐ **B.** $120,000

☐ **C.** $130,000

☐ **D.** $525,000

Answer: C. If college costs rise 5 percent annually for the next decade—and remember, inflation is compounded—an education will cost about 63 percent more than it does today.

CONSULTANT: Ronald Rogé, RW Rogé & Co. Inc.

tinely publish rate surveys. Consumers can often get a better deal if they go out of state, says Robert Heady, publisher of *100 Highest Yields,* a weekly newsletter based in North Palm Beach, Fla.

It's easy to ignore inflation because it's like an invisible termite, silently eating away at your buying power. But that would only undercut your efforts to save for the future, like the way Joe Cizauskas allowed his money to lose value by burying it in his yard.

Banking Savvy

Or How to Avoid Being Nickel-and-Dimed to Death

In 1991, Ricardo Dopwell became fed up with his bank. It seemed that every time he opened his monthly statement, there was a notice that fees were going up or the minimum balance to avoid fees was rising.

"You end up paying the bank to take your money and lend it out and make a profit," says Dopwell, a 35-year-old electronics technician who lives in New York City with his wife and two children. "And then they give you a pittance in interest."

When Dopwell saw an ad in the newspaper for a free checking account at First Federal Savings & Loan, he couldn't quite believe it.

"I don't want to be nickel-and-dimed to death," Dopwell recalls telling a First Federal employee. Assured that the account was free and had no minimum balance requirement, he switched his business there.

Today, Dopwell says that he's happy with the S&L. His biggest complaint now is that First Federal has only one automated teller machine near him and it is often out of service. Yet if he uses an ATM at another bank, he is charged a fee.

Dopwell's experience is not unique. In the decade since interest rates were deregulated, there has been a proliferation of bank products and an explosion in fees. A recent study by the Consumer Federation of America and the U.S. Public Interest Research Group found that in the past three years, bank fees grew four times faster than inflation.

If consumers are not careful, the money they earn in interest could be siphoned off to pay fees. In fact, depositors with low monthly balances lost money at three-fourths of the banks in New York City, according to a 1992 survey.

Not all banks are alike. Yet experts say that consumers generally don't shop around for a bank in the same way they shop for groceries or a car. Many people are apathetic, says Robert Heady, publisher of the *Bank Rate Monitor* newsletter. They don't realize that by shopping around they may earn a half point or more in interest on their savings account, or they could cut four to five percentage points from their credit card rates.

One reason for the apathy is that consumers are confused by the array of bank products, says Chris Lewis, director of banking policy at the Consumer Federation of America until December 1994.

What Is Your Banking IQ?

1. It's legal to write a check in pencil.

   a) true   b) false

2. How long does a check remain valid?

   a) 6 weeks   b) 6 months   c) 6 years

3. Which of the following savings would be most easily accessible in an emergency?

   a) money invested in a certificate of deposit
   b) money in a bank savings account
   c) money invested in stock
   d) money invested in an Individual Retirement Account

4. How long would it take to double $200 in a savings account paying 8 percent?

   a) 2 years   b) 5 years   c) 9 years   d) 10 years

5. If interest on a savings account is compounded daily and credited quarterly, how long must a person keep the account open to receive any interest?

   a) 1 day   b) 3 months   c) 1 month   d) 1 year

6. Which of the following products sold at banks are covered by federal deposit insurance?

   a) mutual funds   d) money market funds
   b) annuities   e) all of the above
   c) money market accounts   f) none of the above

7. Under new federal regulations, what does it mean if a bank advertises a checking account as "free"?

   a) no monthly fee and no per check charge if you maintain a minimum balance
   b) no monthly fees, no minimum balance, no charges at all
   c) no monthly fees, no per check charge, no minimum balance, but the bank may charge for such things as bounced checks, check printing, travelers checks and cashier checks

Answers:

   1. a, but risky because check could be altered
   2. b, but bank has the option to cash an older check
   3. b   4. c   5. b   6. c   7. c

SOURCES: Meridian Corp., Consumer Federation of America, American Express, *Money* magazine, *Sylvia Porter's Money Book*

You'd Better Shop Around

Average minimum balances and fees for various bank transactions:

	National	*New York*
Minimum balance to earn interest on a NOW checking account	$571.00	$624.00
Minimum daily balance on NOW account to avoid fees	$1,023.00	$1,771.00
Monthly fee on NOW account if you fall below minimum balance	$7.56	$7.76
Fee to use another bank's ATM linked to national network	$1.10	$1.79
Fee for bounced check	$18.35	$14.82

SOURCES: New York City Dept. of Consumer Affairs, Consumer Federation of America, New York Public Interest Research Group

In 1993, however, a new federal law took effect that is designed to make it easier for you to compare products at different banks. It standardizes the way banks quote interest rates on deposit accounts and requires full disclosure of fees and minimum balance requirements, among other things.

When you shop for a new bank, Lewis says you should first assess your needs:

• How many checks do you write each month?
• How many times a month do you use an ATM machine?
• Does your checking account balance vary a lot during the month? If so, what is the lowest amount you usually have on deposit at one time?
• What other services, such as direct deposit and telephone banking, do you expect to use?

Then, find the banks with convenient branches and compare their products and services. Ask for disclosure statements for the accounts you are interested in and read them carefully to find out about interest rates and fees.

Lewis says the most important thing to find out about is minimum balance requirements, because many fees hinge on that. Ask about monthly account fees, as well as item processing fees, such as ATM fees. Some banks are even charging teller fees, Lewis notes. Conversely, find out what benefits you will receive if you keep a large amount on deposit in several accounts.

Many banks offer low-cost accounts for senior citizens and low-income

---

You Can Bank on Them

Who to call when you have questions or complaints about your financial institution:

For state chartered banks, savings banks and credit unions, call your state banking department or the nearest Federal Reserve Board office.

For nationally chartered banks, call the Office of the Comptroller of the Currency: 202-874-4820.

For savings and loans and federally chartered savings banks, call the Office of Thrift Supervision: 1-800-253-2181.

For credit unions, call the National Credit Union Administration, with regional offices around the country.

---

customers, often called lifeline accounts. These alternatives to regular checking generally charge a fee each month regardless of the customer's balance and allow the customer to write a certain number of checks without an additional charge. But these accounts are not always a good deal. Lewis cautions that they can become quite costly if consumers exceed the number of checks allowed each month.

If, like Dopwell, you've lost patience with new charges and constantly increasing fees, don't rush to leave your current bank without asking the right questions. If you close out an account in the middle of an interest cycle, you may forfeit all the interest for that period.

Know Your Bank

Don't Assume Your Money Is Safe—
Do Some Checking

WHEN AMERICAN SAVINGS BANK failed in June 1992, Kay Ankenbrand didn't think she had anything to worry about. She didn't have more than $100,000 in her accounts, the limit for federal deposit insurance coverage. And there was no interruption in service because her branch was acquired by Bank of New York.

But Ankenbrand soon discovered that the failure of American Savings was going to cost her money. Although her IRA had been invested in a certificate of deposit earning 9.9 percent interest, Bank of New York informed her it was slashing the rate to 5.5 percent. She was stunned.

"The part that really bugged me is that no one warned me," says Ankenbrand, a retiree who lives with her husband in a suburban community. "I had no way to protect myself. I thought IRAs were sacrosanct. I thought the acquiring bank would have to keep the rate."

Unfortunately for Ankenbrand, that's not the case. After a bank fails, the acquiring institution is allowed to lower CD rates. This is just one example of how a bank failure can inconvenience you and cost you money.

When it comes to protecting the money you keep on deposit at a bank, savings and loan or credit union, the first thing you need to do is to make sure your institution is insured by the Federal Deposit Insurance Corporation or the National Credit Union Administration. Then you need to know if all the money in your accounts is covered by the insurance. But that's not necessarily an easy matter. Sometimes even bank personnel aren't well-versed in the law.

When *Money* magazine assigned a team of reporters to telephone 273 banks in 14 states and ask the same five questions about deposit insurance, the results were dismaying. Only 12 percent of the bank personnel were able to answer all five questions correctly.

The moral of the story is to not rely on your bank for information about deposit insurance. As unfair as it may seem, there is no recourse if you lose money during a bank failure because a bank employee led you astray about FDIC rules.

Before you have an anxiety attack about the safety of your money, total up the deposits in all your accounts at any one bank. If you don't have anywhere near $100,000, then you're insured. It's as simple as that.

Even if your deposits add up to more than $100,000, they may be insured.

Are You Sure You're Insured?

If you have a question on whether your bank deposits are fully insured, call the Federal Deposit Insurance Corp. consumer hotline at 800-934-3342. Some basic rules:

Accounts under your name: Deposits in all accounts under your name at one bank, such as CDs, money market accounts, savings accounts and checking accounts, are lumped together and insured up to $100,000.

Joint accounts are insured separately from your individual accounts. That gives you another $100,000 of coverage. But remember, each person is entitled to only $100,000 of coverage no matter how many accounts he or she holds.

It works like this: Say you and your spouse may have a joint savings and checking account. If so, the deposits in these accounts together would be insured up to $100,000.

But say you and your spouse have $80,000 on deposit in a joint account; you and your son have $80,000 on deposit in a joint account; and you and your daughter have $80,000 on deposit in a joint account. So your half of each joint account is $40,000, for a total of $120,000—only $100,000 of which would be insured.

- Retirement accounts: All of your retirement accounts, such as IRAs and Keogh accounts, are added up and separately insured for up to $100,000.

- Trust accounts: Certain accounts opened in trust for a child or spouse are insured up to $100,000.

Check with the FDIC to be sure you understand rules for insurance coverage so that your hard-earned money is not at risk.

Insured or not, you should not be complacent about the financial condition of your bank, many experts says. For one thing, service may suffer and mistakes may occur when employees are concentrating on keeping an unprofitable institution afloat, says Warren Heller, research director at Veribanc, a bank research firm.

Also, new federal rules impose restrictions on weak banks, which often result in them cutting back on their lending, says Paul Bauer, president of the Bauer Group, a bank research firm. So, for example, an ailing bank may suddenly reduce its customers' home equity lines of credit.

Bauer also notes that weak banks generally charge much higher fees. If they can't make money on traditional loan income, they try to make it up in fee income.

Once a bank fails, there are a number of ways in which you might be hurt. For example, an acquiring institution is not bound by the contracts of the failed bank. That's why it can lower your CD rates. In addition, it can freeze your home eq-

Safety Ratings

Where to order a report on your bank:

• **Veribanc Inc. (800-442-2657)** classifies financial institutions into three basic categories: green (healthy); yellow (some problems, merits your attention); red (serious problems, deserves your close attention). Veribanc offers many types of reports, from an instant rating on a bank, S&L or credit union for $10, to a list of banks in your region that operate conservatively for $35.

• **Bauer Financial Reports (800-388-6686)** uses a star system to rate financial institutions. Bauer offers a number of reports along with financial highlights and star ratings on institutions in your state for about $29. For $10 you can receive the same information on one institution.

• **Sheshunoff Information Services (800-456-2340)** offers a five-page rating report on a specific bank or S&L for $25. Rated by letter grades A through C, along with a percentile ranking against the bank's peers.

uity line of credit, demand payment on some auto loans and cancel a mortgage application prior to closing, in which case you may never get your fees and points back.

If no buyer can be found for a failed bank, regulators will liquidate it and pay off the depositors. Such refunds are generally prompt, but in rare cases it's possible that you might lose access to your money for a few days while the feds untangle the mess.

To avoid getting caught up in a failure, you need to know something about your bank's financial condition. But that is not easy. Although regulatory agencies routinely rate banks according to their financial health, these ratings are never made public for fear of causing a run on the low-rated ones.

You can always ask a bank for a copy of its quarterly report of condition and income, but unless you know how to decipher bank accounting, it will read like a foreign language. A better approach might be asking your branch manager what independent rating companies say about the bank. If it is in good shape, the bank will probably be happy to share the information with you. If bank employees seem evasive, then you might wonder what they have to hide.

In that case you could try another alternative—ordering a rating report from a bank research firm. You will have to pay for the report and it will be based only on the most recent quarterly bank filing with federal regulators. But it will alert you to any major problems.

Credit Cards

*Menagerie of Rates, Terms
Can Leave You in a Quandary*

IT'S ONLY A SMALL piece of plastic. But it comes with about as many features as a new car. In fact, in some cases it can give you rebates on a new car. But if you're not careful, it can drive you straight into debt.

It's a credit card, of course. And it's as American as apple pie and automobiles. Look in almost any adult's wallet and you'll find eight to 12 credit cards, according to industry experts. And these cards are not sitting there idly.

Sixty-seven percent of all cardholders keep a running balance on their bank cards that they don't pay off, according to Robert McKinley, president of RAM Research Corp., a credit card consulting company. And, he says, the average balance for those cardholders is $1,722—an amount that has been increasing each year.

The experts say it's not a very wise way of life, considering its cost. But if you're paying monthly finance charges, now more than ever is the time to reevaluate your credit card and get a better deal.

> ### Where to Order Lists of Low-Rate and No-Fee Cards
>
> **BankCard Holders of America**
>
> Low rate/no fee list, $4
> Call: 1-703-389-5445
>
> **RAM Research**
>
> CardTrak list, $5
> Call: 1-800-344-7714

The reason: Competition has heated up among card issuers, which means there are more choices available to you. There are numerous low rate, no fee cards, as well as cards that offer you rebates and other bonuses. Picking the right card depends on how you plan to use it. And there are pitfalls.

Some shopping suggestions from the experts: Check to see what credit card rates are averaging. You may be able to do better than that. But, many times the cards with the lowest rates are available only to consumers with the best credit history. And even then, these cards often have only very small lines of credit.

What's more, cards with lower rates may have high annual fees. And some of the low rates are teaser rates that will go up in several months. McKinley doesn't see any advantage to these cards unless you plan to increase your payments and pay off your debt during the introductory period.

If you are one of the few who pays off your credit card bill every month, you'll probably want to find a no-fee card with a grace period—usually 25

A Free Lunch?

Those credit cards that offer you rebates or frequent-flier miles may or may not be a good deal. The answer really depends on how you use the card and how many perks you intend to use. Here's how they work. No annual fee is charged unless noted otherwise and the cards have a 20- to 25-day grace period before interest charges begin.

These Give You a Rebate

You must be a high-spender to earn the maximum benefit from these cards—and except for Discover, the benefit evaporates if you don't buy their products. For instance, you must spend $10,000 in a year on the GM card to earn the full $500 rebate. The average consumer charges $2,200 a year.

Card: Discover
Issuer: Discover 800-347-2683

Notes: Uses a less favorable method of calculating interest. Cash rebate is 0.25% for first $1,000 in purchases, 0.50% for second $1,000 in purchases, 0.75% for third $1,000 in purchases and 1% for purchases above $3,000.

Card: Ford MasterCard or VISA
Issuer: Citibank 800-374-7777

Notes: Each dollar charged earns a rebate of 5% of the item's purchase price (up to $700 per year, $3,500 over five years), which can be applied toward the purchase or lease of a new Ford, Lincoln or Mercury car or light truck; $50 rebate bonus every year card is renewed. Annual fee is $20 after the first year.

Card: GE Rewards MasterCard
Issuer: Monogram Bank 800-437-3927

Notes: When purchases total $500 cardholders receive a $10 GE Rewards check good at participating GE Rewards retailers. Four times a year the cardholder also receives $250 in savings certificates for discounts at participating GE Rewards retailers.

Card: General Motors MasterCard
Issuer: Household Bank 800-947-1000

Notes: Every dollar charged earns a rebate of 5 percent of the item's purchase price (up to $500 per year, $3,500 over 7 years), which can be applied toward the purchase or lease of a new GM car or truck.

Here's What It Costs You

To find out if you're better off with a rebate card or a low-rate card, like Wachovia Visa or MasterCard,* check these examples. They're based on one year of interest costs and take into account annual fees and the rebates. If you don't use the full rebate, you'll save more with a no-frills, low-rate card.

You charge $2,200 a year and carry a monthly balance of $1,100.

	Discover	Ford	GE	GM	Wachovia
Your Cost after Rebate:	$154.90	$29.40	$145.90	$70.40	$136.90

You charge $2,200 a year and make only the minimum payment—2.5% of your monthly balance.

	Discover	Ford	GE	GM	Wachovia
Your Cost after Rebate:	$297.03	$177.02	$310.27	$229.16	$136.90

You charge $4,000 a year and pay off the balance in full each month. (No interest charges incurred).

	Discover	Ford	GE	GM	Wachovia
Your Cost after Rebate:	– $25	– $230	– $80	– $200	$39

These Give You an Airline Ticket

In most cases, each dollar charged on a frequent-flier credit card earns you one frequent-flier mile. You will probably want to choose a credit card linked with an airline on which you already earn frequent-flier miles. These cards are best for people who charge a lot and pay it off every month; the high annual fees and interest rates make it a bad deal for most others.

Card: American Airlines AAdvantage MasterCard or VISA
Issuer: Citibank 800-248-4636
Notes: One mile earned for every dollar charged; 20,000 miles required for free ticket.

(continued next page)

Card: Membership Miles American Express or Optima.
Issuer: American Express 800-297-6453
Notes: One mile earned for every dollar charged. Miles can be used in four frequent-flier programs (Continental, Delta, Northwest, Southwest) plus affiliate airlines (a total of 14 airlines); 5,000 miles required before miles can be used.

Card: Continental One Pass, MasterCard or VISA
Issuer: Marine Midland Bank 800-446-5336
Notes: One mile earned for every dollar charged; 2,500 bonus miles on application and 2,500 more when approved; 20,000 miles for a free ticket.

Card: Diners Club
Issuer: Citibank 800-243-6377
Notes: One mile earned for every dollar charged; 1,000 miles required before miles can be used. Miles can be redeemed on 12 airlines and at nine hotels.

Card: Northwest Worldperks VISA
Issuer: Bank One 800-945-2004
Notes: One mile earned for every dollar charged; 20,000 miles required for free ticket.

Card: United Airlines Mileage Plus VISA
Issuer: FCC National Bank 800-537-7783
Notes: One mile earned for every dollar charged; 20,000 miles for free ticket. Limit of 10,000 miles per billing period, 50,000 per year.

Card: USAir VISA
Issuer: NationsBank 800-759-6262
Notes: One mile earned for every dollar charged; 2,500 bonus miles the first time the card is used; 20,000 miles for free ticket. Limit of 10,000 miles per month, 50,000 per year.

Here's What It Costs You

Which is cheaper, using the frequent-flier cards or getting a no-frills card like Wachovia's and simply buying your airline tickets outright? The examples are based on one year of interest costs and take into account annual fees. But they don't account for the value of an airline ticket, which varies by destination. Note, too, that American Express and Diners Club have no interest charges and therefore can earn a ticket for the cost of the annual fee.

You charge $20,000 a year and pay off the balance in full each month. (Earns a free ticket for a small cost.)

	Amer. Air AAdvantage	United Mileage Plus	Northwest Worldperks	Continental One-Pass	USAir	Wachovia
Your Cost:	$50	$60	$55	$45	$80	$35

You charge $20,000 a year and carry a balance of $10,000 a month. (Earns a free ticket, but you'll pay for it in extra finance charges.)

	Amer. Air AAdvantage	United Mileage Plus	Northwest Worldperks	Continental One-Pass	USAir	Wachovia
Your Cost:	$1,590	$1,650	$1,630	$2,040	$1,829	$925

You charge $2,200 a year and carry a balance of $1,100. (In most cases, it would take 10 years to earn a free ticket.)

	Amer. Air AAdvantage	United Mileage Plus	Northwest Worldperks	Continental One-Pass	USAir	Wachovia
Your Cost:	$219.40	$234.90	$228.25	$264.45	$232.34	$136.90

*Wachovia Bank, 800-842-3262. For other low-rate cards see "Best Bets" chart.
SOURCE: BankCard Holders of America

days—so you won't be charged interest between the time you buy and the time you're billed.

You might also consider cards that offer rebates or special services, such as the General Motors or Ford cards, or the airline travel cards. The airline cards give you frequent-flier miles; the auto company cards give you credits toward their brand of car. Other cards offer discounts or rebates on consumer goods.

If you pay your bill in full each month and charge a lot, these can give you something for nothing, says Gerri Detweiler, former executive director of Bank-Card Holders of America. Of course with the rebate cards, you have to want the product or it's worthless.

When comparing credit cards, don't forget to read the disclosure statements. They will tell you about other costs, such as the late-payment fees and cash-advance fees. Also look at the statement to make sure the card uses the average daily balance method of calculating interest charges. It is the most commonly used method. If the card uses the two-cycle method, like the Discover card, it

Best Bets

Credit-card issuers with lowest rates in recent years, where consumers have best shot of being approved.

- **Wachovia Bank**
  Atlanta
  800-842-3262

- **USAA Federal Savings Bank**
  San Antonio
  800-922-9092

- **AFBA Industrial Bank**
  Colorado Springs
  800-776-2265

- **Bank of New York**
  New York City
  800-235-3343

SOURCE: RAM Research Corp.

means you may end up paying higher interest charges, especially if you sometimes pay your bill in full and sometimes carry over a balance.

When it comes to shopping for the best deal, remember you're in the driver's seat. If you already have a card, start by calling up the bank that issued it. Tell them you don't like the rates and fees. Threaten to cancel your card, McKinley says. If they want your business, chances are they will waive your annual fee on the spot.

What's more, your bank may have low-rate cards available, McKinley says. For example, Bank of New York has a Consumers Edge card with an interest rate several percentage points lower than its ordinary card.

If you can't get satisfaction from your bank, look for places you already do business with that may offer discounted credit card rates, such as credit unions or labor unions, McKinley says.

If that doesn't work, compare credit cards across the country for the best deal. For a small fee, you can find out about the best rates from a number of different services.

Finally, if you sign up for a low-rate bank card, ask how to transfer any balances you may have on higher rate cards. Many cards have simple no-fee transfer procedures.

Credit Chaos

There Are Ways to Dig Yourself Out of Charge Card Debt

LUTHER GATLING'S OFFICE in downtown Manhattan is filled with containers of cut-up credit cards. "You should see them," he says enthusiastically. "They make really nice decorations."

It's no surprise that Gatling, president of the non-profit Budget & Credit Counseling Services, views the cut-up cards as a thing of beauty. His mission is to help people get out of debt. Last year, about 25,000 people came into his office for counseling. Many of them ended up tossing out their credit cards and following a strict debt reduction plan.

"The problem is people don't know how to use them properly," he says. "People have no understanding of credit."

"The majority of cardholders who carry a balance from month to month don't even realize that every time they use a bank card they are effectively taking out a personal loan. A lot of people end up financing things they shouldn't be putting on a card, such as groceries, gasoline and dinners out," says Gerri Detweiler, former executive director of BankCard Holders of America, a nonprofit consumer protection group. "They can still be paying interest on a restaurant meal months after they've eaten it."

> ### Need Professional Help?
>
> For the nearest location of the nonprofit Consumer Credit Counseling Service, call 1-800-388-2227.
>
> For information on Debt Zapper, the debt-control plan from BankCard Holders of America's Debt Zapper, call 1-703-389-5445.

But you don't have to let credit card debt give you an ulcer. If you're in trouble, there are some practical steps that can help you reduce your debt more quickly while cutting your interest payments considerably.

The first thing to do, experts say, is to take a good look at how you got into the predicament in the first place. If you don't already have a budget, now's the time to write down your monthly expenditures and compare that with your take-home pay. Then figure out exactly how much you owe on all your bills.

Too often, credit-card spending is just impulse spending. That's why experts suggest that you cut up your cards. Many people don't want to do that because they're afraid they'll need them in case of an emergency, Detweiler says. So lock them up, or give them to someone you trust to hold for you.

Once you stop making new charges, you should develop a plan for reducing your debt.

Debtonation Warning!

Are you in trouble? Credit card debt problems frequently develop over time, catching consumers by surprise when they finally realize the enormity of their problem. If you answer yes to two or more of the following questions, you've got a problem and need to seek help.

1. Are you borrowing to pay for items you used to pay for with cash?

2. Is an increasing percentage of your income going to pay off debts?

3. Is your savings cushion inadequate or nonexistent?

4. Can you only make the minimum payments on your revolving charge accounts?

5. Are your lines of credit at or near the limit on your credit cards?

6. Have circumstances forced you to take out a loan to make payments on a previous loan?

7. Are you unsure about how much you owe?

8. Are your monthly credit bills, excluding rent or mortgage payments, more than 20 percent of your take-home pay?

9. If you lost your job, would you be in immediate financial difficulty?

SOURCE: National Foundation for Consumer Credit Inc.

Start by increasing your monthly payments. Many credit cards have such low minimum monthly payments that your debt load may seem deceptively light. But while these low payments allow you to have more money left over for monthly living expenses, they ultimately prolong your payments and increase your interest charges.

For example, BankCard Holders of America figured out what would happen if you made only the minimum payments on a $1,000 credit card bill, assuming your card charges 17 percent interest and requires a typical minimum payment of 2.5 percent of the current balance. In that case, the group found that it would take 12 years to pay off the $1,000 bill and you would end up paying an additional $979 in interest charges.

Some credit card issuers may allow you to skip a month's payment, but don't think they are doing you a favor. The interest clock keeps ticking and your bill just goes up.

If you owe money on so many different cards that you feel confused and hopelessly mired in debt, you may need professional help. It doesn't have to cost you an arm and a leg. Bankcard Holders of America has a new computerized service called Debt Zapper. For a $15 fee, the organization will help you set up a

Get Control!

If your credit card bills are uncomfortably high, here's how to rid yourself of the debt:

1. Pay more than the minimum payment.

2. Send in your payment as soon as you get your bill. The sooner the card issuer gets your payment the less interest you will pay.

3. Pay off the cards with the highest interest rates first.

4. When you pay the final bill on one card, add the money you were using for that card payment to your payment on another card, thereby paying off debt more quickly.

5. If possible, consolidate all your credit card balances on one low-interest card.

6. Consider using your savings to pay off your high-rate credit card balances. This can be a good investment if the money in your savings account is earning a much lower interest rate than the rate you're being charged on your credit card.

SOURCE: Bankcard Holders of America

schedule for paying off your cards as fast as possible, based on budget information that you give them.

But if you lack discipline and need someone to help you sort out your financial mess, you might want to stop by one of the more than 850 Consumer Credit Counseling Service offices around the country. Gatling's Manhattan office is one of them.

Gatling's counselors will help you set up a budget and a debt repayment schedule. Then, if you still need assistance, they will take over your debt payments—but only after you cut up all your credit cards. (The only exception is a corporate credit card, if it is absolutely necessary for your job.)

The payment service, called BuCCSPLAN, works this way: You make a monthly payment to the counseling service. They use the money to pay your creditors on a timely basis. Because of their experience, they are often able to negotiate a better payment plan with individual creditors.

The service helps take the pressure off of clients, Gatling says, because they don't have to deal with collection companies and creditors. It also simplifies their finances and helps them learn to live on a budget.

There is a $50 initial consultation fee, which entitles you to receive ongoing counseling services for a year. If you choose the BuCCSPLAN payment service, there is a $25 monthly administrative fee.

The ABCs of Investing

Lesson One Is Learning That Every Investment Comes with Some Risk

IN CASE YOU HAVEN'T looked lately, the money in your savings account is earning somewhere around 3 percent interest. The rates on certificates of deposit are better. But factor in inflation and taxes and any bank fees you're paying, and the money you worked so hard to save may be shrinking before your eyes.

Before you throw up your hands in despair, you might want to look at other ways to make the most of your money. Millions of Americans already have ventured out of insured CDs and into mutual funds. They realize it is not enough to be a saver; they are becoming investors.

There is, of course, one major difference: more risk. If you are considering investing for the first time, or if you already have taken the plunge, you need to be sure you have a sound investment plan and an understanding of how much risk you're willing to take.

After you've grown accustomed to insured bank accounts, the more volatile world of investments can give you nightmares. "When I mention the stock market to some people, I can see their eyes pop open," says Ann Diamond, a New York City financial consultant. "People often tell me, 'I work very hard for this money and I'd rather make less than worry about losing it.' But I explain there is risk to any investment.

"You can't escape risk. There is a risk to putting your money in a mattress; your house could burn down or the money could be stolen. So the question is not whether to take a risk with your money, but what kind of a risk you should be taking."

The least risky investments are bank accounts, government bonds and money market funds. Corporate and municipal bonds fall somewhere in the middle. Stocks and junk bonds are among the riskiest types of investments. The proportion of your money you invest in any one category of investment will depend on your age, tax bracket, goals and your personal tolerance for risk.

When deciding how much money to put into a stock or stock fund, it's wise to imagine the worst-case scenario. How would you feel if your investment lost value steadily for a year? Could you afford to lose most of the money?

And what would you do if there were a market crash and your investment suddenly was almost worthless? Would you abandon the investment and take a loss, or stick with it and hope to ride out the downturn?

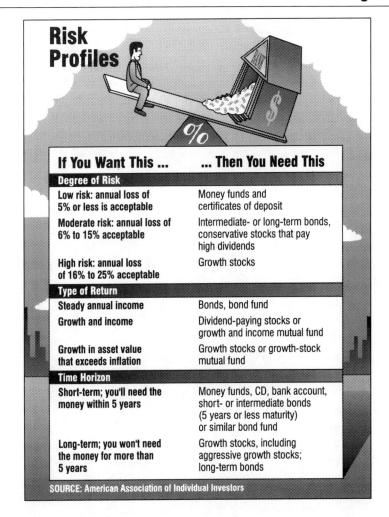

Risk Profiles

If You Want This ...	... Then You Need This
Degree of Risk	
Low risk: annual loss of 5% or less is acceptable	Money funds and certificates of deposit
Moderate risk: annual loss of 6% to 15% acceptable	Intermediate- or long-term bonds, conservative stocks that pay high dividends
High risk: annual loss of 16% to 25% acceptable	Growth stocks
Type of Return	
Steady annual income	Bonds, bond fund
Growth and income	Dividend-paying stocks or growth and income mutual fund
Growth in asset value that exceeds inflation	Growth stocks or growth-stock mutual fund
Time Horizon	
Short-term; you'll need the money within 5 years	Money funds, CD, bank account, short- or intermediate bonds (5 years or less maturity) or similar bond fund
Long-term; you won't need the money for more than 5 years	Growth stocks, including aggressive growth stocks; long-term bonds

SOURCE: American Association of Individual Investors

Generally speaking, experts say that the time to take the most risk is when you are young. The reason: Young people have time to make up for any mistakes they make. Conversely, as you approach retirement, you don't want to jeopardize the money you need to live on.

The amount of risk you take with your money also should depend on how soon you intend to use it. As a rule of thumb, financial advisers say, the stock market should be used only for long-term investing. It's good for retirement or a young child's college education fund. It isn't the place for money you plan to spend next month. That's because, in the short term, stocks can fluctuate greatly in value. You don't want to be forced to sell because the rent is due but your stock is in the dumps.

The Risk Factor

No sense trying to fool Mother Nature. If you aren't cut out for risk-taking you'll end up with ulcers instead of a nice nest egg. There are investments at every risk level and it's better to find options more suited to your risk tolerance. What route should you choose? Take this quiz to find out.

1. Which best describes your feelings about investing?

    A. "Better safe than sorry."
    B. "Moderation in all things."
    C. "Nothing ventured, nothing gained."

2. Which is most important to you as an investor?

    A. Steady income.
    B. Steady income and growth.
    C. Rapid price appreciation.

3. You won! Which prize would you select?

    A. $4,000 in cash.
    B. A 50 percent chance to win $10,000.
    C. A 20 percent chance to win $100,000.

4. The stocks in your 401(k) statement have dropped 20 percent since last quarter. The market experts are optimistic. What would you do?

    A. Transfer out of stocks to avoid losing more.
    B. Stay in stocks and wait for them to come back.
    C. Shift more money into stocks. If they made sense before, they're a bargain now.

5. The stocks in your 401(k) statement have suddenly gone up 20 percent. You have no further information. What would you do?

    A. Transfer out of stocks and lock in my gains.
    B. Stay in stocks, hoping for more gains.
    C. Transfer more money into stocks. They might go higher.

6. Would you borrow money to take advantage of a good investment opportunity?

    A. Never.
    B. Maybe.
    C. Yes.

7. How would you characterize yourself as an investor?

    A. Conservative.
    B. Moderate risk-taker.
    C. Aggressive.

How to determine your score.

For each "A" answer, give yourself one point. For each "B" answer, give yourself two points. For each "C" answer, give yourself three points. If your total score is:

7–11 points, you're a conservative investor and your options include blue-chip stock funds, bonds and U.S. Treasury bills.

12–16 points, you're a moderate risk-taker and your options range from growth and income stock funds, domestic or global, to intermediate bond funds.

17–21 points, you're an aggressive investor and options include growth funds, small-company stocks, high-yield "junk" bonds.

SOURCE: *Standard & Poor's Guide to Retirement Planning*

And although you may be attracted to the latest hot mutual fund category, be careful. It's dangerous to think you can put your money in and make a fast profit. That could happen. But it's just as possible that as soon as you invest, the market could head for a prolonged slump.

Real investing takes time to pay off. History shows that stocks become less volatile over time. So experts say that your minimum commitment to the stock market should be five years. That means if you are saving for a down payment on a home and you plan to buy it in three years, the stock market is not a good place for those funds. For that, you might be better off investing in money market funds or intermediate-term bonds, says Lewis Altfest, a financial planner.

If you don't already have a list of your financial goals, you should sit down and make one. Include everything from saving for retirement and buying a second home to paying for your child's college education and buying a car. Figure out which goals are short term and which are long term. Your investment plan should reflect these goals, and the time needed to achieve them.

You also need to figure out how taxes affect your investment decisions. If you are in a high tax bracket, you may want to opt for triple-tax-free municipal bonds or tax-deferred investments. If you are in a low tax bracket, you might do better in taxable Treasury bonds.

In the end, however, one of the most important things to consider is your tolerance for risk. Everyone is different. You can't make money without some measure of risk, so you'll have to get used to it. But experts say an investment that causes you constant worry probably isn't right for you.

Even wealthy people may be reluctant to take chances. "There are plenty of people with millions who are very aggressive in their own business, but they are conservative in their investments," Altfest says.

And not without reason. "Let's face it, you can and probably will lose money at some point in your investment career." David Sweet, a retired salesman from Forest Hills, Queens, has been playing the stock market for two decades. About five years ago, he invested in an oil and gas stock that was recommended to him. "I lost money," he says. "It turned out to be a dud."

Sweet continues to invest in mutual funds. But he admits he is more cautious today, in part because of the loss, and in part because his needs have changed now that he is retired. Although he hasn't quite achieved his goal of becoming a millionaire, he says he's happy to keep pace with inflation and make a couple of bucks.

A Recipe for Success

How to Choose the Elements for Your Financial Plan

M OST PEOPLE WOULDN'T bake a cake without a recipe. They wouldn't take a vacation without making plans. And they wouldn't buy a car without doing some research. But many people jump into investments because of a tip they received from a neighbor or relative, even though they don't know what they're getting into.

One of the most important things you can do to protect yourself, consumer advocates say, is never to invest in anything you don't understand. Ask questions and find out where to get more information if you need it.

Once you have taken stock of your investment profile—based on your age, tax bracket, goals and risk tolerance—you should come up with an investment strategy.

But before you begin, don't forget to set aside an emergency fund that is equal to three to six months of your living expenses. This money should not be put at risk and it should be easy to get at. You might want to stash it, for example, in a short-term, federally insured bank certificate of deposit.

Now you need a plan of action for the rest of your money. First of all, diversify. That means, for instance, don't put all your money into stocks just because you are eager to make money quickly. Generally speaking, the higher the return, the higher the risk. But putting all your money in riskless certificates of deposit and federal bonds isn't a good idea, either. In the long run your investments may barely keep up with inflation.

So, even if you don't have a lot of money to start, experts say you should divide it among several types of investments. The goal is to spread out your risk—to diversify—so that if one thing goes wrong, something else will take up the slack.

For example, say that a young, single advertising executive has $5,000 to invest. Lewis Altfest, a financial planner in New York City, says he would advise the person to invest $1,000 in three different no-load stock mutual funds and two bond mutual funds. He says he would pick a long-term bond fund, an intermediate-term bond fund, an aggressive domestic stock fund that takes a fair amount of risk, a more conservative growth stock fund, and an international stock fund. Mutual fund companies will tell you which one is which in their brochures.

"That would give you good balance," Altfest says. "And it sets structure for the future." After the initial investment, the young ad executive should add to the funds in equal ratios, he says.

Financial planners generally recommend mutual funds to people who don't have a lot of money to invest. If you were going to buy individual stocks, you would need a lot more cash and knowledge about the financial condition of corporations in order to properly diversify. By definition, mutual funds allow you to own a piece of many different types of companies without a big investment.

And most municipal bonds and corporate bonds are sold in lots of $5,000 to $10,000 or higher. To have a diversified portfolio of bonds, then, would require a substantial investment.

Diversification has another purpose: Some of your money can be invested for short-term goals and some can be invested for the long term. Your portfolio should balance out these needs. Even young people who are saving for a family and a home should also be setting aside some money for retirement.

In fact, one of the best ways to learn about investing and to save for retirement at the same time is to participate in a company-sponsored 401(k) retirement plan if your company offers one. Such plans divert money from your paycheck into mutual funds that you get to choose.

"It's an easy way to get your feet wet," says Ann Diamond, a New York City financial consultant. Usually the company does half the work for you, she says, and gives you a menu of investment options. And you may have an added benefit if your company matches some of your investment. One other bonus: You don't pay taxes on your profits until you retire, which means your investments grow much faster.

Going Long

While your year-to-year return may prove more chancy—you might even lose money once or twice—the best long-term investments are in stocks. Assuming all proceeds are reinvested, here's how several types of investments have performed since 1926.

	Average Total Return Per Year
Small-company stocks	12%
Common stocks in general	10%
Long-term corporate bonds . . .	5%
Intermediate-term government bonds .	5%
Long-term government bonds .	5%
U.S. Treasury bills . . .	4%
Average annual rate of inflation	3%

SOURCE: Ibbotson Associates

Financial advisers emphasize that once you start investing, be sure to reinvest your interest and dividends. This is the way to make your investment build momentum. Most mutual funds will do it automatically for you if you ask.

At the same time, add to your investments regularly. Decide on an amount that you can afford to set aside, and if possible have it automatically deducted from your salary. This is often referred to as dollar-cost averaging. It not only establishes a discipline for saving, but it also helps you avoid putting your money into the market at the wrong time, because you're constantly buying shares in both good times and bad. If you invest regularly and for the long term, any losses you incur from the ones you buy at high prices should average out.

Keep in mind, however, that while a mutual fund's diversity protects you against a sharp drop in any one stock or industry, it can't protect you from a general market decline—in other words, a bear market. Only in very rare cases can a mutual fund manager stay even while everyone else shows a loss.

Other things to consider when choosing among investments are convenience and the amount of time and attention they will require. Many people like mutual funds, for example, because they are easy to buy and because an experienced manager is keeping a eye on the fund. If you're like most people, you want to spend all your free time relaxing, not worrying about gyrations in the stock market or poring over prospect uses.

Know Your Bonds

Interest Rates Rise, Your Return Drops—
And You Can Even Lose Principal

MURIEL SIEBERT, head of a discount brokerage firm that bears her name, warned bondholders that they were in for a shock when rates began to rise.

That was in 1993, and Siebert, a former New York State superintendent of banks, was saying that many people who invested in bonds and bond funds during the stretch of sagging interest rates didn't fully understand what could happen to the value of their investment when the trend finally reversed.

"Boy are they going to be yelling," she said. And indeed, when rates began to rise in 1994, many investors opened their bond fund statements and were horrified to see big losses.

"I think bond funds showed one thing," Siebert says now. "You can get in and get out of them easily."

Many people apparently found that out for themselves. In 1994 the amount of money invested in bond funds dropped dramatically.

When rates on certificates of deposit were languishing, bonds and bond funds appeared to be a good alternative for risk-adverse investors. But experts say that, too often, these people believed their principal would be totally safe. And that is not necessarily true. Even Treasury bonds fluctuate in value. If you need to sell your bonds before they mature, you could be in the unenviable condition of selling at a loss.

On the surface bonds seem like a straightforward, relatively safe investment. A company, a municipality or the federal government needs money. So it issues bonds, which are like an IOU. You pay the issuer for the bonds and it agrees to pay you a fixed amount of interest, usually every six months. The issuer agrees to buy the bond back from you at the initial price after a set period of time.

Most bonds are negotiable. That means that if you want to sell them before the date of maturity, a broker may be able to find another investor who is in the market for them.

But you need to remember a crucial rule of bonds: Their price, or market value, moves in the opposite direction of interest rates.

Think of it this way: Investing in bonds is like riding on a seesaw. On one end is the price you paid for your bond and on the other is the prevailing interest rate. If rates begin to go up, your bond will be worth less to another investor, so the market price of your bond goes down.

A Bond Translator

Face value

The value of the bond when it is issued, usually $1,000 per bond. Face value is also called par.

Market value

The price you pay for a bond. On any given day you may purchase a bond for more or less than the face value; if the price is higher than the face value, it is selling at a premium, but if it is low, it is said to be selling at a discount.

Maturity

The day the bond expires, and all your principal is be returned to you.

Coupon rate

The fixed interest rate on the bond. For example say a bond has a coupon rate of 8 percent.

Current yield

If you bought a bond for more or less than face value, discount, then your current yield will not be the same as the coupon rate. Say, for example, you paid $1,367 for a $1,000 bond that has an interest rate of 8 percent. Because you paid a premium, your current yield is 7.7. percent.

Yield to maturity

The return you will receive if you hold the bond to maturity. In the example above, if you paid $1,367 on a bond with an 8 percent coupon rate, your yield to maturity would be 6 percent. That's less than your current yield, because at maturity you would only receive $1,000 back on your original investment

Call provision

Some issuers have the right to redeem bonds early. This usually happens if interest rates go down. You would be paid the face value of the bond, but you would be stuck seeking another place to invest your money in a low-rate environment.

Convertible bond

Some corporations issue bonds that have a provision allowing the bond to be converted into stock if the stock price reaches a certain level. The bonds generally pay less interest than other corporate bonds. Investors accept the low rate on the bonds because they are betting the company will flourish and they will be able to convert their bonds at some point.

Zero coupon bonds

Like savings bonds, these bonds do not make interest payments. Instead, they are sold at a discount from the face value; you get your money at maturity when they pay off at full face value.

Do-It-Yourself Treasuries

Many commercial banks can get you a Treasury security for a modest fee. If you want to save the commission and buy original issues of Treasury securities, you can go to the New York Federal Reserve on auction days or more conveniently you can open a Treasury Direct account by mail. To set one up call your local Federal Reserve Bank. The process works like this:

You submit a noncompetitive bid in writing. This means you agree to accept the average price paid by competitive bidders, which tend to be large financial institutions. Your tender offer should state the face amount of the securities you wish to purchase and the maturity. It must be postmarked by midnight the day before the auction and received by the Fed by the issue date or it will not be accepted for that auction.

Your offer must be accompanied by the following:

- A check made out to the New York Federal Reserve Bank for the full face value.

- Your name and mailing address, you Social Security number and a daytime phone number.

- If you have not already established a Treasury Direct account, include the name of your bank and its nine-digit routing number for direct deposit (your banker can supply it), as well as your account name, number and type of account (checking or savings). Once you have established an account, the semiannual interest payments on Treasury notes and bonds can be electronically deposited in your account.

- A W-9 certificate, or a statement in writing, certifying that you are not subject to backup withholding tax.

Treasury bill are similar to savings bonds because the bills are sold at a discount from their face value. However, because the purchase price is determined at the auction, you must send in the full face value ahead of time. You will be reimbursed for the difference between the purchase price and face value of the bill, which is in effect your interest.

Through Treasury Direct, you will receive a notice 45 days before your securities mature asking you if you want to reinvest your money or have the principal deposited in your bank account.

Three and six-month T-bills are auctioned every Monday (unless Monday is a holiday, then auction day is Tuesday). The schedule for 12-month T-bills and Treasury notes and bonds, which are auctioned much less frequently, can be obtained from the Fed.

This doesn't matter if you hold the bond to maturity. In that case, you will get back the face value of the bond that is, unless the company or municipality that issued you bonds goes bust and can't pay you back. No company is immune to financial problems. Recent history shows that even such venerable companies as Kodak and IBM can flounder.

As a rule, the higher a bond's interest rate, or coupon rate, the riskier the investment. You will also receive higher interest rates on long-term bonds because there is the risk that before the bond matures, interest rates will go up and you will be locked into the lower rate.

If you are considering investing in bonds, there are many kinds to choose from:

Government bonds: These are usually considered the safest of all bonds because they are backed by the government, and their interest usually isn't taxed by states.

U.S. Savings Bonds are the most convenient because they can be purchased at your bank for no fee. And they come in denominations as small as $50. They are bought for one-half of their face amount. The interest rate determines how many years it will take the bond to mature to its face value.

Treasury bills must be bought in minimum amounts of $10,000, and they can be bought without a broker directly from the government. They are sold in maturities of three months, six months and one year.

Treasury notes have maturities ranging from two to 10 years. And Treasury bonds have maturities of as much as 30 years. They are sold at a minimum of $1,000, except for notes with terms of less than four years, which are sold at a minimum of $5,000.

Some government and quasi-government agencies, such as the Federal National Mortgage Association (Fannie Mae), also issue bonds.

Municipal bonds. These bonds are issued by states, cities and localities. In most cases, you need to buy them through a broker. Their coupon rates are relatively low but they have tax advantages for some people. In light of the recent tax bill, municipal bonds have become increasingly popular. More about them in the next chapter.

Corporate bonds. These bonds are also bought through a broker. Be aware that when you buy a bond, you don't pay a brokerage commission. Instead, the cost to you is built into the price you pay for the bond. This is referred to as the margin, or spread, between the selling price and buying price. If you are buying a bond partway through its interest period, don't be surprised if you have to make an upfront accrued interest payment. This reimburses the previous owner for the portion of the next coupon payment owed to him.

Buying individual municipal and corporate bonds is a tough task for beginners. It requires a sophisticated knowledge of the credit quality of the issuer. Bond rating firms, such as Standard & Poor's and Moody's, are in the business of analyzing the credit risk of a bond issuer and assigning a rating that sums up the bond quality. Although rating systems can vary, in the case of Standard &

Poor's, the ratings range from AAA (the best quality) to D (issuer has defaulted or is in bankruptcy). Although bonds rarely drop from a AAA rating to a D rating overnight, the condition of a company can change rapidly and there may be a lag before the rating is adjusted.

Bond terminology can be confusing. Before buying a bond, be sure to ask your broker about its yield to maturity, which is the most accurate reflection of what you will earn if you hold the bond for its full term. While you will often see the current yield cited in bond listing, it does not factor in the gain or loss you receive at maturity when you are paid the face value.

Some bonds contain provisions that allow the issuers to redeem the bonds before they mature. So, you will also want to ask your broker what the yield to call would be in that event.

Most financial planners recommend buying bonds in different maturities, often called laddering, to spread out your risk. Laddering will better assure you that the average rate of return on your bond portfolio will beat inflation, without locking up all your money in long-term investments.

Because of the difficulty of buying individual bonds, many people have turned to bond funds. Your investment is pooled with others to buy bonds that have been selected by a manager. You can choose short-term funds. And you can select corporate, municipal and Treasury bond funds.

The advantage of a fund is that they are convenient, you can invest in small amounts and they are managed by a financial expert. But Ronald Rogé, a financial planner, says there is a downside to bond funds too.

When you own a bond, you have a contract with the company that says it will pay you back the face value of the bond on a certain date, Rogé says. With bond funds, you lose that guarantee because they are constantly trading bonds and do not hold them to maturity.

And Joel Issacson, a financial planner, cautions that you should carefully consider the fees and expenses associated with a bond fund. "The return is so low on bond funds, why pay 4 or 5 percent?" he says.

The Lure of Munis: Seeking Shelter

They Can Reduce Taxes, but Taxable Investments May Be Better for Some

P RESIDENT BILL CLINTON may have trouble selling Congress on some of his proposals, but he seemed to know just how to sell the public on municipal bonds: raise taxes.

When Clinton started talking about a tax hike early in his term, accountants and financial planners across the country began receiving calls from anxious clients who wanted to know how to reduce their taxes. The answer in many cases was tax-exempt municipal bonds, or, in industry parlance, munis.

Many of the people who recently have rushed to buy munis were not even affected by changes in the tax law, says James Cooner, who heads the tax-exempt bond division at the Bank of New York. There is an obvious incentive for those people whose taxes are going up, he says. But the tax increase also created an incentive for others who felt they may be vulnerable to a tax increase in the future.

But before you rush in, look closer. Financial experts say munis are not for everyone. Sometimes, you're better off with a taxable investment.

Cooner says that municipal bond investors should be in the 28 percent federal tax bracket or higher to benefit from the tax exemption. And, he emphasizes, investors should never put a penny of their IRA or company-sponsored 401(k) retirement account in municipal bonds because those plans are already sheltered from taxes.

Municipal bonds are issued by cities, states, counties and localities to pay for such things as bridges, roads, schools and public office buildings. There are two basic kinds: general obligation and revenue bonds.

General obligation bonds are backed by the faith and credit of the local government that issued them. If necessary, a municipality can raise taxes to pay back investors.

In contrast, revenue bonds are guaranteed by the revenues produced by the project that the bonds are issued to finance. For example, if bonds are issued to build a toll road, then the tolls will be used to make the bond interest payments and pay back the investors when the bonds mature. The safety of these bonds depends on the financial soundness of the individual project.

Like corporate bonds, municipal bonds are rated according to their underly-

WORKSHEET: Is Tax-Free a Savings?

Say you have a certificate of deposit that is coming due. You're tired of paying taxes; you're thinking about switching to municipal bonds. But they pay a lower interest rate, perhaps leaving you with less money than if you stayed with the CD and paid your taxes. How do you know which one is a better deal? Get out your calculator; here's how to figure it out:

1. Estimate your tax bracket by adding together your federal, state and local income tax rates.

> *Example:*
>
> Federal tax rate . . . . 31 percent
>
> New York State rate . . . . + 5 percent
> _____
>
> Total tax bracket . . . . 36 percent

2. To find out how much of your CD interest goes for taxes, put a decimal point in front of your tax bracket and multiply that figure by the interest rate on a CD.

> *Example: A five-year CD with a yield of 5.49 percent*
>
> Your tax bracket . . . .   0.36 percent
>
> CD yield . . . . X 5.49 percent
> _____
>
> Tax bite . . . .   1.98 percent

3. Subtract the tax bite from the CD rate to get your after-tax yield.

> *Example:*
>
> CD yield . . . .   5.49 percent
>
> Tax bite . . . . – 1.98 percent
> _____
>
> After-tax CD yield . . . .   3.51 percent

So, in our example, to do better than a 5.49 percent CD, a person in a 36 percent tax bracket needs to find a municipal bond with an interest rate of at least 3.52 percent. Remember, to be equivalent, the municipal bond should be for the same term as the CD.

ing credit quality. Bonds with low ratings are considered more likely to default. They will pay the highest interest rates.

Some bonds are insured, so if the issuer defaults, the insurance company will guarantee the interest and principal payments. Insurance will boost a bond's rating and reduce the return to investors. However, many experts caution that insurance is only as good as the financial condition of the insurance company.

The big attraction to munis, of course, is that they are usually exempt from federal, state and local taxes. The triple-tax exemption only applies to bonds issued in your home state, however. If you live in New York and purchase municipal bonds issued by Texas, you will pay state and local taxes. There is an ex-

A Mini Muni Quiz

True or False?

1. Municipal bonds are as safe as Treasury securities and U.S. Savings Bonds.

2. Not all municipal bonds are exempt from federal, state and local taxes.

3. Municipal bonds don't make financial sense for everyone.

4. It is always better to choose a non-callable bond over a callable bond.

5. Municipal bonds are a good place to park the money you've saved for a down payment while you look for a home to buy.

6. Long-term municipal bonds are always a better investment because they have higher yields.

---

1. False: Treasuries and Savings Bonds are backed by the Treasury Department, which has the authority to print money, if necessary, to back its bonds. But if a town is having financial problems, it may not have the tax revenue necessary to back general obligation bonds. Or if a hospital is badly managed, it may not be able to pay back revenue bonds.

2. True: It generally depends on whether you are buying bonds issued in your home state. In addition, if you are subject to alternative minimum tax, you may be taxed on certain types of municipal bonds.

3. True: If you are in a 15 percent federal tax bracket, you may be better off putting your money into a taxable investment. Retirees who drop into a lower tax bracket also need to reevaluate the wisdom of municipal bond investments. The only way to be sure, however, is to determine your combined state and federal tax bracket and figure out what a particular taxable investment would yield after taxes.

4. False: You need to evaluate a bond on a number of criteria. For example, if you are a conservative investor, a high-quality municipal bond that is callable may be a better for you than a riskier bond that is not callable.

5. False: There is not an active market for municipal bonds. If you have to sell them when interest rates are low, you may lose money. Experts don't advise investing in munis unless you can hold them until maturity.

6. False: The reason long-term bonds pay a higher yield is because you are locking up your money for many years. If interest rates rise in that interval, the long-term bond yields may not look so good to you.

ception: bonds issued by Puerto Rico, Guam and the Virgin Islands are tax exempt in all states.

There is no active market for trading munis, as there is for stocks. They are only traded in large lots, so you usually have to buy individual municipal bonds in minimum amounts of $25,000 through a broker.

To properly spread out your risk, most financial experts suggest owning several different bond issues in varying maturities. Ronald W. Rogé, a financial adviser, also recommends that his clients have no more than 10 percent of their portfolio in any one bond issue. In that case, a municipal bond portfolio would contain $250,000 worth of bonds.

Most investors don't have that kind of money. So they invest in municipal bond funds, which have minimum investment requirements as low as $1,000. The tax advantage will depend on the types of munis in the portfolio. If a fund contains munis from many different states, you will pay state and local taxes on the interest from the out-of-state bonds. Single-state municipal bond funds are also available.

As with any mutual fund, you need to consider the fund's fees, its historical record, and the kind of bonds in the portfolio. The rule for diversification also holds true for bond funds: Don't invest all your money in one fund, experts say.

Although very few munis actually default, their value will go down as interest rates rise. That means your principal may be fairly safe, but there is no guarantee that you will receive a certain return on your investment. Many investors discovered this the hard way when interest rates began to rise in 1994, and suddenly they were faced with negative returns on their bond funds.

There is another alternative for small investors. Some cities and counties in New York have begun selling minimunis, which can be bought in amounts as small as $5,000. If you decide to buy them, financial advisers say to keep the amount to a small fraction of your total investments. And don't buy them if you can't afford to tie up the money until the bonds mature. It may be difficult to trade them and you may have to sell them at a loss.

One disadvantage to municipal bonds is that most of them are callable after 10 years. At that point, the issuer may choose to redeem them, especially if interest rates have gone down.

Investors today do not actually receive the bonds they have bought. Instead the bonds are registered through their broker. Interest payments are automatically deposited in the investor's brokerage account, and if the bonds are called, the investor will immediately be notified.

However, people who bought bonds before 1983 may still have bearer bonds with the attached coupons that must be clipped to receive interest payments. They need to be vigilant, because the only way for the issuer to notify them if the bonds are called is to advertise in the local newspapers. But it is easy for bondholders to miss such call notices. "They might only find out the bonds have been called six months later when they go to cash in their interest coupon," Cooner says. "And bingo, they discover they're out the interest payment."

Going Shopping at the Stock Market

Do Your Homework and Be Prepared for a Letdown

EVEN VETERAN INVESTORS occasionally make mistakes. Just ask Stephen Beer.

Beer, a Manhattan accountant, has belonged to investment clubs for more than a decade. He spends a couple of hours a week reading company quarterly reports and stock analyst reports. Yet when it came to IBM, Beer says, he tripped up. He held onto the stock despite the company's mounting financial problems.

"I let myself get fooled into thinking IBM was going to turn around," Beer says. "I relied on an analyst report that said the worst was over."

Unfortunately, most small investors must rely on analyst reports or stock broker tips because they don't have the expertise to evaluate individual stocks. But, as Beer discovered, there is no guarantee that the advice will be accurate. This can put novice investors at a particular disadvantage, consumer advocates say.

They are going up against seasoned professionals who spend all their time analyzing stocks, says Barbara Roper, director of investor protection at the Consumer Federation of America. For a professional to buy low and sell high, someone else has to buy high and sell low. Nine times out of ten, it will be a small investor.

Yet despite the pitfalls, the prospect of big gains has attracted a flood of individual investors to the stock market. Many of them have turned to stock mutual funds, which are managed by professional stock pickers. Others have jumped directly into the market, choosing and buying their stocks themselves. And still others, like Beer, have joined investment clubs to pool their resources and research with a small group of investors.

When you buy a share of stock you become an owner of a small piece of the company. There is no guarantee that you will receive a return on your investment or even get your money back. As a stockholder, you are betting that the company is going to do well.

There are two ways for you to make money on your stock: dividends and capital gains. Some companies take a portion of their profits and share them with stockholders in the form of quarterly dividends or cash payments. Dividends are taxable in the year in which you receive them. Although some companies pay

A Reader's Guide to the Stock Market

Common Stock: A share of ownership in a corporation.

Bid: The highest price you are willing to pay for a stock.

Ask: The lowest price at which someone is willing to sell a stock.

Spread: The difference between the bid and the asking price.

Specialist, or Market Maker: Person in charge of trading particular stocks. If, for example, a broker can't immediately find a seller for a bid, then the specialist takes charge of completing the transaction.

Close: The price of the last transaction of the day for a particular stock.

Confirmation: A written receipt that you receive after you buy or sell stock.

Dividend: Some companies share their profits with stockholders on a per-share basis. This payment is usually made quarterly.

Bull Market: A rising market.

Bear Market: A falling market.

Price/Earnings Ratio, P/E Ratio or Multiple: The price of a stock divided by its earnings per share. A high P/E ratio usually indicates that stockholders expect a company's earnings to rise.

Book Value Per Share: The net worth of a company divided by the number of shares on the market.

Total Return: The dividends you have received, plus any gain or loss on the price of a stock since you bought it.

Growth Stock: Some companies reinvest all their profits to help fuel their growth. Stockholders in these companies usually do not receive, but instead hope for earnings growth and a rapid rise in their stock price.

Blue Chip Stocks: A highly regarded company that can be counted on for regular dividend payments, as well as long-term growth.

Income Stock: Some companies, such as utilities, can be counted on for a steady dividend payment but do not provide stockholders with exciting growth prospects.

Penny Stock: Cheap stocks from new companies without a track record that don't sell on the traditional exchanges. They often sell for less than a dollar a share and are considered the riskiest kind of stock.

Stock Split: When a company increases the number of shares and lowers the stock price. In a two-for-one split, a stockholder gets twice the number of shares but the price of each one is cut in half. This helps encourage investors to buy the stock because it is less expensive.

Preferred Stock: Not exactly a stock or bond, but a hybrid of the two. These stocks pay a fixed dividend, which does not rise if the company's profits soar. In return for accepting the fixed dividend, the preferred stockholders receive preferential treatment. If the company is liquidated, they have a claim on the company's assets before holders of common stock.

Odd Lot: An order to buy an odd number of shares. Shares are usually sold in multiples of 100, called a round lot. Brokers usually charge a higher commission to make an odd lot trade.

Securities and Exchange Commission: The SEC is the U.S. government agency that regulates the stock market.

Short Selling: A risky transaction in which the investor bets that a stock is going to fall in price. The investor borrows stock and sells it, hoping to replace the borrowed shares later when the price is lower.

Program Trading: When institutions trade a number of stocks at once, usually by computer. Some stocks are automatically triggered when prices hit certain levels. After the 1987 stock market collapse, some limits were placed on program trading.

Buying on Margin: Basically, this refers to borrowing some money from a broker to buy stock.

dividends year after year, the payments are not guaranteed. If the company runs into trouble, its directors could decide to cut the dividend.

Other companies plow their profits back into the company so that it will grow more quickly. If that happens, the stock should gain in value. That capital gain only exists on paper until you sell your stock. Once you sell, the profit is taxable. Capital gains are even less of a sure thing than dividends.

It's not always an either/or proposition. Some stocks—traditionally the blue chip stocks—pay dividends and produce capital gains. The term blue chip is reserved for the most respected corporations in America. They usually are considered safe investment bets.

That isn't necessarily true, however. Just look at IBM. Its stock fell from a high of $175.90 in the summer of 1987 to $42 in September 1993. "Some of the worst performers are blue chips," says James Cloonan, chairman of the American Association of Individual Investors. "There is really no stock that is safe."

Stocks are commonly bought and sold in open auctions on the trading room floors of different exchanges, where orders from stockbrokers pour in. The New York Stock Exchange, or Big Board, tends to handle the largest corporations. Investors often use the Dow Jones Industrial Average—based on 30 blue chips—as a proxy for the NYSE. When investors talk of the market rising or falling 10 points, they are referring to the movement of the Dow. The American Stock Exchange handles more mid-sized corporations. There are a number of regional exchanges as well.

However, many stocks—especially small-company and start-up company stocks—are not traded on an exchange. Instead, they are traded by individual dealers through an electronic marketplace called the Over-the-Counter Market. The most actively traded OTC stocks are listed in newspapers under the heading NASDAQ, the National Association of Securities Dealers Automated Quotations.

There are lots of different theories about how to get started in the stock market. Cloonan says that if you decide you want to begin investing in individual stocks, you should start with a minimum of between $25,000 and $50,000. He arrives at that amount in two ways.

First, you must buy stocks through a broker, who will charge you a commission. Even discount brokerage houses will charge a minimum commission of about $30 to $40. That can be steep if you are only buying a small amount of shares. So to offset the commission, he recommends buying a minimum of 200 or 300 shares.

Second, to protect yourself against a bad choice, Cloonan says you should have no more than 10 percent of your stock portfolio in any one company. So, you should be prepared to invest in about 10 different stocks.

To properly diversify you also should invest in different types of stocks. For example, don't have more than one or two stocks in the same industry. And while there is some advantage to having a mix of large and small company stocks, Cloonan says the novice investor should stick to well known corporations. That's because it is often harder to get analyst reports and other financial information on small companies.

In particular, beware of penny stocks. These speculative stocks usually sell for less than a dollar and are issued by new companies. "Most penny stocks lose money," Roper says. "Buying them is equivalent to going to Las Vegas. And there has been a tremendous amount of penny stock fraud."

Okay, so you've done your homework and you're ready to invest. Still, something is bothering you. Is this a good time to get into the market? Isn't the market too high?

Analysts agree there is no way for a small investor to predict market trends. They advise staggering your investments over intervals of several months. Then, be prepared to stick with them for a minimum of five years.

History shows that stock market volatility evens out over the long haul. Even if the market crashes you are better off holding onto your stocks, experts say. In time, your investment should recover more of its value than if you bolt when the market is down.

That doesn't mean you should keep a particular stock if the company is steadily losing money and has no prospect of improving. At some point, you should cut your losses and put your money into a better stock.

Mutual Fund Investing

*Millions Plop Down Money,
but Don't Know the Risks*

MORE THAN 40 MILLION AMERICANS own a mutual fund today. Chances are you are one of them.

If so, you have helped pour more than $2.2 trillion into one of more than 5,500 different mutual funds. And while that would seem to be good news for the industry, it has some people worried.

"We don't believe all investors are aware of the risks," says Brian Mattes, vice president of the Vanguard Group, one of the largest mutual fund companies in the nation. "There needs to be more awareness that these are not bank vehicles. They are not going to be stable."

Richard Schmidt agrees. "Many people don't read the fine print or the prospectus," says Schmidt, editor of the *Risk Report,* an investment advisory newsletter. "They don't understand that mutual funds are not a panacea in a low interest rate environment. They need to become educated investors."

This is important because it's nearly impossible to anticipate trends in the stock market. At the same time, many people don't take into account how interest rate trends can affect their investments. Sudden changes in the stock market or interest rates can throw you for a loop if you're not prepared for them, and you'll have a tendency to overreact. You may see your fund is losing money and sell at the worst possible time—at the very moment that experts say you should be buying.

So now is the time to be sure you know something about how your mutual fund investment works.

Mutual funds simply pool the money of many people to invest in stocks, bonds or money market securities—or some combination of these three. For the small investor, there are a number of advantages to owning mutual funds:

- Their minimum investment requirement usually is small.
- They are diversified, because they invest in many securities.
- They have professional management.
- They are easy to purchase and redeem.
- They allow you to automatically reinvest your dividends and capital gains to build your investment more rapidly.
- They have a performance record, which allows you to compare many funds before picking one.

Playing the Mutual Funds

Mutual funds offer a variety of choices varying in risk. The riskier options offer the greatest potential gains, but also are the most volatile.

Low Risk					High Risk
Money Market	Fixed Income	Balanced	Growth & Income	Growth	Aggressive Growth

Selection: Money market
Objective: Liquidity, preservation of capital
Means: Bank accounts, short-term debt securities
Potential gain: None

Selection: Fixed income
Objective: Stability
Means: Corporate, municipal and Treasury bonds
Potential gain: Low

Selection: Balanced
Objective: Income and long-term growth
Means: A mix of bonds and stocks that pay high dividends but offer little appreciation in price
Potential gain: Low to moderate

Selection: Growth and income
Objective: Price appreciation and income
Means: Stocks that offer consistent dividend payments and steady but not outstanding appreciation in price
Potential gain: Moderate

Selection: Growth
Objective: Long-term price appreciation
Means: Stocks of established companies that reinvest profits in the business
Potential gain: Moderate to high

Selection: Aggressive growth
Objective: Maximum capital gains
Means: Investments in stocks of fledgling companies and new industries
Potential gain: High

• They often are inexpensive; many have no up front commissions and low annual fees.

Unfortunately, as mutual funds have proliferated, investing in them has become more confusing. Too many people just grab the hot mutual fund of the

Fundamentals

Annual rankings of mutual funds published by major magazines this year:

Consumer Reports	**May**
Business Week	**February 15**
Forbes	**August 30**
Kiplinger's	**September**
Money	**February**

Offerings from trade groups and associations:

• *The Individual Investor's Guide to Low-Load Mutual Funds,* by the American Association of Individual Investors, an independent, nonprofit group. Cost: $24.95 for non-members. A quarterly report costs another $30 a year; call 800-428-2244 or write to AAII at 625 North Michigan Ave. Suite 1900, Chicago IL 60611.

• *Directory of Mutual Funds,* by the Investment Company Institute, the main industry trade group. It covers basics of mutual fund investing and services, and lists major fund names, objectives, addresses and toll-free phone numbers. Cost: $8.50, and on request you can get a free booklet on the pitfalls of bond fund investing. Send a check to The Investment Company Institute, P.O. Box 27850, Washington, DC 20038–7850.

• *The Investor's Guide to Low-Cost Mutual Funds,* by the Mutual Fund Educational Alliance, a trade group promoting funds that don't use brokers. Cost: $7. To order, send a check or money order to the alliance at 1900 Erie St., Suite 120, Kansas City, MO 64116.

month, experts say. They don't consider how much the funds really charge—good times can hide an enormous commission—or how the fund achieved its hot ranking—was it through consistent management or one lucky bet?

"People may spend three weeks finding the right toaster," Schmidt says. "They read *Consumer Reports.* They shop around for sales. They look for the best value for their money. Yet when it comes to mutual funds, they will see an ad for a fund that is up 17 percent. They'll call for a prospectus and without reading it, they'll send in a check."

As the investment climate changes, investors will need to be more discerning, financial planners say. With rising interest rates and a volatile stock market, the quality of the management of your fund has become more important.

Before you invest in a mutual fund, you need to evaluate your goals. Are you saving for your child's college education, for your retirement, or to buy a home? Is there a chance you will need to redeem your mutual fund investment in a year or two? Or are you able to hold onto your investment for at least five years?

If you are saving for a down payment on a home or some other short-term goal, you should not invest in stock or bond mutual funds, experts say. The only

No-Brainers

If you can't decide which funds to pick or how to divide up your money, try these:

Index Funds: They are designed to duplicate the performance of a particular market index, such as the Standard & Poor's 500, an index of 500 industrial stocks. They are often low-cost funds, since little management is needed.

Fund of Funds: These spread your money among various mutual funds. Big mutual fund families pitch them to investors who don't have the experience or the inclination to pick the individual funds themselves.

Balanced Funds: They generally split their portfolio into 60 percent stocks and 40 percent bonds. The bonds are supposed to help offset problems in the stock market and vice versa; considered less volatile than straight stock funds.

Asset Allocation Funds: Similar to balanced funds except they split the money in no particular ratio. The fund manager tries to anticipate market changes and is free to put as much as 100 percent of the fund's assets in one type of securities.

mutual fund that might be appropriate is money market funds, they say. These funds generally invest in Treasury bills, certificates of deposit and other highly liquid investments.

Ideally, you should decide on an amount of money you can invest for the long term, and divide it among several mutual funds with different types of investments so that your portfolio is diversified. The proportion of your portfolio that you put at risk will depend on your goals, age and tolerance for risk.

Most funds require minimum investments of between $1,000 and $3,000, but there are ways around this. The majority have lower minimum investment requirements for IRA accounts and trust accounts for children. Vanguard has a balanced fund, the Star Fund, that requires only $500 to start so that first-time investors can participate.

Most funds today also offer automatic investment plans that allow you to have as little as $50 a month deducted from a bank account or from your paycheck and invested in a fund of your choice. Many financial experts recommend these programs because they help you become disciplined about saving money. And they give you the protection that comes with investing at regular intervals. That way, you aren't as vulnerable to the ups and downs of the market.

And there are bound to be downs, so remember—you're in it for the long term. Experts say you have a better chance of recovering from them if you hold on to your investment, but it may take years.

Once a decline starts, you should ride it out, says John Markese, president of the American Association of Individual Investors. What's more, he adds, be prepared to plunge back in: "What makes it palatable is to understand that a decline is a buying opportunity. You should continue to invest and accumulate more stock at lower prices."

Investing in Mutual Funds

Choosing a Good One
Involves More Than You Think

BRUCE DAVIS, who works for the enforcement division of the New York Stock Exchange, says he decided to invest in Fidelity's Contrafund after he read a column about it in *GQ* magazine. "I've done well with it," he said when he stopped by a Fidelity office in downtown Manhattan.

Other people are more systematic shoppers. William Martin, who works for a Wall Street brokerage firm, says he regularly reads *Money* magazine and *Kiplinger's Personal Finance* magazine, keeping an eye out for high-performance funds to invest in. "I look at returns over a five- and 10-year period," he says.

Still others pay firms like the one where Martin works to select mutual funds for them.

With thousands of funds to choose from, the task of finding the best for your needs can seem overwhelming. But it need not be if you follow some general guidelines.

Experts say that when you pick a fund, you should consider cost, performance and service. Beyond that, you need to know how to monitor the performance of your funds and how to keep records for tax purposes.

To get started, you must choose between load and no-load funds. This decision boils down to how confident you are at making your own investment decisions. Generally speaking, load funds are sold by brokerage firms, banks, insurance companies and some financial planners who charge a sales commission, called a load, in return for their advice. The load is a percentage that comes off the top of your investment and therefore lowers your return.

Many consumer advocates favor no-load funds, noting that brokers might push high-commission funds that don't perform as well as some no-load funds. Yet some novice investors may be better off paying a small commission if a broker can save them the legwork and come up with a top-performing fund.

"A load might make sense for the reluctant investors who are just coming to mutual funds from bank CDs," says Don Phillips, publisher of *Morningstar Mutual Funds* newsletter. "They are often less enthusiastic about investing and need help making decisions."

If you prefer a no-load fund, then you must do your own research and invest directly with the mutual fund company.

Your first priority, experts say, is to find mutual funds with above-average returns. Many financial publications annually rank mutual funds, and you may be able to find such magazines at your local library.

Find the category that matches your needs, such as growth funds or income funds. "Compare a fund on a quarter-to-quarter and year-to-year basis to its peer group," says John Markese, president of the American Association of Individual Investors. "Look for consistency over time. Ideally, this means you should look at a fund's record over a five to 10-year period so that you can see how it has performed in both good and bad times." Markese says to avoid new funds unless the manager has an exceptional reputation.

After you've found several good performers, send for their prospectuses. These statements will tell you about each fund's objectives and performance.

They also will list the fund's annual expenses. Here you'll learn that even the no-load funds aren't free; the managers and their expenses have to get paid, and this is how they collect from you.

The prospectus will tell you whether a fund has an up-front load or a deferred load—sometimes called a back-end load or exit fee—which is charged when you redeem your investment. Typically these fees start at 5 percent in the first year and decline each year by 1 percent, so there is no fee if you hold the investment for more than five years.

All funds charge an annual management fee, which they do by deducting a percentage of your assets. But there are a host of other potential expenses you should be aware of.

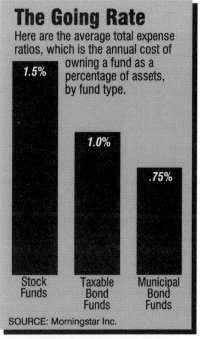

The Going Rate

Here are the average total expense ratios, which is the annual cost of owning a fund as a percentage of assets, by fund type.

1.5%

1.0%

.75%

Stock Funds

Taxable Bond Funds

Municipal Bond Funds

SOURCE: Morningstar Inc.

Some funds charge a fee to reinvest dividends. Others charge you to switch from one fund to another in the same family of funds. And many now charge annual 12b-1 fees, another percentage of your assets which the fund uses to pay for its own advertising and distribution of literature. These annual charges can actually be more onerous than an up-front load if you hold a fund for many years.

To compare the cost of different funds, look in the prospectus for the total fund operating expenses. This expense ratio shows what proportion of the fund's assets goes to pay for expenses, excluding up-front loads. Every prospectus also will give a hypothetical example of what you would pay in expenses on a $1,000 investment, assuming a 5 percent annual return.

You may be tempted to ignore the expenses if a fund is a top performer. But

Fees, Please

Here's the range of mutual fund fees charged. Ask lots of questions if your fund seems to always be at the high end.

Front-end load. A sales commission charged at the time of purchase, usually 1% to 3% of your investment. Some funds range as high as 8.5%.

Back-end load. A commission charged when you sell your shares of the fund. Range is from 0.5% to 6.0%.

Redemption fee. Also a commission of 1% to 2% charged when you sell your shares of the fund, but the fee is often waived if you hold your shares for a specified number of years.

12b-1 fee. An annual charge ranging from 0.1% to 1.25% of the fund's assets to pay for advertising. Since this is charged each year it can be more costly than load charges.

Management fee. A fee of 0.2% to 1.6% of fund assets charged each year for managing the fund.

Other expenses. Administrative and other expenses amounting to an annual fee of 0.2% to 1.0% of fund assets.

Total expense ratio. Allows you to compare the annual cost of various funds and is disclosed in the prospectus. (This excludes one-time load charges.) The ratio is calculated by dividing the value of the fund's assets by the total annual expenses charged to you. The higher the ratio, the more costly the fund.

SOURCE: American Association of Individual Investors; *Mutual Fund Fact Book; Money* magazine

Phillips says it is important to keep track of fund costs. In the 1980s, expenses rose rapidly. Although they have begun to ease, he says that if the market begins to decline, cost will eat up a greater percentage of an investment.

Next, you should consider what services a fund has to offer. Some offer lower minimum investments than others, which is important if your nest egg or the amount you save each week isn't very large. Many families of funds make it easy to switch from one fund to another at no extra charge. Others have 24-hour phone service to allow you to conduct transactions at any time. Some allow you to write checks, and a few offer detailed end-of-the-year statements to help you keep track of all your transactions for tax purposes.

When you've finally picked a fund, don't rush to send in your check. First find out when it makes its annual capital gains distribution. This usually occurs near the end of the year. Lewis Altfest, a financial planner, cautions against investing right before such a payment because, under the quirky tax rules that govern mutual funds, you'll get clobbered with a taxable gain before your investment begins earning any money.

As soon as you've invested in a fund, set up a file of your statements for your

---

The Bottom Line

Here's how to calculate the total return on your mutual fund.

Multiply the number of shares you own by the current net asset value per share (the price per share). Then subtract your original investment from the result. Add any capital gains or dividend/interest distributions paid that were not reinvested. Divide that total by the original investment and multiply it by 100 to convert the decimal answer to a percentage.

For example: Assume that two years ago you paid $5,000 to buy 100 shares of a mutual fund. The current net asset value of each share is $6.50, so your shares are now worth $6,500. Also, suppose that you were paid $500 in distributions (which you did not reinvest) over that two-year period. Your total return consists of the $1,500 increase in the share value plus $500 in distributions for a total of $2,000. Dividing by $5,000, you get 0.4. Multiplying that by 100 results in a total return of 40 percent for the two-year period.

SOURCE: The Mutual Fund Education Alliance

---

tax records, and keep them until well after the account is closed. If you're sloppy, you could pay unnecessary taxes.

Don't be complacent about your investment. Monitor its performance quarterly, comparing its returns with funds in the same category. If your fund dips below average in one quarter, don't automatically jump ship, Markese says. You should expect such things, especially in stock funds.

So when should you sell? Markese says you should think about it when your fund has four consecutive quarters of below-average returns. Phillips says you might want to switch if a new manager comes in and the fund changes its philosophy. That might become apparent if a relatively conservative stock fund suddenly changes many of the stocks in its portfolio.

Another reason to switch funds is if your goals have changed. Say, for example, you are suddenly laid off and need to tap into some of your long-term savings. "Investments are a means to a goal," Phillips says. "You might be saving for a college education or retirement. Your investment choices should depend on where you are in achieving those goals."

Study the Fine Print

Read the Prospectus, Read the
Prospectus and Read the Prospectus

THE FIRST THING an investor must do before buying shares in a mutual fund is to order a prospectus. Unfortunately, the last thing many investors are likely to do is to sit down and read it.

It's no wonder. Prospectuses are often packed with industry jargon about covered call options and forward foreign currency exchange contracts.

But don't be put off. It is in your interest to figure out how to read a prospectus. Sure, magazine articles or reports by mutual fund rating companies might be easier to understand. But that information might not be complete and there is no guarantee it is accurate.

The prospectus, on the other hand, is a legal document. It must be accurate, and it must detail certain key facts you need to know.

For example, if you don't read the prospectus, you may not realize that a fund has certain limitations on its check-writing privileges. Or that your fund charges a fee to reinvest dividends. In either case, you would have no one to blame but yourself for not being informed.

Fortunately, you don't need a degree in finance to read a mutual fund prospectus, if you know what to look for.

Before you dive in, check to see that you have the most recent copy. And then make sure you can afford the minimum investment required by the fund. There's no reason to go forward if you haven't done these two things, says Michelle Smith, managing director of the Mutual Fund Education Alliance, an industry trade group.

Then you should look for the fund's goal and investment strategy. Usually the prospectus will contain a brief summary statement in the front. For example, it may say that the goal of the fund is capital appreciation, and the strategy is to invest in common stock of U.S. and foreign companies of all sizes. If you are primarily seeking dividend income, this is not the fund for you.

Every prospectus will contain a uniform table of expenses, which is also in the first few pages. This is a great help, because in recent years there has been a proliferation of fees and different ways to shuffle fund costs, says Don Phillips, publisher of Morningstar Mutual Fund newsletter. This makes it easy to get a grip on the fees and to compare different funds.

The prospectus will also give you a hypothetical example of what you would pay in fees, assuming you invested $1,000 in a fund that earned 5 percent a year. This is particularly helpful in illustrating how different combinations of expenses will cut into your investment.

Next you should check the standard table of financial performance. If you are looking for a simple statement of total annual return, you won't find it here. Instead, the table will tell you the value of a share, called net asset value, over time. What's important here is the trend. Conservative investors, for example, will want to avoid funds with very volatile net asset values. If they have to sell one day, they don't want to do it during one of those downdrafts.

Several lines are also devoted to the distributions paid by the fund. This will give you an idea of what kind of dividend and capital gains payments the fund has made in the past. Remember, this is historical information and not a guarantee of what will happen in the future, says Stanley Altmark, a financial planner at Joel Isaacson & Co.

Prospectuses printed after July 1993, have to include a 10-year comparison of a fund's performance to a market average. This is very helpful because a fund may sound less attractive after you compare it to a benchmark. If it constantly underperforms the average, you'll want to look for another fund.

> **Prospecting**
>
> A checklist of what to look for in a prospectus:
>
> • Minimum amount required to open an account
> • The investment goal of the fund
> • The fees
> • The past performance
> • The risk
> • How to purchase and redeem shares
> • What services are offered

You may be impressed with a fund's high return, but before you invest, be sure you understand its risks. In discussing its investment strategy, the prospectus will describe the principal risks associated with investing in the fund, as well as in the general fund category. If you're considering a biotechnology fund, the prospectus should point out that sector funds, which specialize in one type of stock, are not very diversified and can suffer sudden losses if the industry falls out of favor.

If you like what you've seen so far, then you should look for the nuts-and-bolts information about how to buy and redeem shares. Find out if the fund offers an automatic investment plan, check its distribution options, and read the section on how your investment will be taxed. Be sure to check what rules and restrictions apply.

Unless a fund is managed by a group of people, the prospectus must tell you the fund manager's name and information about his or her background and tenure at the fund. If, for example, you learn that a fund with a great track record recently hired a new manager, you might want to reconsider your purchase.

"It would be unthinkable for a fund manager to buy stock in IBM without knowing the name of the company's chief executive officer," Phillips says. "So this is very important information for investors."

How to Read A Mutual Fund Table

After you've read the prospectus and bought your fund, you'll want to keep track of its performance. The daily charts vary from newspaper to newspaper, with some offering basic price movements and others, such as the *Wall Street Journal,* rotating the kind of information they offer from day to day. A typical listing:

Part I

1. Funds are listed alphabetically by fund company with individual funds listed under each company heading.

2. Some newspapers list the investment objective: This is a category based on the fund's investment goals. Look for an explanation of what each category abbreviation stands for.

3. NAV: Net Asset Value shows how much each share in a fund is worth. It is the value of the securities in the portfolio divided by the number of its shares. Data is provided by the National Association of Securities Dealers.

4. Offer Price: The amount you would pay to purchase a share in the fund. It is the NAV plus any sales commission. NL means it is a no-load fund and you would pay the same amount as the NAV.

5. NAV Chg: Gain or loss in NAV based on previous trading day.

Part II

6. Total Return: A performance calculation that assumes dividends and capital gains distributions are reinvested. It does not factor in sales commissions. Data are provided by an independent rating service.

Total return may be calculated for various time periods, such as year-to-date, four weeks, 39 weeks, one year or five years. Some publications rotate data so that the five-year return, for example, is always listed on one day of the week. NS means the fund did not exist at the start of the period.

7. R: Some newspapers, including the Journal, assign a rank, based on fund performance within its category (during the longest time period listed on that day). In this case, A = top 20 percent, B = next 20 percent, and so forth.

Optional data: Some publications also list risk ratings, expense ratios, maximum sales charge.

Part III

Footnotes: The mutual fund listing will contain a number of footnotes. Some refer to different types of fees a fund may charge, such as:

r: The fund charges a redemption fee

p: The fund charges a 12b-1 fee*

t: The fund charges both a redemption fee and a 12b-1 fee

Check your newspaper for an explanation of its footnotes.

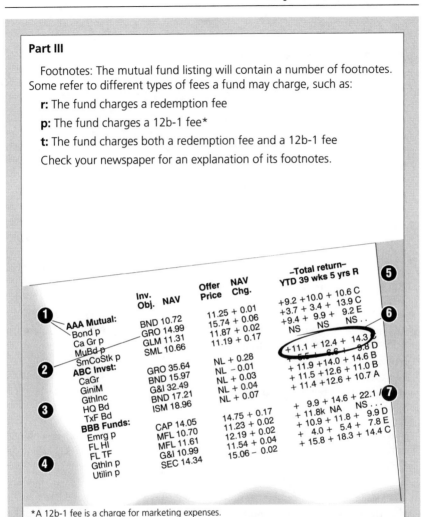

*A 12b-1 fee is a charge for marketing expenses.

In addition to changes mandated by regulators, some fund companies, such as Fidelity Investments, are taking the initiative to make their prospectuses easier to read. Such efforts, in and of themselves, are not a reason to invest in a fund. However, Phillips says the way a fund communicates with investors is important because it indicates whether the shareholder is just an afterthought.

You can find out even more about a fund from its annual report and statement of additional information. And for an independent appraisal, check to see if your library carries any reports from rating agencies, such as Morningstar.

It's Quiz Time
Sharpen Your No. 2 Pencils and Get to Work

Are you on your way to fiscal fitness? In the past 16 chapters, we have covered some of the basics of record keeping and budgeting, banking and using credit cards, drawing up a financial plan and selecting the right investments. Now, before we tackle new subjects, test yourself on some of the principles you've read about.

Part I

What would you do in the following situations?

1. A newly married couple is saving for a down payment on a home, which they plan to buy within five years. Which of the following would be an appropriate place to invest their savings?
A) Stock mutual fund
B) Individual stocks
C) Long-term bond mutual fund
D) Money market mutual fund

2. A young, single Wall Street broker wants to start planning for retirement. The majority of the broker's retirement portfolio should be invested in which of the following?
A) Municipal bond mutual fund
B) Domestic and international stock mutual funds
C) Money market mutual fund
D) None of the above

3. A 63-year-old businessman wants to shift some of his savings into a relatively safe investment that will provide him with income for his retirement and beat inflation. Which would be most appropriate?
A) Bank certificate of deposit
B) Bond mutual fund
C) Growth stock fund
D) Money market mutual fund

4. A young publishing executive wants to invest in mutual funds but doesn't have enough money to spread out among a number of different funds in order to

Portfolio Pie

Draw your own pie chart, based on your age and financial situation. Divide your assets among the following categories, in percentages. Remember it all has to add up to 100 percent.

Cash

Bonds

Large-company stocks

Small-company stocks

International stocks

Now compare your results with some suggested breakdowns on the next page.

SOURCE: American Association of Individual Investors, Chicago.

have a diversified portfolio. Which of the following would be an appropriate alternative?
A) Growth and income fund
B) Asset allocation fund
C) Municipal bond mutual fund
D) Global stock fund

5. A 40-year-old office manager can't stomach the idea of putting her hard-earned savings at risk. Which of the following will guarantee her principal investment?
A) Short-term bond mutual fund
B) Municipal bond mutual fund
C) Bank certificate of deposit
D) GNMA mutual fund
E) All of the above

Part II. True/False

1. Passports should be stored in your safe deposit box.
2. You should maintain an emergency fund equal to three to six months' worth of your salary, which should be kept in a liquid, easily accessible account.
3. If you calculate the impact of inflation, fees and taxes, you may be losing money by keeping your savings in a low-rate bank account.
4. Mutual funds sold by banks are federally insured.

5. If your bank fails and is acquired by another bank, the acquiring institution can arbitrarily lower the interest rate on your certificate of deposit.

6. In general, the higher the return of an investment, the greater the risk that you could lose money.

7. If you invest in a stock mutual fund right before it makes its capital gains distribution, you stand to make an immediate windfall.

Part III. Multiple Choice

1. If you are weighed down by credit card debt, you should:
A) Consolidate all your credit card balances on one low-interest card, if possible.
B) Consider cutting up all your cards and paying for purchases by cash and check.
C) Pay more than the minimum payment.
D) All of the above.

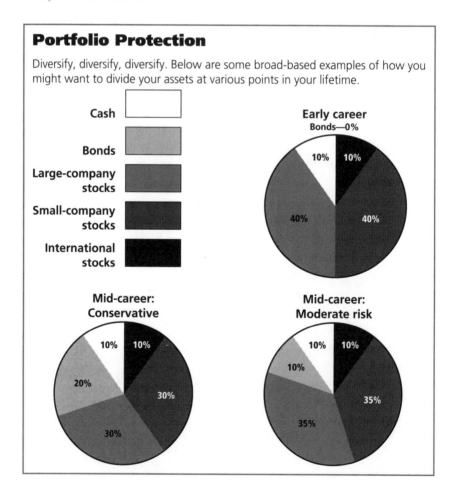

Portfolio Protection

Diversify, diversify, diversify. Below are some broad-based examples of how you might want to divide your assets at various points in your lifetime.

Cash

Bonds

Large-company stocks

Small-company stocks

International stocks

Early career
Bonds—0%
10%   10%
40%   40%

Mid-career: Conservative
10%   10%
20%
30%
30%

Mid-career: Moderate risk
10%   10%
10%
35%
35%

2. What is dollar-cost averaging?

A) A new way to calculate the return on your mutual-fund investment.

B) A plan for making regular investments so that if you are investing in both good times and bad, any losses you incur will average out.

C) A way to calculate whether, on average, your investment is beating inflation.

D) None of the above.

3. If you own a bond and plan to hold it to maturity, which is the best measure of its projected return?

A) Current yield

B) Yield to maturity

C) Coupon rate

D) None of the above.

4. If a bond has a call provision it means that:

A) After a certain number of years—usually 10—the issuer can reduce the coupon rate.

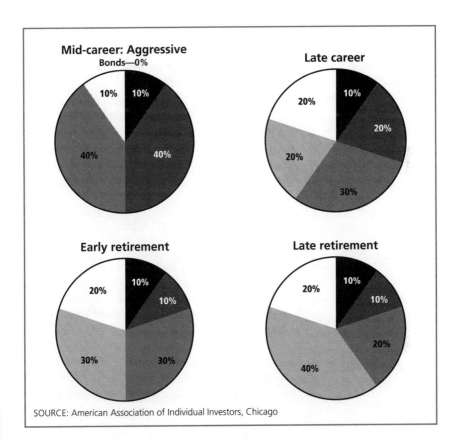

SOURCE: American Association of Individual Investors, Chicago

B) After a certain number of years—usually 10—the issuer can redeem the bonds even though the bond hasn't matured yet.

C) Either of the above.

D) None of the above.

5. Which best describes a growth stock?

A) Stock in a new company.

B) Stock in a company that is reinvesting profits for growth rather than paying dividends.

C) Stock in a company that has recently acquired another company.

D) None of the above.

Part IV

Match the number with the letter

1. Index fund	A) Change in the cost of living
2. Bear market	B) Exit fee
3. General obligation bonds	C) New York Stock Exchange
4. Zero coupon bonds	D) A mix of stocks and bonds
5. Big Board	E) A mix of bank accounts and high
6. Balanced fund	quality, short-term bonds
7. Back-end load	F) Pay steady dividends
8. Income stocks	G) Falling market
9. Inflation	H) Backed by faith and credit of local
10. Money market fund	government issuing them.
	I) Make no dividend payments
	J) Designed to duplicate the S&P 500
	or other market standard

ANSWERS

Part I

1. D) A money market mutual fund is the only one of the four choices that is safe and liquid, allowing you to withdraw your money at any time without penalty. Stocks are a volatile investment, especially in the short run. Bond mutual funds, though less volatile, also fluctuate in value depending on interest rates. So if you suddenly find the home of your dreams, you don't want to be stuck selling your stocks or bonds at a loss.

2. B) Experts say that when you are young and are saving money for a long-term goal, such as retirement, you should invest heavily in stocks or stock mutual funds. The reason is that stocks tend to have a higher return over time than other investments. Despite their volatility, you have a better chance of recovering from any downturns in the market or bad stock picks if you start investing at a young age.

3. B) Bond mutual funds have lower returns than stocks, yet they usually outperform money market funds and bank CDs. They are relatively safe, and can provide a steady source of income. Experts often advise people who are about to retire and will need to live on their investment income to consider bond funds.

4. B) An asset allocation fund is designed to do the job of diversifying for you by investing in both stocks and bonds. Other funds that do the diversifying for you are balanced funds and fund of funds, which spread your money among various mutual funds.

5. C) The only choice that comes with any guarantee is a bank certificate of deposit, which is insured by the Federal Deposit Insurance Corp. Some people mistakenly believe that investments in Government National Mortgage Association funds are guaranteed by the federal government. The government backs the mortgages that the funds hold as assets—but the market value of the mortgages may change, so the value of your investment may also change.

Part II. True/False

1. False. People who store their passports in their safe deposit box and suddenly need to travel abroad on a weekend will find themselves in a pickle if their bank is not open.

2. True. This money should be reserved for emergencies, and not used to pay for an impulse purchase. It should not be invested anywhere that would put the money at risk.

3. True. As banks add transaction fees and increase minimum deposit requirements, you need to be sure you're not paying the bank to keep your money.

4. False. Mutual funds are never insured by the FDIC. Banks are increasingly getting into the investment business, so when in doubt about a product they are pitching, ask if it is FDIC-insured. If they say it is, get it in writing.

5. True. As cruel as it may seem, acquiring banks are allowed to lower the rate on your CDs.

6. True, in other words, if it seems too good to be true, it probably is. You usually don't get a fantastic return on an investment without taking some added risk.

7. False. The opposite is true. If you invest right before a fund makes a capital gains distribution, you will receive a payment. That sounds good, but it cuts the value of your original investment—and even if you choose to reinvest the capital gains payment, you pay taxes on it.

Part III. Multiple Choice

1. D) These and other strategies can help you get off the treadmill of credit card debt.

2. B) Few people can figure out the best time to invest in the market. But if you are investing the same amount of money at regular intervals, you don't need a crystal ball because your gains and losses should average out.

3. B) Yield to maturity will tell you what to expect if you hold the bond to maturity. But if a bond has a call provision (see next question), you also want to look at the yield to call so you know what the return would be if the issuer calls the bond.

4. B) Municipal bonds frequently have call provisions that allow the locality to redeem the bonds after 10 years. They will usually do this if rates have gone down since the bonds were first issued.

5. B) Growth mutual funds, for example, seek out companies that are using their profits to help fuel growth. These have capital appreciation instead of dividends.

Part IV. Matching

1-J; 2-G; 3-H; 4-I; 5-C; 6-D; 7-B; 8-F; 9-A; 10-E

The Basics

• If you still need more help on how to manage your money, consider buying a copy of *Money Management Basics* by Howard Sutton and the editors of Consumer Reports Books. Published by an arm of Consumer's Union in Yonkers, N.Y., it includes many helpful worksheets. It costs $14.95; to order a copy call 800-272-0722.

So You Want a Loan, Huh?

If You Need Money, Make Sure You Can Pay It Back

For MANY PEOPLE, borrowing money is a fact of life; they couldn't go to school or buy a car or furnish a home without a loan. But for too many of them, borrowing has become a way of life.

Some people see borrowing money as a rite of passage to adulthood, says Paul Richards, vice president of the National Center for Financial Education, a non-profit group based in San Diego. But it also can be a passage into serious debt.

Richards speaks from experience. When he was 17, his father cosigned his first loan to buy a car. After that, his debts mounted steadily until he filed for bankruptcy eight years later. Today Richards owns no credit cards and teaches other people how to avoid getting hooked on credit. The key is to make yourself an informed borrower.

It may seem obvious, but before you even bother filling out a loan application, be sure you can really make the loan payments.

It's not as simple as it sounds. Bob Lovinger, president of the Debt and Credit Center in Long Island, N.Y., says you should start with an objective analysis of your monthly income and expenses. He stresses the word objective because many people simply list their major bills and ignore what they spend on out-of-pocket expenses, such as movies, newspapers, and takeout food. But the little things add up, and many times they put you over the edge, he says.

Maybe you can afford the loan. But you still should ask yourself if it's a wise idea. Richards says you should never go into debt for anything that will lose value before the loan is repaid. Take new cars, for example: Three years into a five-year loan, it's possible to owe more than a car is worth.

Likewise, it makes no sense to put a restaurant meal on a credit card unless you intend to pay the bill in full when it comes. Otherwise you'll be paying interest on the meal for months after you ate it.

On a practical level, however, you probably can't pay cash for a new car or a college loan. So if you need to borrow, consider all your options. Financial consultant Ann Diamond recommends making a list of potential lenders. Among the options:

• **Your relatives.** Lots of times, they will be more flexible than a bank, Diamond says. But if you're the one doing the lending, she cautions, be sure to charge interest; otherwise there's little incentive for the borrower to pay you

Advice for Loanlyhearts

If you've never had a loan and need one now, you may get the cold shoulder from lenders. That's because they usually want proof that you've borrowed and paid back money before—a real problem if this is your first loan. If that sounds like a Catch-22, well, it is. Here's how to build up a credit record and break out of the cycle:

• Open a checking account and savings account. They prove you have money and know how to manage it. Canceled checks can be used to show you pay utility bills or rent regularly, a sign of reliability.

• Apply for a department store credit card, and pay up on time.

• Find a bank that will give you a secured credit card, in which you agree to deposit money as collateral.

• If you're new in town, write for a summary of any credit record kept by a credit bureau in your former town. Ask the bank or department store in your old hometown for the name of the agency it reports to.

• If you don't qualify on the basis of your own credit standing, offer to have someone cosign your application.

• If you're turned down, find out why and try to clear up any misunderstandings. You're entitled to contest wrong information and insert explanations into the record.

SOURCE: Federal Reserve

back in a timely way. And watch out: In some circumstances if you lend money to relatives, the IRS may dun you for taxes.

• **Your employer.** Diamond notes that some companies offer emergency loans to workers. More frequently, companies allow employees to borrow from their 401(k) retirement account. There are limits on how much you can borrow and how quickly it must be repaid, but the interest you pay goes back into your own retirement account.

• **Your home.** It may make sense to borrow against the equity in your home because the rate is often lower and the interest is almost always tax deductible. Be aware, however, that if you fail to pay, you could lose your home.

• **Your credit union.** Experts say that among different types of lenders, you will probably get the best deal from a credit union. They are nonprofit organizations, owned by their members, and so loan rates are usually lower than at banks. And they're more apt to bend the rules because they know their members, says Gail Lieberman, editor of *Bank Rate Monitor,* an industry newsletter.

After credit unions, try the banks and savings and loans in your area. If you have no alternative, you may have to go to a finance company. But, experts warn, they usually charge the highest rates.

A Borrower's Checklist

Things to find out before you sign for a loan or buy on credit. Remember, get it in writing and read the contract.

☐ What will the loan or credit actually cost in dollars and cents?

☐ What penalties are imposed for late payment?

☐ What other charges may be imposed?

☐ Are interest charges and insurance premiums refunded if you pay off the loan early?

☐ Do you get a notice before repossession? Can charges for repossession be assessed against your account?

☐ Understand exactly what security or collateral you are giving the lender to secure your loan or credit. Determine if it includes other merchandise you may have bought earlier.

☐ Does your creditor have the right to deduct money from your wages?

☐ Do not sign away your legal rights, or waive certain defenses under collection or foreclosure proceedings.

☐ Question all insurance charges. Some are strictly for the benefit of the dealer or lending institution and are not required by law.

☐ Determine exactly what insurance you are buying and what it covers. Get it in writing.

☐ Make certain all the figures are listed correctly on the contract.

☐ Do not leave any blank spaces. Draw a line through those blanks that do not apply.

☐ Make certain that you will receive a monthly statement, invoice or coupon book to send in with your payment.

SOURCE: NCFE's Home Study Course in Personal Finance

When it comes to actually applying for a loan, don't let banks and financial institutions intimidate you. Remember, it's a business transaction, and they're not doing you a favor. So, be prepared to shop around for the best rates.

"It always pays to haggle," Liberman says. "Banks have a lot of discretion." Sometimes, for example, a bank will give you a better rate if you open an account there.

Once you've agreed on a rate, get everything in writing and carefully examine the terms of the loan. Don't look just at the interest rate, which is referred to as the annual percentage rate or APR. Ask about any fees and service charges, and whether you will be penalized for paying off the loan early.

Also consider the length of the loan and what the total cost will be when it's all paid off. The longer the loan, the more you will pay in interest. You might be surprised to find out that you're paying $12,000 for an $8,000 car, Richards says.

Being a smart borrower also means anticipating the standards you will have to meet to be approved. Most lenders will look for the three C's:

• **Character** is an assessment of how reliable you are. In other words, are you a stable member of the community? Do you have good credit references to show that you pay your rent and utility bills on time? You'll look bad if you change jobs a lot, constantly move from place to place, or often pay bills late.

• **Capacity** refers to your ability to pay back the loan. Banks have specific formulas; they usually say that no more than 20 percent of your income should go to pay for consumer debts other than a mortgage.

• **Collateral** is something the lender can take from you if you don't pay up. In the case of an auto loan, it's the car. Banks don't like to give out unsecured personal loans because there is no collateral. They are reserved for the cream of the crop, Lovinger says.

Banks also will order a copy of your credit report. They want to see a record of how you repay your debts. Sometimes having no credit history is as bad as having a record of late payments, experts say.

Finally, know your rights under the law. Despite all the personal detail they ask for, banks cannot discriminate simply on the basis of sex, race or age. And they cannot hold up your application on those grounds. They must notify you within 30 days after you have applied whether your loan has been approved. If credit is denied, they must say why, in writing.

Bright Ideas

• **FYI:** If you want more information on your rights as a borrower, write to the Federal Reserve and ask for a free copy of the pamphlet *Consumer Handbook to Credit Protection Laws.* The address is: Publications Services, Division of Support Services, Board of Governors of the Federal Reserve System, Washington D.C. 20551

Romantic? No, But . . .

*Financial Planning Helps Keep You
Together after Honeymoon's Over*

Pᴇᴏᴘʟᴇ ᴀssᴏᴄɪᴀᴛᴇ ᴍᴀɴʏ ᴛʜɪɴɢs with love and romance, but financial planning is not usually one of them. Yet a little time spent on basic money matters can go a long way toward building a lasting relationship.

Consider this: According to a recent Gallup poll, 57 percent of divorced couples said disputes over money were a contributing cause of their breakup, and an additional 10 percent said it was the main cause.

Hopefully, couples talk about finances long before they talk about getting married, says Kathleen Stepp, who teaches a Citibank MasterCard and Visa seminar on money matters for newlyweds. Unfortunately, that's often not the case.

Couples should begin by simply talking about their financial goals. Do they want to buy furniture or a new house? Do they want to go to college or get a graduate degree? Do they eventually want to have children? Do they hope to retire early?

"They need to open the lines of communication," Stepp says. "They don't have to agree on everything. Usually one person is more interested in taking care of the finances. But that doesn't mean one person should make all the decisions."

It's increasingly common for both husband and wife to work. So when it comes to managing day-to-day expenses, couples need to decide whether they will pool their money. "Personally, I would recommend having a joint checking account for household expenses, but keeping separate personal accounts," Stepp says. "Everyone needs some money to call their own."

And it's a good idea for each person to maintain his or her own credit cards. Even nonworking spouses should have credit cards in their own name, experts say. That helps provide a credit record in the event of divorce or death of a partner.

Before tying the knot, couples should also take stock of their debts and credit histories. Does either person have any loans outstanding? Are they weighed down by big credit card bills?

If so, before they start dreaming of a new car and home, they need to develop a plan for paying off the debt. It's not very romantic, but dealing with financial realities before the marriage will help newlyweds get off to a better start.

It's never too soon for couples to begin saving for future goals, and some special programs are designed to help. For example, BankAmerica Mortgage has developed a new twist on a traditional bridal registry. Participating couples ask

Please Pay at the Altar

Thinking about marriage? Well, family values don't come cheap. The IRS won't come bearing gifts, but a hefty annual marriage bill. And the higher your income, the more you'll pay. Here are two examples:

Donald & Marla

As singles, Donald and Marla have a combined income of $74,000, itemized deductions of $6,362 and are entitled to a personal exemption of $2,350 each. As single taxpayers, their combined federal and state tax bill is $15,766.

But as a married couple, they must pay the higher joint income tax rate. Even though their income is the same, their federal and state tax bill now is $17,184.

SOURCE: Grant Thornton

Ted & Jane

As singles, Ted and Jane have a combined income of $318,000 (includes $30,000 in capital gains) and itemized deductions of $18,000. However, their itemized deductions are reduced by a total of $3,034 because each of their adjusted gross incomes exceeds $108,450. The personal exemption allowed is reduced as income increases. Ted and Jane are allowed a total of $2,726. As single taxpayers, their combined federal and state tax bill is $109,353.

As a married couple, their itemized deductions are reduced even more—$6,287—and they are allowed no personal exemptions. This, combined with the higher joint tax rate, results in a tax bill of $118,632.

guests to contribute to a Home Bridal Registry. The program allows them to buy a home with a minimum 5 percent down payment, all of which can come from wedding gifts from friends and relatives.

Because it's hard for couples to say, "Don't give us crystal, give us cash," the mortgage company gives them engraved cards to send to guests, saying that they are registered with BankAmerica for a down payment and explaining how to contribute to the interest-bearing account.

Although some couples prefer an informal approach to finances, an increasing number are choosing prenuptial agreements. These contracts specify how their property will be divided in the event of a divorce. Peter Bienstock, a matrimonial lawyer at the Manhattan law firm of Beigel & Sandler, says prenuptials are most common among couples who are marrying for a second time and have assets and children from their first marriage.

Anyone who stands to inherit a family business may also want a prenuptial pact. Although inheritances are not considered marital property, any increase in the value of a business may be viewed as marital property, says Elliot Samuelson, a matrimonial lawyer and author of *Unmarried Couples: A Guide to Your Legal Rights and Obligations.*

Even young couples without many assets sometimes opt for prenuptials. "There is a good chance the marriage isn't going to last," Samuelson says. "A prenuptial agreement is a good way to avoid divorce court and litigation."

But it also can be a good way to take the romance out of a relationship, especially if one person is imposing a heavy-handed agreement on the other. Bienstock says couples sometimes find they can't go through with the agreement and simply tear it up. It has to be handled with delicacy, because a prenuptial agreement tends to emphasize financial aspects of a relationship at the expense of emotions.

Many newlyweds soon discover marriage can have its financial pitfalls: They may have to pay much more in taxes than they did when they were single. Stuart Kessler, a senior tax partner at Goldstein Golub Kessler & Co, says that high-income couples, in particular, suffer from the marriage tax. When planning a wedding, he says, some people will change the ceremony from December to January in order to avoid the marriage tax penalty for a year.

Of course, higher income taxes are not necessarily a reason to stay single. Ralph Warner, coauthor of *The Living Together Kit,* points out that inheritance tax law favors married couples. That's because the law allows married spouses to leave their estates to each other tax-free.

Couples who do decide to forgo marriage and simply live together have even more reason to carefully plan their finances. Warner says that many people mistakenly assume that if they live together long enough, they are automatically married. In fact, most states, including New York and California, do not recognize common-law marriages. In lieu of a marriage license, couples may need to draw up a living together contract, sometimes called a cohabitation agreement.

Such contracts are a good idea if an unmarried couple purchases a home together. This is especially true, Warner says, if one person contributes more to the down payment or to the mortgage than another. If both people work, but one earns more money than the other, they may want a contract to specify how they will divide their property if they break up.

Contracts are particularly important for gay and lesbian couples because they don't have the option of getting legally married. "If they want to leave property to each other, they will have to draft a will," says Robin Leonard, a lawyer and coauthor of *A Legal Guide for Lesbian and Gay Couples.* "If they want their lover to handle their affairs in case of illness, they will need a durable power of attorney for health care and for finances."

Helpful Publications

• For a free copy of *Money Matters for Newlyweds,* a 24-page booklet sponsored by Citibank, call (800) 967–6777 or send a postcard to: Keeping your Financial Balance, Citibank Processing Center, P.O. Box 17029, Baltimore, Md., 21203–7029.

• Couples who don't take the marriage route may want to order *The Living Together Kit,* available through Nolo Press for $17.95. Nolo Press also publishes *A Legal Guide for Lesbian and Gay Couples,* available for $21.95. Both may be ordered by calling the Berkeley, Calif., publisher at (800) 992–6656.

Home Buyers, Beware
Even in "Buyer's Market" There Are Pitfalls to Skirt

"**A**FFORDABLE DREAM," trumpets a recent real estate ad.

"Great rates. Low payments. A home of your own," boasts another ad.

Although the ads sound alluring, there is no doubt that buying a home can be one of life's most nerve-wracking experiences. Few decisions are as complicated, costly and emotional. And many potential home buyers soon discover that in the world of bankers and brokers, few of those people have the consumer's interest at heart. So the most important rule to remember is Buyer Beware!

"I've been putting myself under tremendous pressure," says Christine Lapidus, owner of a women's apparel manufacturing firm in Manhattan, who worries that interest rates will climb even higher before she finds an apartment she wants to buy. "I finally said I can't keep pressuring myself like this."

In the end, the headaches involved in buying a home usually prove worthwhile. Owning a home provides an emotional and financial base that most Americans want. Here are some basic things to consider before you begin shopping for your dream home.

Start with a reality check on your finances. You can't buy a house or apartment unless you can get a mortgage. And lenders have strict guidelines on how much they will lend, depending on your credit history and income, among other things.

In general, lenders say that no more than 28 percent of your gross monthly income can be spent on housing-related expenses, such as mortgage payments, insurance, taxes or co-op maintenance payments. Another measure banks will look at is your total debt load. As a rule, they don't want your mortgage payments, credit card bills and other consumer debts to exceed 36 percent of your gross monthly income.

Next, you have to determine if you can afford the down payment and closing costs. A down payment typically ranges anywhere between 5 percent and 25 percent of the purchase price. Closing costs can add up to another 7 percent.

Imagine this scenario: You're buying a home for $150,000. The bank wants a 20 percent down payment, and you need another $4,500 for various fees and closing costs.

Then, don't forget to count how much it will cost to move and get settled in your new home. You might want to paint. You'll need new curtains and possibly carpeting. First-time home buyers like to buy new furniture and decorate,

You'd Better Do the Math!

Don't let others tell you how much you can afford to pay for a house. Grab your calculator and figure it out for yourself.

	Your Financial Figures	*Example*
Step 1: Gross monthly income Combined annual incomes of all people listed on the application.	$_____ ÷ 12	$51,816 ÷ 12
Gross monthly income	$_____ (A)	$4,318

Step 2: Affordable monthly PITI
Generally lenders allow you to allocate up to 28 percent of your monthly income to payments, interest, taxes, and insurance (PITI).

Gross monthly income	$_____ (A)	$4,318
	x .28	x .28
Affordable monthly PITI	$_____ (B)	$1,209

Lenders will allow about 33 to 36 percent of your gross income for debts such as your mortgage, credit card, car loans, installment loans, etc.

Gross monthly income	$_____ (A)	$4,318
	x .36	x .36
Affordable monthly PITI with debts Minimum actual debt payments other than for housing. (Example uses monthly car payment of $270 and annual credit card debt of $864, divided by 12.)	$_____ –$_____	$1,554 – $342
Affordable monthly PITI	$_____ (C)	$1,212
Enter the smaller PITI (figure B or C)	$_____ (D)	$1,209

Step 3: Affordable monthly principal and interest

Affordable monthly PITI	$_____ (D)	$1,209
Minus estimated taxes and insurance. (Example uses annual property taxes of $4,000 plus annual insurance of $490, divided by 12.)	–$_____	– $374
Affordable monthly payment for principal and interest	$_____ (E)	$835

Step 4: Maximum amount of mortgage loan
Use the amortization table below to estimate the maximum loan for which you can qualify, based on current interest rates for a fixed-rate mortgage. (Example uses 6.75 percent interest rate on a 30-year fixed mortgage.)

$_____ ÷ Rate and Term factor = $_____
 (E)   (F)

Example: $835 ÷ 6.486 = $128.739

$_____ x 1,000 = $_____
 (F)   (G)

Example: $128.739 x 1,000 = $128,739

Enter the maximum amount for your mortgage $_____ $128,739
                                            (G)

Interest rate	15-year term	30-year term	Interest rate	15-year term	30-year term
3%	6.906	4.216	5%	7.908	5.368
3.25%	7.027	4.352	5.25%	8.039	5.522
3.5%	7.149	4.491	5.5%	8.171	5.678
3.75%	7.272	4.631	5.75%	8.304	5.836
4%	7.397	4.774	6%	8.439	5.996
4.25%	7.523	4.919	6.25%	8.574	6.157
4.5%	7.650	5.067	6.5%	8.711	6.321
4.75%	7.778	5.216	6.75%	8.849	6.486

(continued next page)

	Your Financial Figures	Example
Step 5: Cash available for a down payment		
Available cash and cash gifts	$_____	$29,300
Sale of assets (CDs, stocks, bonds, etc.) +	$_____	+$11,000
Total cash to be raised	$_____	$40,300
Minus closing costs. (Estimate 7 percent of the amount of the mortgage.)	– $_____	– $9,012
Total cash for down payment (5 percent to 25 percent of purchase price for a conventional loan. Example uses 20 percent.)	$_____ (H)	$31,260
Step 6: Maximum purchase price		
Enter down payment	$_____ (H)	$31,260
Add maximum mortgage	+ $_____ (G)	$128,740
Estimate maximum purchase price	$_____	$160,000

This is the maximum home price a lender will allow. However, you may not be comfortable sacrificing your lifestyle (vacation, new car, financing college, etc.) for this maximum payment. You may start with lowering the PITI in Step 4 to your maximum comfortable payment and work from there.

SOURCE: *How to Buy Your First Home* by Peter Jones. Copyright Lee Simmons Associate

which can be very expensive, says Ron Rogé, a financial planner. And if they're buying a home, they'll probably need to landscape.

So, in this case, your cash outlay to buy the house could easily total $40,000.

Even if you believe you can qualify for a mortgage and afford the up-front costs, you need to be sure buying is a better choice than renting. Lewis Altfest, a financial planner, says you should take stock of your plans: Do you hope to switch jobs in a few years? Do you think your company may transfer you to another city in a year or two?

Experts say it usually doesn't make financial sense to buy unless you'll be in the home at least four or five years. If you have to sell before then, your home may not have appreciated enough for you to recover your initial costs.

Most financial experts today say that while a home can be a good financial investment, there is no guarantee you'll make a killing when you finally sell. "It's a matter of supply and demand," Rogé says. "If there's no demand, prices won't appreciate."

In the 1970s and 1980s, there was plenty of demand. Real estate was booming, and just about every house or apartment was along for the ride. Home buyers didn't have to be very discriminating. Now, however, you need to be sure that you're not overpaying for a home by researching average prices in the neighborhood of your choice.

Buying a home still offers you a tax advantage over renting. You can deduct the interest on your mortgage and your property taxes. And don't forget that as you pay off your mortgage, you build equity in your home—something you can borrow against later to help pay for a child's college education or to remodel your home.

By the time you approach retirement, you probably will have paid off your mortgage. So even if you don't stand to make a windfall from selling your home, you will have the security of owning it free and clear.

If you've done your soul searching and budget analysis and decide to pursue buying a home, be sure to order copies of your credit reports right away. You want to find out if old credit problems are still haunting you. And you want to make sure there aren't any mistakes on your credit reports that could hold up your mortgage approval.

"The wife of a friend of mine has a common name," Rogé says. "She found out information from someone else's credit report ended up on hers." The problem took so long to clear up, it delayed the closing on their house.

Begin to familiarize yourself with the terms involved in buying a home or condominium or cooperative apartment. If you are considering buying a co-op you need to understand that you will be purchasing shares in a corporation. So you will have an added hurdle: getting approval from the co-op's board of directors.

If you buy a condo, you are buying an apartment; each condo owner also owns a share of the common areas. A condominium board can't prevent you from buying an apartment. It simply rules on matters related to the operation of the building.

Buying a home can be a scary proposition, so be sure you know who's on your side. Most real estate brokers represent sellers. Even if a broker shows you a lot homes and develops a cozy relationship with you, remember that his or her job is to get the best deal for the seller—not you.

Today, however, there is a new development: buyer's brokers. Although there aren't very many of them, their job is to represent buyers and help negotiate the lowest purchase price.

Buyer's brokers get paid in different ways. Some require a flat fee. Some get paid according to the reduction in list price they are able to negotiate. Still others receive a share of the commission that the seller pays. If you hire a buyer's broker, just be sure you know what the terms are, and get a copy of the form stating that the broker is working for you.

Lapidus decided to retain a buyer's broker, Michelle Barshay in Manhattan, to help her weed through the apartments that are on the market and to save her the trouble of researching the financial condition of apartment buildings. "Usually the broker's No. 1 priority is the seller," Lapidus says. "But Michelle makes me her priority."

When It's Time to Make the Big Move

Flexible Mortgages, Lower Rates Are Making Home Ownership Easier

I N THE PAST, qualifying for a mortgage was a matter of fitting into one-size-fits-all requirements. If you didn't have enough money for a 10 percent down payment or if you didn't have the right kind of credit history, you were out of luck.

But now, new flexible mortgage products make owning a home possible for more people than ever before. If someone is paying high monthly rent, there is practically no reason they can't buy a home, experts say. Maybe not right now, but perhaps in six months or so.

But before you rush out to take advantage of the opportunity, do your homework.

Too often, prospective home buyers don't even think about the mortgage until they've already picked out a house or apartment. "Making a few panicked phone calls after you've found a home can lead to bad mistakes," says Keith Gumbinger, an analyst at HSH Associates, a Butler, N.J., mortgage research firm. "Your real estate agent may say he or she knows a place where you can get a great deal on a mortgage. Maybe it's true. But if you haven't done some research, you take the chance of getting taken advantage of."

As soon as you've calculated how much you can afford to borrow, start researching mortgages. Talk to friends who have recently gone through the mortgage application process. You might want to attend a seminar on home buying; community groups and banks frequently offer them. And there are services that for a fee can help you shop for a mortgage.

When you select a loan, it's important to consider how long you plan to live in the home. For example, if you're buying a home large enough to accommodate an expanding family, you probably want a fixed-rate mortgage. But if you know that in four years you'll be transferred to another state, an adjustable-rate loan may be best suited to your needs.

If you opt for an adjustable-rate mortgage, or ARM, there are a number of features you will need to evaluate:

• The adjustment period. This is the amount of time between changes in the interest rate. Adjustment periods range from six months to five years, but one year is most common.

• The index. This is the benchmark rate that lenders use to set ARM rates. Most ARMs are linked to the one-year Treasury note. The important thing is to be sure the index is not too volatile.

• The margin. This is the percentage that is added to the index rate each time your loan is adjusted. The total of the two is the rate you pay. These days, margins typically range from 2.75 percent to 3 percent.

• The introductory rate. This is the rate you pay for the first period of the ARM. Sometimes lenders offer you a so-called teaser rate, which is arbitrarily set below the rate determined by the index and margin. If you aren't aware you have a teaser rate, you can be in for a shock when the rate is adjusted for the first time.

• Caps. ARM loan agreements should place limits on how much the rate can rise or fall when it's time for an adjustment. One-year ARMs are commonly capped at 2 percent a year and 6 percent over the lifetime of the loan.

During the real estate boom, there were many complicated varieties of mortgages, such as balloon payment loans. Fortunately for consumers, Gumbinger says, plain vanilla mortgages are the rule today.

If, like most home buyers, you decide on a conventional, fixed-rate mortgage, then you need to choose the term. The longer the term, the lower your monthly payment. As a result, thirty-year loans are the most popular. If you can afford the higher payments of a 15-year mortgage, you will save a considerable amount on interest over the life of the loan.

Keep in mind, however, that mortgage interest payments are tax deductible, says Joel Isaacson, a Manhattan financial planner. On balance, some high-income people would prefer a 30-year term because they can invest the money they save from the lower monthly payments and also benefit from the tax deduction.

You also need to consider whether you'd rather pay points up front, or forgo points but pay a higher interest rate. A point is 1 percent of the loan amount and is tax deductible. If the points are added into the loan, they will be reflected in an annual percent rate, or APR, that is higher than the interest rate you are quoted on the loan.

Experts say that each point will add about an eighth of a percent onto the APR, so that a 7 percent loan with two points, for instance, will be equal to a 7.25 percent loan with no points.

When you finally settle on a type of mortgage, the next step is to see what's available. Start by making a list of questions to ask lenders. You need to know about the interest rate, the application costs and points. Be sure to find out if application fees are refundable. And ask about a lender's lock-in agreement, which tells you how long the rate is guaranteed.

Always beware of loans that have penalties for paying off early. And make sure the loan you are considering does not lead to negative amortization—an arrangement that caps your adjustable rate, but makes up for it by increasing the loan size if rates go up.

When shopping around for a mortgage, it's a good idea to check first with the bank or credit union where you normally do business. Robert Heady, publisher of *Bank Rate Monitor* in West Palm Beach, Fla., recommends consulting five to eight lenders in your area. And you should check with a mortgage broker, because they sometimes offer better deals than banks.

If you don't have much money for a down payment or if you've already been turned down for a mortgage, don't give up. There are a number of government loan programs with flexible rules that are offered through many lenders. Be sure to ask if you qualify for them. Some allow down payments as low as 2 percent. Others have discount rates. A new program introduced in 1994 by Fannie Mae, a federally chartered corporation that purchases mortgages from lenders, has more relaxed rules for obtaining co-op loans.

If you're getting a cold shoulder from banks, you may want to take advantage of free loan counseling offered by community groups in many cities. At ACORN, a nonprofit group in New York City, counselors not only teach home buyers about mortgage terms and formulas, but they also shepherd the applicant through the loan process.

"We advocate for them and don't let the application die," says Bertha Lewis, director of ACORN's loan counseling program in New York. What's more, the group has negotiated exclusive contracts with banks that provide borrowers with more flexible terms.

Fight Back!

*Credit Report Errors Can
Cost You Time and Money*

WHEN CELESTE YAZZETTI applied to refinance her mortgage several years ago, she was surprised to learn that she didn't qualify for the bank's 8 percent loan.

The reason? She was a poor credit risk, the lender said. If she wanted a new mortgage, she was told she would have to pay an interest rate of 12 percent.

Yazzetti, the manager of office services for the Consumers Union in Yonkers, was perplexed and angry. "What are you talking about?" she asked. She soon discovered that the source of the problem was a TRW credit report that said she had failed to pay a $220 bill.

In fact, Yazzetti had paid the bill years earlier. She was able to get a letter verifying that fact. But clearing up the error proved to be more difficult than she ever anticipated. As a result, Yazzetti, who lives with her husband and four children, was stuck with the 12 percent loan and years later, the $220 bill still had not been deleted from her credit report.

This is not an isolated case. Between 1989 and 1993, the leading cause of complaints to the Federal Trade Commission was credit bureaus, according to a report by the U.S. Public Interest Research Group. Despite industry promises to reform itself, the report found that the consumers who complain are worse off than ever: In 1993, it took 31 weeks, on average, to clear up a complaint against a credit bureau, up from 23 weeks in 1991. In 1994, Congress considered a bill that would have made credit bureaus legally liable to correct errors within a certain period of time. Despite bipartisan support, the legislation was killed because of a procedural maneuver by one senator. Currently there is no deadline mandated by federal law.

The bill's failure only underscores the importance of keeping track of your credit reports. The stakes are high: A bad credit report can hurt your chances to get a new job or a promotion, to borrow money, to buy life insurance or even to rent an apartment.

A credit report is more than just a description of your credit and debt repayment history. It will list your name, address, Social Security number, and birth date. It may also mention the name of your spouse, your employer, former employers and an indication of whether you own your home or rent. And it may note any lawsuits, judgments or tax liens against you.

Credit reports usually list your credit cards and any loans you've taken out and their outstanding balance. It should indicate whether you are behind in any payments or if you've filed for bankruptcy. In addition, it will probably note the largest amount of credit you have had and the maximum you are allowed to borrow on a line of credit.

The credit report also will note anyone who has requested your file for credit-granting reasons in the past six months and anyone who has seen your file during the past two years for employment purposes. For example, if you apply for a credit card from a bank, the bank will ask for a copy of your file to help determine your credit-worthiness. If there are many such inquiries without any indication that credit was subsequently granted, then other creditors may assume you've been turned down.

Even if your credit record is unblemished, you may want to closely monitor your files to be sure the information is not being improperly disseminated.

"We recommend routinely reviewing your credit reports, not just to fix mistakes but also to see who's looked at your file and make sure it's a legitimate request," says Michele Meier, counsel for government affairs at the Consumers Union.

There are three major national credit bureaus—TRW Information Services, Trans-Union Credit Information, and Equifax—as well as many smaller local agencies. They maintain credit files and sell them to their clients.

"Credit bureaus get paid by subscribers, who are banks and finance companies," says Paul Richards, vice president of the National Center for Financial Education, a nonprofit group. "That is why they have little interest in helping consumers."

In fact, credit bureaus are notoriously difficult to deal with. "Every time I called TRW, I would get a recording telling me where to write," Yazzetti says. "There was never any way to get human contact."

One of the biggest headaches for consumers has been caused by the so-called mixed files. This commonly occurs when a credit bureau mistakenly combines the files of individuals with the same or similar names. In 1991 the problem became so flagrant that the New York State attorney general, along with 17 other states, sued TRW. The states subsequently negotiated settlements with all three major bureaus. Among other things, they require the agencies to write reports in plain, easily understandable language, and to attempt to obtain more complete identifying data.

Credit report problems also frequently plague recently divorced people, who find that debts belonging to their former spouses may appear on their own credit reports. Richards says that if you are about to divorce, make sure you cancel any joint credit cards and settle any accounts held in both names.

If there is one mistake consumers often make when dealing with credit bureaus, it is not keeping good records, Richards says. When you discover a problem on your credit report, set up a file immediately. Take notes of any phone conversations you have with the agency. And Richards suggests that you send letters to credit bureaus and creditors by certified mail, return receipt requested.

How to Fight Back

If you have a problem with your credit report:

Send certified letters to the credit bureau and your creditor, return receipt requested. Explain the problem and provide copies of any documents that support your side of the story. Ask both of them to correct the problem.

If that doesn't work, here are some places to go for help:

• Contact your state attorney general's office. Include copies of the letters you have written to the credit bureau and creditor.

• File a complaint with your Better Business Bureau.

• File a complaint with the Federal Trade Commission. The FTC can't resolve individual disputes. However, it will take action against a credit agency if it sees a pattern of abuse, and you can help document such a pattern. Also, the FTC will attempt to answer your questions. Write to the Federal Trade Commission, Correspondence Branch, Washington, D.C. 20580. You can also call 202-326-3758 to listen to a recording outlining your rights under the law and how to dispute an item on your credit report. You will be able to leave your name and address if you want to receive more information.

If you believe the credit bureau has failed to comply with the law or you believe people are illegally obtaining your credit report, you may want to consider legal remedies. Depending on state law, you may be able to sue in small claims court. A small claims court is unable to force a credit bureau to correct your report, but it can award small amounts of money in damages. Also, credit agencies illegally releasing reports or people illegally requesting reports may be fined up to $5,000.

Despite the problems some consumers have dealing with credit agencies, you do have rights under the Fair Credit Reporting Act. If you are turned down for a job, an insurance policy, or a loan in whole or in part because of your credit report, you must be notified that it played a role.

The law, enforced by the Federal Trade Commission, also says you must be told which agency was the source of the report. You then have 30 days to obtain a free copy.

If you have a legitimate credit problem, it should not plague you for the rest of your life. The law says that credit agencies can report most kinds of negative information for seven years. Personal bankruptcy can be reported for 10 years. However, in certain circumstances—for example, if you apply for a loan for $50,000 or more—there are no time limits on releasing negative information.

Finally, if you have an unresolved dispute with a creditor, you have the right to write a 100-word statement telling your side of the story, which will be added to your credit file.

Calling for Your Report

If you have been turned down for credit or other benefits because of a credit report, you must be notified. You can receive a free copy of the report if you request one from the agency within 30 days. Here's how to obtain copies of your credit report:

TRW Information Systems

Toll-free number: 800-682-7654
Headquarters: Orange, Calif. 714-385-7000
Cost: One free copy a year; other copies are $2 to $8.66, depending on your residency. New York residents pay $8.66.

Equifax

Toll-free number: 800-685-111
Headquarters: Atlanta, 404-885-8000
Cost: $8 in all states except Maine, where a copy is $3, and Maryland and Vermont, where residents can receive one free copy a year.

Trans Union Credit Information

New York office: 718-459-1800
Headquarters: Chicago, 312-408-1050
Cost: $8

For more details on how to handle problems with your credit report:

• *The Do-it-Yourself Credit Repair and Improvement Guide* by Paul Richard, published by the National Center for Financial Education, can be ordered by sending a check for $10 to NCFE, P.O. Box 34070, San Diego, CA, 92163-4070 (add $2 if you want to receive the guide by first-class mail).

• *The Credit Repair Kit* by John Ventura, published by Dearborn Financial Publishing is $19.95 and available at bookstores or by calling the publisher at (800) 829-7934.

Time for Some Advice on Advisers

What to Look for when Picking a Financial Planner

So, YOU'D LIKE some help managing your money.

Why not? You probably work long hours and you want to spend your free time with family and friends. Financial planning is time-consuming, the number of investment choices is mind-boggling and with college tuitions and retirement to plan for—admit it—you're confused.

And, of course, there is an overabundance of experts out there who would like to help you with the job.

There are financial planners, financial consultants, certified financial planners, chartered financial analysts, brokers who are also financial planners, and accountants who are personal financial specialists. Some of them charge commissions. Some charge fees. Some charge both. Some give you a choice. Some are licensed to give investment advice. Some are not. Most of them can draw up financial plans, but some cannot implement them.

How do you figure out who is best suited to help you? More importantly, how do you know whether to trust them with your hard-earned money?

Ask Barbara Roper about financial advisers and you'll get an earful. As the director of investor protection for the Consumer Federation of America, Roper believes the financial planning industry is riddled with potential conflicts of interest. As she puts it: "Objective advice is a pretty rare commodity."

It's not that Roper thinks all financial planners are bad. She just believes the commission system is at odds with the best interests of the consumer. And, she notes, there is little or no industry oversight. Anyone can set up shop as a financial planner.

The financial planning industry may think Roper's appraisal is too harsh. Yet the professional associations themselves recognize many of these problems and have been attempting to address them. They have set standards, established codes of ethics, and, in some cases, they even have begun to police themselves. To make sure you receive good advice, they encourage you to ask many questions and shop around before you settle on a financial planner.

Who really needs a financial adviser? Roper believes many people can do the job themselves. Everyone needs financial planning, she says. "The question is, can you afford a competent financial adviser? If you don't have a lot of money and don't have a particularly complicated financial situation, you can probably do the job yourself."

Roper says that you should never blindly follow the advice of a financial planner. That means you must educate yourself enough so that you can monitor your adviser. In some cases, the work involved in doing that is roughly equivalent to doing the planning yourself, Roper says.

There are certainly many people who do need professional advice, however. Some people need help getting on track. They might be well served by paying an adviser to develop a financial plan for them. Other people with chronic financial problems or complicated financial situations may need someone to manage their money on an ongoing basis.

Whatever the case, there are three main things you need to consider before hiring a financial adviser: their qualifications, their specialty and how they will be compensated.

Not all financial advisers are alike. Some recommend specific investments. If a planner says he or she will be helping you select stocks and bonds and mutual funds, then you should ask if they are registered with the Securities and Exchange Commission as an investment adviser. If they say they are not, ask why, says Gene Gohlke, associate director of compliance in charge of inspection at the SEC. There may be a legitimate reason, he notes. For example, if they have fewer than 15 clients, they don't need to register. Or they may be a registered broker/dealer instead of an investment adviser.

You should know that registered investment advisers are required to fill out what's called an ADV form. This is a public document. Part II of the form includes information on such things as fees, educational background and the type of service offered. Gohlke says that advisers are required to give a copy to new clients. The information may be repackaged into a glossy brochure.

Part I of the ADV form contains information on the adviser's disciplinary history. This is also a public document, although the adviser is not required to give you a copy. You can obtain the disciplinary history from the SEC. But Gohlke suggests that you ask advisers directly for a copy. If they have nothing to hide, they shouldn't object to showing it to you. You can also request disciplinary history from your state securities regulator.

When you interview a planner, don't be afraid to ask about his or her education and to request references. You should look for advisers who have a track record. For example, Roper suggests finding planners who have been in business at least through a business cycle—about five to seven years—so they have the perspective that comes from riding out the ups and downs of the stock market and dealing with different interest rate environments.

Ask if a planner has a particular expertise and a philosophy of investing. Some specialize in serving wealthy clients. Some are conservative in the way they select investments and others are risk-takers. Find one that matches your own risk tolerance. And take into account your own particular needs; for example if you have tax problems, you may want to find a planner who is also a CPA.

One of the most important things to consider before choosing a financial adviser is the method of compensation. Some planners charge no fee for their service, but earn commissions by selling you investment products.

Then there are fee-only financial planners. Because they have no financial stake in the investments they recommend, many consumer groups consider their advice more objective than commission-based advisers. They may charge you a flat fee to draw up a financial plan. Or they may charge you an hourly rate, or an annual fee equal to a certain percentage of the assets they manage for you.

The fee for a financial plan can range anywhere from $75 to $10,000, depending on the planner and the complexity of the client's financial situation, according to Christine Grillo, director of communication for the International Association of Financial Planners. It is important to ask if a fee-only planner will implement the plan they draw up for you. They can do this by setting up accounts for you at no-load mutual fund companies or at discount brokerage houses.

It is much more common for a planner to charge a fee plus commissions. In this case, planners charge a fee for the advice they give and then earn commissions on the products they sell you. Sometimes the commissions are deducted from the up-front fee. One way to evaluate these planners is to ask what proportion of their earnings comes from fees as opposed to commissions. There is always the danger that planners who are very reliant on commission income may steer you to the investments that generate the most money for them.

Some of the industry associations do not believe commissions are necessarily bad, especially if the consumer is informed of the planner's fee structure. Norma Restivo, an official at the Institute of Certified Financial Planners, says that her organization advocates full disclosure of fees in advance. That includes telling the consumer the commission a planner will earn on the sale of a particular product. "We believe this allows consumers to make a more educated decision," she says.

What if you hire a financial planner and then discover they aren't registered with the SEC as you believe they should be? Or what if you lose money because a planner misled you about the risks associated with an investment? Depending on the type of planner, you can file complaints with SEC and your state securities commission, as well as with some professional organizations. In some cases, the planner may be publicly censured and you may recover your losses.

Keep in mind, however, that just because you lose money on an investment doesn't mean you have a claim against your planner. If you sign off on investments, you'd better know what you're getting into and be prepared to accept the consequences.

Questions to Ask Before You Choose

Here's a checklist of factors for you to consider while shopping for a financial planner.

Services Provided

1. Which of the following financial planning services are offered by your firm? (You want to make sure that the planner will be able to meet your specific interests.)

____ Goals and objectives	____ Cash management, budgeting
____ Tax planning	____ Investment review and planning
____ Estate planning	____ Retirement planning
____ Education planning	____ Other
____ Insurance needs	

2. Do your financial planning services include specific investment recommendations? (Some planners will draw up a plan with only broad objectives.)

_____

_____

3. Will you help me implement your recommendations? (Some planners leave the implementation of a plan up to you. You must then seek out a broker, insurance agent, tax adviser or other professionals.) _____

_____

4. Do you offer ongoing financial planning services? (Some firms draw up a one-shot plan; others actively manage your money and periodically call you with recommendations.) _____

_____

Background and experience

You want a financial planner who has a solid foundation and is committed to staying current.

1. Licenses and Certifications

(Insurance)

(Insurance)	*(Securities)*
____ Life insurance	____ General securities
____ Disability insurance	____ Mutual funds
____ Property/casualty	____ Limited partnerships
____ Fixed annuities	
____ Variable annuities	

(Other)

____ Certified public accountant

____ Lawyer

____ Accredited financial planner specialist (AFPS)

____ Certified financial planner (CFP)

____ Chartered financial consultant (ChFC)

2. Professional associations _____

_____

3. Education
Degree: _____   Area of Study: _____

4. How long have you been offering financial planning services? _____

5. How many financial planning continuing education units (CEUs) have you completed in the past year? _____

6. Will you provide me with references? _____

_____

7. Have you ever been cited by a professional or regulatory governing body for disciplinary reasons? _____

Method of Compensation

You want to know how the planner is paid. Some planners charge you a fee. Others receive commissions or referral fees based on the recommendations they make to you, which could lead to a conflict of interest.

1. How will I pay for financial planning services and implementation of a plan provided by you or your firm?
_____Fees _____Commissions _____Other

2. Does your firm or any member of your firm receive compensation from investments that you may recommend to me? _____

3. Do you or any related parties receive any compensation from any people or companies to whom I may be referred? _____

SOURCE: International Association for Financial Planning

Deciphering the Alphabet Soup

Here's some help in figuring out what all those letters behind a financial planner's name mean:

CFP or Certified Financial Planner
Designation issued by International Board of Standards and Practices for Certified Financial Planners to those who meet certain education, examination, experience and ethics standards.

PFS or Personal Financial Specialist
Designation issued by the American Institute of Certified Public Accountants to accountants who meet certain examination and experience requirements.

CFA or Chartered Financial Analyst
Designation issued by the Association for Investment Management and Research to anyone who completes a program on investment analysis.

CLU or Chartered Life Underwriter
Designation issued by the American College to anyone who completes a specialized insurance course.

ChFC or Chartered Financial Consultant
Designation issued by the American College to an insurance specialist who is trained in all aspects of financial planning.

Who'll listen to a complaint:

• If you have a complaint about an adviser who is a registered broker/dealer, you can avoid legal bills by asking the National Association of Securities Dealers to arbitrate the dispute. All NASD members agree to abide by the arbitration. For more information on how to file a complaint, call 212-480-4881.

• The Certified Financial Planner Board of Standards has the power to suspend or revoke a planner's right to use the Certified Financial Planner designation. To file a complaint call 303-830-7543 or write to the board at 1660 Lincoln, Suite 3050, Denver CO 80202.

Handling the Pitch for Life Insurance

Grit Your Teeth, but Be Sure to Shop Around

For most people, life insurance is part of growing older. It's about as much fun, and as inevitable, as receding hairlines and middle-age spread.

Never mind that most life insurance policies are indecipherable, that many of them have costly commissions and surrender charges or that some people may not need a policy. When the agent comes calling, many adults just grit their teeth and sign on the dotted line.

"There is an old saw in the industry," says Jim Hunt, a director of the National Insurance Consumer Organization. "Life insurance is sold and not bought."

But you can turn that cliché on its head by shopping around for your life insurance policy and not buying anything you don't understand or need.

Start by asking yourself some basic questions:

What is the purpose of life insurance?

Although it may seem obvious, remember that life insurance is a death benefit, not a way to get rich. It is intended to provide for your loved ones after you die.

True, many insurance policies also have a savings component. But this is optional. You don't necessarily need a life insurance policy to help you save.

• Who needs life insurance? You need it if you have children, especially if you are the only bread-earner, says Mary Griffin, insurance counsel for the Washington office of Consumers Union. If you are single but have a dependent parent, you also may want to have life insurance. And even if you have no children, you might want life insurance to help your spouse pay bills in the event of your death.

• What should a life insurance policy pay for? It commonly serves a number of purposes, such as paying off funeral expenses and estate taxes, paying for children's education or providing monthly income for a spouse and for children until they are grown and out of school.

How much life insurance do you need?

First figure out your family's living expenses in the event of your death. Add the estimated costs of the things you earmarked above, such as funeral expenses and your children's college education.

Life Goes On

And your family is going to have to pay for it. Here's how to figure out how much life insurance you'll need to help them if you die prematurely. Some current figures will need to be multiplied by the number of years to be provided. For example, if you have seven years remaining on your mortgage, your survivors will need to pay off the balance entirely at your death or have money available to meet the payment for the next seven years. Figure your calculations as if you were to die tomorrow.

Money needed after you die	Today's Dollars	No. of Years	Total
Settlement expenses (Funeral, estate taxes, etc.)	$_____		$_____
Mortgage payment	$_____	_____	$_____
Other debt payments	$_____	_____	$_____
Emergency fund (3 to 6 months of living expenses).	$_____		$_____
Inheritance for children	$_____		$_____
Living expenses for survivors			
While children are at home	$_____	_____	$_____
After they leave home	$_____	_____	$_____
Education expenses	$_____	_____	$_____
Miscellaneous needs	$_____		$_____
TOTAL DOLLARS NEEDED			$_____ **A**

Money available after you die	Today's Dollars	No. of Years	Total
Investments outside retirement accounts	$_____		$_____
Retirement investments of deceased (IRA, 401(k), Keogh plan)	$_____		$_____
Life insurance from employer	$_____		$_____
Social Security			
While children are at home	$_____	_____	$_____
After they leave home	$_____	_____	$_____
Pension	$_____		$_____
Spouse's earned income	$_____	_____	$_____
Other	$_____		$_____
TOTAL DOLLARS AVAILABLE			$_____ **B**

DOLLARS NEEDED	**A**	$_____
MINUS DOLLARS AVAILABLE	**– B**	$_____
***LIFE INSURANCE NEEDED**	**=**	$_____

*This figure may be adjusted up or down by as much as 25 percent, depending on your lifestyle and investment strategies. For example, if money is tight, it is more important to put funds aside for your retirement rather than buy a great sum of life insurance. Also, consider your investments. If they aren't keeping pace with inflation, your survivors will need more insurance; if they are outpacing inflation, your survivors will need less.

SOURCE: Glenn Daily, insurance consultant; *Consumer Reports*

Then, subtract any income that your family will continue to receive after your death, such as your spouse's salary, your Social Security benefits, and your pension and retirement plans. This will give you an idea of how much they will need in insurance benefits to cover the shortfall. See the worksheet on page 97.

Hunt says that as a rule, you will want a life insurance policy that is seven to eight times your gross annual income.

What kind of life insurance do you need?

Here is where it can get complicated if you don't understand the basic types of insurance.

The simplest policy is term insurance. You pay a premium, and if you die during the term period, your beneficiaries receive the face value of the insurance policy.

This is the least expensive type of life insurance and the easiest type of policy to compare if you are shopping around. The premiums for term policies are lowest when you are young and get progressively more expensive as you get older. However, many people can reduce their life insurance when they approach retirement age because their children are grown and can support themselves.

You can buy term insurance for a set period, such as five, 10 or 20 years, and lock in your premium. Or you can buy annual renewable term insurance, in which case the premium usually rises each year.

While many consumer advocates recommend term insurance, insurance agents are unlikely to do so. The reason, Hunt says, is that agents make more money in commissions by selling you the other major type of life insurance, cash value insurance.

There are two types of cash value insurance, whole life and universal life. The premiums for these are much higher than rates for term insurance, but you're also getting more: A portion of your premium pays for the death benefit, just like term insurance, and the rest, called the cash value, is invested and grows in a tax-deferred account. In most cases, you pay taxes only when you cash in the policy.

Glenn Daily, a Manhattan-based, fee-only insurance consultant, says you can consider a cash value policy the way you think of an interest-bearing checking account. "You pay premiums; the insurer deducts insurance and expense charges and then credits interest."

An advantage of these policies is that you can borrow against them at a favorable rate. And if you cancel the policy, you will receive a cash value payment.

In theory, it sounds good. But it is very difficult to find out the rate of return on an insurance company's investment portfolio, which is what determines your cash value.

Insurance agents will usually provide you with a sales illustration—it's actually a long computer printout of numbers—when they sell you the policy. This is supposed to show you what you can expect to pay for a policy and what the investment account should earn in interest year by year.

But be forewarned: the sales illustration is nothing more than a projection. It is not a guarantee!

In a three-part series of articles about life insurance, *Consumer Reports* magazine examined more than 100 sales illustrations. Among other things, the magazine found they often failed to say what kind of policy they represented; they were often incomplete and routinely filled with confusing labels and terms.

Make sure you ask about surrender charges; that's what you lose if you drop the policy early. Typically, these surrender charges are highest in the first few years and gradually decline over the life of the policy.

People who drop their policies after a couple of years may be shocked to find that despite the high premiums they have been paying, they will receive little or nothing back from their cash-value account. Unfortunately, this happens all too often—Hunt says about half of all cash value policyholders drop them during the first seven to eight years. As a result, experts say, you should consider a cash value policy only if you can be sure of keeping up the payments for about 20 years.

But before you sign up for a cash value policy, ask yourself if you have other tax-deferred savings plans available, such as a 401(k) plan through your employer. If so, Daily recommends using them as a savings vehicle, and buying a term life insurance policy. Then, only if you need additional tax-deferred investments, should you consider a cash value policy, he says.

How do whole life and universal differ?

Whole life is the most common type of life insurance. You pay a set amount in premiums for the life of the policy. With a universal policy, you can adjust the premium, or adjust how it is allocated between the death benefit and the cash value. You can even skip premium payments. Daily says that if your needs change as you grow older, a universal policy allows you the flexibility to adjust it.

How can you shop for a life insurance policy?

First of all, experts say, recognize that agents get a commission, and therefore have a financial stake in what you buy. Don't buy anything you don't understand and don't let them sell you more insurance than you need.

Consult more than one agent and consider policies from various companies. Daily says the best advice he can offer is to buy a low-load policy. These policies, sold by a handful of insurance companies, have much lower expenses and commission charges than typical policies because you generally buy them directly from the company.

Some financial planners and insurance consultants will help you select among the low-load products and charge a flat fee—perhaps $150 an hour—with no commission. There are also some services that for a fee will analyze sales illustrations from insurance companies and estimate the rate of return.

Finally, you should check on the financial health of the insurance company you are considering. After all, you don't want the insurer to die before you do. There are a number of rating firms that analyze each insurance company and then assign a letter grade to reflect its financial condition. Although the rating systems vary, the strongest companies will have ratings that range from AAA or A+++, to A or A3. Ask for A.M. Best's guide to insurers at your public library.

Pop Quiz

It's Time to Take a Midterm Fiscal Fitness Exam, and It's OK to Look at the Answers

STAYING WITHIN A BUDGET is like trying to stay on a diet. Old habits die hard—and setting realistic limits isn't easy. But once the results start to show you'll be glad you stuck with it.

Let's review what you've learned over the past 24 exercises.

1. If you need to borrow money, one advantage of a home equity loan is:
A) You don't have to fill out any applications.
B) The interest is tax deductible.
C) You can skip loan payments.

2. But one disadvantage of a home equity loan is:
A) You risk losing your home if you fail to pay the loan.
B) You can only use the money for certain things.
C) You will have to pay back the loan in two years.

3. When is it a good idea to have a prenuptial agreement?
A) When either party has been married before and has children from a previous marriage.
B) When either party stands to inherit a family business.
C) When either party has a considerably higher income and more assets than the other.
D) A & C
E) All of the above

4. If you lost your job, and then fell behind on your $150,000 mortgage, how long can the information about your delinquent loan remain on your credit reports?
A) Seven years.
B) Ten years.
C) Fifteen years.
D) No limit on large loans.

5. What requirements must be met before people can call themselves financial planners?
A) They must register with the Securities and Exchange Commission.
B) There are no requirements.

C) They must be certified by a professional organization, such as the Institute of Certified Financial Planners.

D) They must hold a two-year degree in financial planning.

6. What does a life insurance sales illustration tell you?

A) How much the company guarantees you will make in interest on the investment portion of a whole or universal policy.

B) It is a booklet describing your rights under the law.

C) It is a sales pitch that includes the insurance company's projections of what you can expect to pay for a policy and what the investment account might earn in interest.

7. If you're having trouble qualifying for a loan because you've never established a credit history, which of the following can help?

A) Open a checking account and use it to pay your monthly bills to show you are reliable.

B) Apply for as many credit cards as possible and charge them up to the limit.

C) Find a bank that will give you a secured card, in which you deposit money as collateral; then pay your bills on time to show you can be a responsible borrower.

D) A and C.

E) None of the above.

8. Credit reports generally contain which of the following information?

A) Your religious affiliation, and memberships in clubs and organizations.

B) Your credit and debt repayment history.

C) Your address, Social Security number and birthdate.

D) Any judgments or tax liens against you

E) B, C and D

F) All of the above

True/False

1. As a rule, lenders say no more than 40 percent of your gross monthly income can be spent on housing-related expenses.

2. The advantage of a 15-year mortgage is that you will pay much less in interest over the life of the loan.

3. Married couples—especially two-income married couples—generally pay more in federal tax than if they were single.

4. If you are turned down for a job because of information in your credit report, you can sue the employer.

5. A cash-value life insurance policy is one that puts a portion of your premium toward the death benefit and invests another portion of your premium in a tax-deferred account.

6. It is important to ask fee-only financial planners if they can implement a plan as well as draw one up.

7. If you buy a condominium apartment, you're buying shares in a corporation.

8. If you can't afford a down payment that is equal to 20 percent or 25 percent of the purchase price of a home, don't even bother applying for a mortgage.

9. If you are considering buying a home, one of the first things you should do is to send for copies of your credit reports to make sure there are no mistakes on them that would prohibit you from qualifying for a mortgage.

ANSWER KEY

Multiple Choice

1. B	3. E	5. B	7. D
2. A	4. D	6. C	8. E

True/False

1. False. Lenders don't want more than 28 percent of your gross monthly income to be spent on housing-related expenses.

2. True

3. True

4. False. If you are turned down for a job because of your credit report, you must be informed by the employer and you have 30 days to obtain a free copy of the report.

5. True

6. True

7. False. When you purchase a condominium you are buying an apartment; when you purchase a cooperative apartment you are buying shares in a corporation.

8. False. Mortgages come in many varieties. Some banks require only a 10 percent down payment. There are also a number of government loan programs with more flexible rules; some allow down payments as low as 2 percent.

9. True

Opportunity Knocks

Well-managed 401(k) Ensures You Have a Leg to Stand On In Retirement

IT IS OFTEN SAID that the retirement system in the United States is like a three-legged stool.

Why? Because by the time you reach retirement, you are supposed to be supported by three things: Social Security, a company pension and individual savings.

This analogy is not only tiresome, it's also increasingly inaccurate. By the time you retire, two of the legs may be shaky at best. The only financial leg you're probably going to be able to rely on is your personal retirement savings.

That is why financial planners urge people to take advantage of 401(k) retirement plans. These plans, which are offered by many employers, allow you to have a percentage of your pretax salary automatically deducted and placed into a tax-deferred retirement account. As a result, your taxable income is reduced, and the money in the plan accumulates tax free until you withdraw it at retirement.

In addition, more than half of all companies that offer 401(k) plans will match at least a portion of your contribution, according to Access Research, a Windsor, Conn., consulting firm. For example, an employer may offer to contribute 50 cents for each dollar you put in, up to 6 percent of your salary. In other words, you make 50 percent on your money with no risk. That's a windfall few people can afford to pass up.

Yet, despite the benefits of 401(k) plans, Access Research says that more than one-quarter of all people eligible to participate in them fail to do so.

And other financial experts say that even when people do participate, they often fail to use the plans wisely, partly because companies have not provided their employees with much information about how the plans work and how to make investment choices.

That is changing, however. In 1994, a new federal regulation took effect that encourages employers to provide 401(k) plan participants with at least three diverse investment options, the ability to switch their funds among these options, and more information about making investment decisions. Complying with the regulation, called 404(c), is not mandatory, but will reduce a company's potential liability.

As a result of the regulation, employers are more frequently subscribing to newsletters and other educational materials, which they distribute to their plan participants. Standard & Poor's, for example, publishes a quarterly newsletter called *Your Financial Future,* which it says has about 500,000 readers at companies with 401(k) retirement plans.

To help you better understand your 401(k) plan, here are the answers to some common questions:

• How much can you contribute? There is a cap, which is adjusted each year for inflation. Last year, the maximum was $9,235, according to the Internal Revenue Service.

A nondiscrimination rule prevents certain highly compensated employees from contributing the maximum amount. The idea is to make sure the top employees do not disproportionately benefit from a 401(k) plan. So the amount upper-income employees can contribute to the plan is linked to the average contribution of lower-income employees at a company. "This puts pressure on companies to encourage lower paid employees to participate," says 401(k) Association president Ted Benna, who pioneered the retirement plan.

• Is your money safe in a 401(k) plan? It is not federally insured. However, if your company goes bankrupt, there should be no risk to your 401(k) funds. Benna notes that employers are required to set aside 401(k) money in a separate account that management can't touch.

Keep in mind, however, that there is a certain amount of investment risk associated with any 401(k) plan. Stocks funds, for example, are more risky and volatile than bond funds or money market funds. But even if you select the safest option, there is some risk. That's because if your contribution grows slowly, it may not keep pace with inflation and you may have less money than you need to live comfortably when it comes time to retire.

• When should you begin participating in a 401(k) plan? The sooner, the better. Because of the power of compounding, if you contribute regularly in the early years of your career, you will have a big head start on those who procrastinate. Even if you have to temporarily stop contributing when you need money for buying a home or paying for a child's college education, the money already in your plan will continue to grow.

• How should you invest your 401(k) funds? That depends on your age and how long you've been contributing to a retirement plan. Your company will provide you with a menu of investments to choose from. Financial planners generally recommend that you divide your retirement savings among several different options. This makes you less vulnerable to losses in any one category.

The way you choose to allocate your money should be based on your particular situation. But many advisers suggest investing more heavily in stocks when you are young. The closer you are to retirement, the less time you have to recover from a major market upset, notes a recent issue of S&P's *Your Financial Future.*

The most common mistake people make, financial experts say, is to invest too conservatively. "They say, 'I don't want to take any chances; I don't want to be a millionaire,'" says Brian Ternoey, a principal at the consulting firm Foster Higgins. "But you can be risky with your future by being too safe with your investments."

Check Yourself Against the Pros

The 401(k) plan turns people into do-it-yourself pension managers, and many are too conservative. Here's how the average participant in a 401(k) plan stacks up against the professional pension fund managers when it comes to asset allocation. The figures are from a 1992 survey; they may not add up to 100 percent due to rounding.

	% of Assets	
Asset	Pros	401(k)
Common stocks	48%	49%
Int'l stock/ bonds	10%	1%
Bonds	29%	10%
Guaranteed investment contracts	1%	30%
Equity real estate	5%	0%
Cash and equivalents	4%	8%
Other	3%	2%

SOURCE: Greenwich Associates

• When should you shift your finds from one investment to another? Financial planners agree that you shouldn't try to anticipate market trends. It's almost impossible for experts to accurately time the market, Ternoey says, so it's unlikely you can do it.

However, you may want to shift some of your 401(k) funds if your employer offers you new options. And as you approach retirement, you will probably want to reallocate your funds. Although you need to know something about how your investments are performing, don't become fixated on the short-term performance of your funds, experts say.

• Can you borrow from your 401(k) fund? It depends on your plan. Access Research says that two-thirds of all plans allow participants to borrow against their funds, but there are restrictions. You can borrow 50 percent of your money, up to $50,000. In most cases you must repay the loan in five years. And you must pay interest on the loan, although the interest goes into your account.

• Can you withdraw the funds whenever you want? Not before you reach age $59^{1}/_{2}$. The only exception is in event of extreme hardship. But if you have a sudden emergency, you can only tap into your 401(k) funds if you have exhausted all other possibilities. And remember, you will pay taxes on the amount you withdraw, as well as a 10 percent penalty.

• What happens when you change jobs or get laid off? If you are not yet $59^{1}/_{2}$ and decide you want to withdraw from your plan, you will be hit with the 10 percent penalty and a big tax bill.

If you want to roll over the money into another retirement plan, you need to be sure to instruct your company to transfer the 401(k) funds directly to another retirement account.

In the past, you could ask your employer to issue you a check and you had 60 days to decide what to do with the money. Now if your employer issues you a check, IRS regulations require them to withhold 20 percent of your money.

So, if you have $100,000 in your account, you will receive a check for $80,000. In order to avoid a tax and penalty on your retirement fund, you must deposit $100,000 into a new retirement account before the 60-day deadline. Unfortunately, the IRS won't give you back the $20,000 that quickly. In theory, you'd get it after you file your next tax return. But in the meantime, you must come up with that missing money to put into the retirement account.

The problem with this convoluted process is that many people don't have enough money on hand to make up for the amount the IRS withheld, and they will suffer the consequences: tax and penalty on the 20 percent.

In addition to unfairly penalizing consumers, Benna says, the withholding rule—along with a number of other new regulations—is driving up the administrative costs for employers. And that is causing some small companies to drop their 401(k) plans. He formed the 401(k) Association primarily to lobby for less government regulation of these plans.

• How soon can you get a lump sum payment after you leave your company? Stuart Kessler, a Manhattan accountant, notes that many will not disburse funds until the end of the plan's fiscal year. So depending on when you resign, you might have to wait many months to get your money.

And Cindy Hounsell, a staff attorney for the Pension Rights Center, a Washington, D.C., public interest group, says it can take up to 60 days after the end of the plan year for your employer to process your disbursement, during which time you will receive no interest. "People become outraged about this," she says.

Baby Steps to Saving

Ideas for Getting a Bundle of Cash So
You Can Send the Bundle of Joy to College

IF YOU'RE EXPECTING a baby, you're probably busy lining up a crib and a stroller and the multitude of other items that newborns require. No doubt you're also debating whether to use cloth or disposable diapers. And you're preparing for the delivery and the sleepless nights ahead.

But have you also started planning for the baby's college education?

That may be the last thing you want to think about now. Yet experts say it's wise to start considering how you're going to pay for college tuition well before your child is in school.

"I always say couples should start saving for college while the baby is still in the womb," says Keith Fevurly, director of academic programs at the College for Financial Planning in Denver.

Just consider the fact that the cost of tuition at four-year public institutions rose 8 percent in 1993—well outpacing inflation. At that rate, the longer you put off saving for college, the bigger the lump sum you'll eventually have to come up with to cover the costs.

And the fact that many people are having children at a later age means that if they don't start saving now, they may have the burden of financing their children's college education and their own retirement at the same time.

Before you faint at the thought of college costs today, you should realize that few people pay for college entirely from their savings. Raymond Loewe, president of Educational Planning Systems Inc., in Marlton, N.J., says there are four main ways to finance a college education: by saving money beforehand, by paying as you go, by borrowing money and by letting someone else pay for it—such as getting financial aid or money from grandparents.

The least painful way to fund a college education is to learn about college financing options while your child is young and develop a disciplined savings plan. Loewe says that means deciding on an amount—even if it's small—that you can regularly save so that you spread the financial pressure as evenly as possible over time. If that's ultimately not enough to pay for college costs, you can apply for financial aid or borrow the rest.

One thing Loewe does not recommend is sacrificing your retirement savings in favor of a college fund. If your company offers a 401(k) retirement plan, you're probably better off putting the maximum amount into it so that you can get any matching funds your company offers, as well as the tax deferral. The key is sometimes to beef up your retirement plan so that you can handle debt when it comes time to pay for college, Loewe says.

If you'd like to start saving for college but feel unsure how to go about it, here are some tips from financial experts:

• You should first consider whether you're likely to qualify for financial aid when it's time to apply for college. This may seem impossible to predict if your child is now an infant. But Fevurly suggests talking to a college or bank loan officer to learn about the current guidelines for financial aid. Then, he says, you should take the income limits today and estimate what they will be in 18 years if they increase 4 percent to 5 percent a year.

Once you have that information, you need to make some assumptions about your own financial situation 18 years from now. That should give you an idea about your future eligibility. If you need help figuring this out, you can consult books on the subject. For example, every year the College Board publishes the *College Costs and Financial Aid Handbook,* which has worksheets on financial aid and advice on how to pay for college. It's a good idea to redo the worksheets every few years to see if you're on track.

Once you have an idea whether you will qualify for financial aid, you can better gauge how much to save now. "If you discover you're not in the ballpark for financial aid, then you jolly well better start arranging your finances now," says Kathleen Brouder, a spokeswoman for the College Board.

• You should decide early on whether to put a college fund in your child's name or in your own. Knowing if you may be eligible for financial aid will help you with this decision. That's because financial aid formulas are designed so that a child's assets are deemed more available to pay for college than the parent's assets.

Loewe gives an example of how this works: If a child has $10,000 in savings, his or her financial aid will be reduced by $3,500; but if the same $10,000 is in the parent's name, the financial aid will only be reduced by $600.

In that scenario, it seems to make sense to keep money in the parent's name. But many people prefer to put college money in their child's name because of the tax advantages.

Joel Isaacson, a Manhattan financial planner, notes that recent changes in the tax law have reduced the incentive to put money in a child's name. If you set up a custodial account for a child under age 14, the first $600 of unearned income is tax-free. The next $600 in unearned income is taxed at the child's rate. But anything above $1,200 is taxed at the parents' rate until the child reaches 14. After that, anything over the first $600 of unearned income is taxed at the child's rate.

One disadvantage of these accounts is that they are irrevocable gifts that become available to your children when they reach adulthood—age 18 or 21, depending on the state. In New York, custodial accounts go to the child at age 18, unless you specify age 21 when you open the account. Once a child has access to the account, he or she can use the money in any way—to go to college, or instead, to travel around the world.

Trusts are more complicated to set up but they can give parents more control over the money. Recent changes in the tax law also have reduced the benefits of trusts, Isaacson says. Check with an accountant or financial adviser about the merits of a setting one up.

Custodial Pros and Cons

If you decide to put money in your child's name with a custodial account:

• **You can save on taxes.** Up to $600 per year of unearned income—in other words, not from a job—is tax-free. And the next $600 is taxed at the child's rate. Unless your kid is a tycoon, that means the lowest bracket of 15 percent. Income above $1,200 is taxed at the parent's top rate.

• **You can't take it back.** The money is an irrevocable gift.

• **You have to let go.** When the child becomes a legal adult, the money is theirs to spend on whatever he or she wants.

• You should carefully consider how to make your investments keep pace with rapidly escalating college costs. "We would think that most of the money ought to go into stocks, preferably into a mutual fund," says Porter Morgan, an investment strategist at Liberty Financial Cos. You can easily establish a custodial account at a no-load mutual fund company. And you can set it up so that a certain amount of money is automatically withdrawn from your salary or bank account at regular intervals and invested in the fund.

However, Morgan cautions that if your child is already in high school when you start planning for college, you need to save aggressively, but invest more cautiously. That means you need a mix of stocks and bonds and money market accounts. Stocks are the most volatile of these investments, so you should gradually shift out of them the closer you get to paying for college. You don't want to get stuck selling your investment at a loss when the market is down.

There are some programs designed especially to fund a college education. For example, the U.S. Treasury Department offers the Education Savings Bond Program, which allows qualified taxpayers to use series EE savings bonds issued after 1989 to pay for tuition and fees without paying federal tax on the interest.

The bonds must be purchased in a parent's name. And there are income limits, which are adjusted annually for inflation, on who can participate in the program. In 1993, couples filing a joint return who earned more than $98,250 were not eligible for the benefit. Couples earning between $68,250 and $98,250 received only partial tax benefits. It's possible you could purchase bonds when your child is small, only to find that a decade later you don't qualify for the tax abatement. And some financial experts say even if you're sure you will qualify, savings bonds should not account for a major portion of a college fund because they typically earn much less than other investments.

• Finally, encourage relatives to contribute to a college fund on birthdays and holidays. "A lot of grandparents have a certain level of financial comfort and can afford several thousand dollars a year to help provide for a college education," Morgan says. A gift of a few thousand dollars when a child is young can make an enormous difference.

College Plans?

Need a brochure offering insights for preparing to meet the rising costs of college education, and that outlines the major advantages of using mutual funds to meet those costs? To receive a free copy write: Consumer Brochures, Investment Company Institute, Dept. ND, P.O. Box 66140, Washington, D.C. 20035-6140.

• *Preparing Your Child for College: A Resource Book for Parents.* Write to: Consumer Information Center, Department 510A, Pueblo, CO 81009. Include your name and address.

• *The 1994 College Costs and Financial Aid Handbook,* published by the College Board, costs $16, (plus $3.95 for handling, if you're ordering by mail). It can be purchased at many bookstores or you can call 800-323-7155 to order by credit card.

• *How to Pay for College without Ruining Your Retirement* is a two-video set from Educational Planning Systems. It sells for $75. To order, call 609-596-4702.

Money, Kid-Style
Start 'Em at 4 and Continue Making Deposits

WHEN DAVID GREENE was a boy growing up in Brooklyn, he learned the value of saving money by opening his own bank account.

"It was a small amount of money, maybe $60 that opened that account," he recalled. "Gradually, I added a few dollars and began accumulating interest. My money increased to my amazement, much like part of the American Dream."

In 1993, Greene decided it was time for his daughter, Rachel, then 9, to open her first account. As it happened, however, she didn't learn the lesson that her father had in mind.

When Rachel recently went to add $40 to her account at Chemical Bank, she discovered that the original $170 she had deposited had shrunk to $156 because the monthly fees exceeded the interest. Upset and disappointed, Rachel last month wrote to the president of Chemical to say she had decided to close her account.

Chemical Bank spokeswoman Judy Walsh said there obviously had been an error. In fact, she said, Greene should have been directed to open a custodial account for his daughter under the Uniform Gift to Minors Act; in such accounts, there are no monthly fees. Chemical will reimburse Rachel for the fees that were taken from her account.

Rachel will now get to see how an interest-bearing account can help her money grow. And in the meantime, she has learned how important it is to be an informed and vigilant consumer.

We live in an increasingly complicated financial world where it is more important than ever to teach children to make intelligent decisions. Yet a survey of the consumer knowledge of college students conducted by the Consumer Federation of America found that most were unprepared to make wise purchasing decisions about financial services.

The biggest mistake parents make is to wrongly assume children are going to learn these things in school, says Paul Richard, vice president of the National Center for Financial Education. There is no uniform program for financial education in the schools and only 20 states have any mandate for consumer or economic financial education.

Other parents fail to teach their children about money because they never learned about it themselves, Richard says.

Janet Bodnar, author of *Kiplinger's Money-Smart Kids,* says: "Parents are

Let's Do a Budget

Use this work sheet to keep track of your money. At the beginning of the month, start writing down the money you receive and the money you spend. At the end of the month, you'll see whether you came out even (you spent as much as you received), ahead (you spent less than you received and have money left over to add to your savings) or behind (you spent more than you received).

The worksheet may help you decide that you want to spend your money differently next month. Maybe you want to increase your income by asking for more odd jobs around the house. Perhaps you will spend less on snacks so you can save up for a new pair of skates. But remember, just because something is listed on this work sheet doesn't mean you have to buy it—or that your parents will let you.

Month _____

Where My Money Comes From

My allowance	$ _____
Odd jobs	_____
Babysitting, paper route, etc.	_____
Gifts	_____
Money borrowed from my parent(s) or someone else	_____

My Total Income = $ _____

What I Spend My Money On

Money I owe my parent(s) or someone else	$ _____
My savings (savings account or piggy bank)	_____
My church or other charity	_____
Gifts for my family and friends	_____
Lunch money	_____
Clothing I help pay for	_____
School supplies and fees (class parties, science, etc.)	_____
Snacks	_____

Fun stuff I pay for

Books, magazines and comics	$ _____
Toys	_____
Things I collect	_____
Special stuff for my room (posters and so on)	_____
Entrance fees (for skating rink, recreation center, etc.)	_____
Club dues & uniforms	_____
Art and craft supplies (including taking pictures)	_____

Holiday costumes	_____
CDs, tapes and records	_____
Video and computer games	_____
Videotapes (bought or rented)	_____
Movies	_____
Other outings (amusement parks, museums, zoos, etc.)	_____
Souvenirs and postcards	_____
Odds and ends	
My Total Expenses	$ _____
My Total Income	$ _____
Minus My Total Expenses	– $ _____
Money Left Over	= $ _____

SOURCE: *Kiplinger's Money-Smart Kids (and Parents, too!)* by Janet Bodnar

often not quite sure how to talk about money. It's a private thing. Some are downright uncomfortable with the subject."

But even when parents don't take time to teach their children about money, children learn from their example. In a survey of junior and senior high school students commissioned by Liberty Financial Companies in 1993, more than 88 percent said they learned everything they know about money from their parents. Nonetheless, nearly half of these students said their parents did not regularly discuss family finances with them, except topics like savings and allowances.

So what's a parent to do? Here are some basic tips:

• Bodnar says that the earliest you can start teaching children about money is around age 4. That's when you can begin to show them that money can be exchanged for something else. Take them to the supermarket and let them see that if they give the checkout clerk money, they can get a treat in return.

• When children get older, you can give them simple responsibilities so they then learn more about the role money plays in supporting the family. For example, Liberty Financial's *Young Investor Parent's Guide* suggests allowing your child to collect bottles that can be returned for a deposit. On your next trip to the market, the guide says, let your child return the bottles and use the money to buy an item of food for the family. The remaining money can be used as he or she sees fit.

• Give young children a piggy bank or jar where they can collect change. Encourage them to save the money until they have enough to buy an item they really want. You can't tell a 6- or 7-year-old to save for college, Bodnar says, but you can say to save for the latest Star Trek figure. You might even cut out a picture of the figure from a catalog, she added, and hang it near the piggy bank to remind them they will get a reward for saving their money.

• When your children reach school age, you can start giving them an allowance. There's a lot of debate about whether to link an allowance to specific chores. Experts say if you decide your child must earn the allowance, you should make the system simple to oversee. Bodnar, who has three children, says she tried putting a chore chart up on her refrigerator, but found she was too busy to monitor what they were doing.

Now she simply gives them a weekly allowance and tells them what they are expected to pay for themselves, such as treats at the movie theater. Richard also gives his children a set allowance, but if they want more money, they have to do a job around the house to earn it.

• Some parents require their children to deposit a portion of their allowance in a bank account. Others encourage their children to donate a portion to charity. To give an incentive to save money, some parents agree to match whatever their child puts into a savings account.

• Teach your children how to become smart consumers by asking them to help you shop for groceries. Kids can be a pain in the neck at the supermarket, Bodnar says. So, she suggests letting children shop for some of the items on your list. When they are old enough, teach them to read labels and look for unit prices. Show them how coupons work and ask them to help look for sales.

Many parents also discuss TV and print ads with their children. This helps them learn to be analytical and better understand the power of persuasion.

• Talk about family finances with your children. This doesn't necessarily mean telling them how much money your earn or how you invest money. But help teach them that running a household is expensive. Kids often have no concept of the value of money and how hard parents have to work to afford things, Richard says. He routinely holds family council meetings where, for example, they look at utility bills and compare them to the previous year.

• Older children should learn about credit cards before they graduate from high school and are bombarded by card applications. They need to understand that when you charge an item on a credit card you are in effect taking out a loan. Some parents try to teach children about credit by lending them money for something they want to buy, say a bicycle, and making them pay the money back on a schedule with interest.

But Richard doesn't believe parents should encourage children to go into debt, even to teach them a lesson. He says that before children go off to college, they should be armed with a budget and a plan for paying expenses instead of credit cards.

You can begin to teach children about investing when they are in junior high school. Start with individual stocks, because they are less abstract than mutual funds. Children can easily relate to buying a share in a company they have heard about, such as McDonald's. You can play an imaginary game where they pick several stocks and together you follow their performance over a period of time. This helps children learn about the risk associated with investing.

If your children are very interested in how the stock market works, you can open a custodial account and buy stocks for them. You also can purchase mutual funds for them through a custodial account. When the account statements come in the mail, go over them with your child.

You may feel unprepared to explain investing to your children. If so, you're not alone. Fortunately, there are many books for parents that can help.

• Finally, if you want to do more to improve financial education in your schools, encourage your bank to participate in the Save for America Program, which is funded by the U.S. Department of Education. The program enlists banks, which then establish partnerships with local schools. The school then is able to open its own savings bank operated by volunteer parents who use special software to keep track of deposits. This is linked to the participating bank, which sends out account statements to the students. Banks get a new generation of customers and schools get materials for a financial education program for kindergarten through eighth grade. And children get a head start on saving money.

A Fraud Survival Kit

Know How to Spot It and How to Prevent It

WHAT'S WRONG WITH this scene? You sit down to pay your bills and you realize you haven't received a credit card bill for the past two months. You congratulate yourself because you've gotten your spending under control.

Answer: Although it's good to curtail your spending, you should immediately become concerned if you haven't received a monthly credit card bill. It may be an indication that you've been a victim of credit card fraud.

Con artists have been known to get hold of credit card account information and call the card issuer to change the mailing address. Then they start charging items to the account, hoping the real cardholder won't report the fraud for a while because he or she doesn't see the bills with the phony charges.

Unfortunately, as technology has produced new ways to deliver financial services, criminals have found ways to exploit them. Right now, most of you have a wallet full of items that could be a treasure trove in someone else's hands: credit cards, ATM card, checkbook, telephone calling card, drivers license and other identification. Some people carry so many of these items that they don't even notice right away if one is missing.

What's the big deal, you may ask. After all, if a credit card is stolen, you can't be liable for more than $50 of fraudulent charges.

Well, depending on the type of credit card fraud, you may not notice right away. If unpaid charges build up under your name, it will create havoc with your credit reports. It can take months or years to clear up these reports and, until they are cleared, you probably won't be able to get a loan.

Don't assume that the $50 limit on your credit card fraud liability applies to other types of financial fraud. Check fraud is governed by each state's uniform commercial code, or UCC. In New York, for example, if you leave your checkbook on your desk at work and it is stolen, you may be deemed negligent and held liable for the losses. So even if a criminal steals your checks and forges your signature, the state could decide it was your own fault they were stolen in the first place, and say tough luck.

Automated teller machine fraud is another matter. According to the Electronic Funds Transfer Act, if you notify your bank within two days of learning of the loss or theft of your ATM card, your maximum liability is $50. But if you wait longer than two days, your liability can jump dramatically.

Real Junk Mail

Some people will use any method—even the mail—to separate you from your money. Here are two ways to protect yourself.

• **DON'T** pay for something that is supposedly "free." Beware of postcards touting "free" or "guaranteed" prizes that are yours in exchange for a shipping, handling, delivery or promotional fee. Often these charges will add up to more than the value of the prizes involved. If you are urged to call a 900 number, recognize that you may end up with a phone bill for $20 or more, even if you decide not to participate. Keep in mind that many postcard deals are shams intended to suck you into buying overpriced products, including vitamins and water purifiers.

• **DO** ignore demands for immediate action. One technique con artists use to overcome objections is to push for a quick response. Do not base your decision on whether to respond to a postcard scheme on references to a "72-hour notification deadline" or a bogus second notice. Be wary of firms that ask for your money to be picked up by a courier or delivered via overnight mail.

SOURCE: National Fraud Information Center

If you use common sense, you can often protect yourself from financial fraud. But sometimes it is out of your control.

For example, thieves often intercept new cards before you receive them in the mail. That means you should be on the lookout for any new or reissued card that you are expecting, says Charlotte Rush, a spokeswoman for MasterCard.

There also have been instances in which criminals have gotten their hands on employment files at a company. They use the information to apply for credit cards under someone's name and Social Security number, but with a different mailing address.

In such cases, the most important thing you can do is to be on the alert and report any sign of fraud right away. In the example above, you might wonder how you would ever know about the fraud. Experts say that one way to try to be sure you're not an unsuspecting victim is to periodically order copies of your credit reports. TRW Information Services will give you a free report each year, while Equifax and Trans Union Credit charge $8 a copy.

Janis Lamar, a spokeswoman for TRW Information Services, one of the biggest credit reporting bureaus, says that when you get the report, examine it carefully and make sure you understand all the items listed on it. TRW also withholds account numbers from credit reports sent to car dealers and employers. Lamar says the idea is to limit access of this information to companies that need it for decision making.

It is always a good idea to review some of the things you can do to help prevent fraud. Although many of them seem self-evident, it is easy to let them slide if you are busy.

Protecting Your Credit Cards

• Never leave cards in your car.
• When your card has expired, destroy it so that no one could alter your card to use it again.
• Guard your card from the view of others in the store, so they can't read the name and number. Someone with a name and number could use your card to charge by phone.
• Make sure sales clerks fill in credit card slips completely, correctly and legibly.
• Cancel credit cards or close your checking account immediately if either is stolen.
• Void or destroy all carbons and incorrect receipts.
• Don't write your card number on a postcard or the outside of an envelope.
• Don't give your number over the phone unless you are initiating a transaction with a company you know is reputable.

SOURCE: American Bankers Association, TRW Information Systems & Services

---

• You should keep track of what's in your wallet so you can easily report something that is lost or stolen, says Gerri Detweiler, former executive director of BankCard Holders of America. That means arranging cards in such a way that you can immediately see if one is missing. And be sure to keep a list at home of all your cards, their account numbers, and the phone numbers to call in case of a problem.

Detweiler advises you to only carry two or three cards. Carrying a wallet full of cards is asking for trouble, she says.

• If you are paying for merchandise by personal check, don't let the sales clerk write your credit card account number on it. This practice is now illegal in many states.

• If you discover an error on your credit card bill, report it immediately. Detweiler says it's not enough just to call about a billing error. You must put your complaint in writing within 60 days.

• Before you toss unwanted offers from your bank or credit card company into the garbage, check to see if your account number or other identification is on it. Gayle Moore, a special agent for the U.S. Secret Service, says there are con artists who specialize in dumpster diving. They go looking through the garbage for credit card carbons and other documents they can use to defraud you. So carefully tear up anything with identifying information on it. Then divide the pieces among several garbage bags.

Fortunately, most credit card transaction slips no longer have the troublesome carbon slips. If you happen to find a merchant still using them, be sure to tear it up or have the merchant tear it up in front of you. And some mutual funds have begun omitting sensitive data like Social Security numbers from their monthly statements.

• Be aware that if you call an 800 telephone number, the company you are calling will have a record of your phone number. Don't forget that if you call a 900 number you can end up with a big phone bill. When you use your telephone calling card at a public phone, don't let other people see you punch in your code. And if you are going to use a public phone to make a hotel reservation or to order merchandise, make sure no one can overhear you giving out your credit card number and expiration date, says Marty Abrams, director of privacy and consumer policy for TRW.

• Both cellular and cordless phones work like walkie-talkies. That means your conversations are not secure. They can easily be picked up by older radio scanners, though it's illegal to build new ones with that capability. Just remember that if you give out sensitive information over these phones, someone may be listening.

• Some con artists excel at stealing cellular phone identification codes and installing them in a tampered phone. If you have a cellular phone, you should monitor your bills carefully. A subsidiary of TRW is planning to sell a system, TRW PhonePrint, that will track, identify and block illegally made phone calls by people using stolen cellular identification numbers. A subsidiary of TRW has developed a system that will identify and block illegally made phone calls by people who are using stolen cellular ID numbers.

• Take a look at the currency you accept to be sure it's not counterfeit. Moore says to look at the clarity and texture of a bill. The real thing will have red and blue fibers, while counterfeit bills are very slick. This is especially important if you are accepting large denominations because if you get stuck with a counterfeit bill, you will be out the money.

• Carefully guard your checkbook and deposit slips. Always use your checks in sequential order and reconcile your account promptly. Don't just let the unopened statements pile up in a drawer, says Edward Alwood, a spokesman for the American Bankers Association. Even if you don't regularly balance your account, look carefully at the statement.

If your checkbook or credit card is stolen, you should file a police report. You are likely to be dunned by collection agencies to cover any fraudulent purchases, but they are supposed to back off after you send them a copy.

• Don't be afraid to ask questions. If someone wants your Social Security number, find out why they need it. If a company, such as a video rental store, asks to keep an imprint of your credit card on file, ask if there is any alternative, such as leaving a cash deposit with them.

• If you receive an unsolicited call from someone trying to sell you something, don't ever give out your credit card number or Social Security number. Also beware of anyone who calls to say you have won a sweepstakes but needs your credit card number to hold your prize.

• The National Consumer League says you should never feel pressured to give out information about yourself or to pay for shipping if you receive a postcard saying you have won a prize but have 72 hours to respond. "The joke in consumer protection circles is that the only time a consumer should take a postcard sweepstakes offer seriously is when Ed McMahon shows up in person at the door," says Linda Golodner, National Consumer League president.

If you believe you have been the victim of fraud but don't know where to go to report it, call the National Fraud Information Center, a service of the National Consumer League. It will help direct you to the right agency. The center also can give you advice about sweepstakes and other offers you receive that sound too good to be true. Call the consumer assistance line at 800-876-7060.

Beware of Scams

Super Rabbits and Get-Rich Schemes Should Raise a Flag

IN THE MID-1980S, a West Coast company was selling partnerships in an exotic rabbit-breeding program. The rex rabbit was a superior breed of bunny that had fur as fine as mink, and meat that was supposed to be freeze-dried and sold to Korean workers guarding Saudi Arabian oil fields.

It was an idea that appealed to investors. Unfortunately, authorities later alleged that the company charged $9,000 to $10,000 for rabbits that actually cost only $50 to $100 apiece. The company had taken in millions of dollars from hundreds of investors before it went belly-up in 1989.

For sheer imagination, the scam has never been topped, says Barbara Roper, director of investor protection at the Consumer Federation of America.

Although outlandish in some ways, the rabbit scam was a fairly typical attempt to swindle people out of their savings. It seems there have always been con artists who lure people into get-rich-quick schemes. The schemes may vary, but the promises of guaranteed riches stay the same.

In addition to garden-variety phone swindlers working out of cheap boiler rooms, there are also unscrupulous brokers operating out of highly regarded Wall Street firms. They can be especially dangerous because unsuspecting clients feel protected by the reputation of the firm.

You may wonder what any of this has to do with you. Only elderly widows are susceptible to investment fraud, right?

Wrong. Doctors, accountants and small-business owners alike have been duped. "I have seen the most educated people who took their retirement money to a broker and lost it all," says John Lawrence Allen, a lawyer who represents victims of dishonest and incompetent brokers.

There is no reason to be paranoid; not everyone is out to rip you off. But there is every reason to learn how to protect yourself from all types of fraud—especially in this low-interest-rate environment when you might be reaching a little too far for extra income. Experts agree that if you are seeking a higher yield for your savings than banks are offering, be wary of unusual investments with promises of high return.

You can get scammed anywhere, in the parking lot of a mall or through a phony mail solicitation. But many con artists ply their trade over the phone; as with legitimate business, they can cover more ground that way.

Here are some suggestions on how to handle an unsolicited cold call from someone you don't know who is trying to sell you an investment:

• Cold callers typically try to pressure people into making a quick decision. They may say that the offer is only good for today, or if you wait, you'll lose the opportunity. This should raise a red flag. "Never invest in something you haven't checked out, or don't understand," Roper says, adding, "Scam artists are adept at building on something that is in the news. Perhaps the caller may tout a new company that has discovered a cure for AIDS. When the company gets approval to market the drug, goes his spiel, the stock is sure to go through the roof—but you can get in now. What he doesn't say is where the stock will go if the drug doesn't work—which is through the floor."

• Don't be afraid to hang up on such a caller, especially if they are using high pressure tactics. The North American Securities Administrators Association (NASAA), which represents state securities agencies, reports that too often con artists exploit the good manners of a potential victim. In these circumstances, it is not impolite to explain that you are not interested and hang up the phone, the association reports. Save your good manners for friends and family members, not swindlers!

• Don't be swayed by callers who tell you they can guarantee a specific return, or they have a sure thing. Ask the person on the phone to send you some documentation. If it's a scam, they probably won't want to give you something in writing, and they may not want to use the U.S. mail because of mail fraud laws. If they do send you some documentation, don't just blindly accept the information. Go to your library and try to find out more about the investment.

• Be suspicious of a stranger who calls and tries to engage you in friendly conversation. Laura Polacheck, a senior analyst at the American Association of Retired Persons, says some con artists try to take advantage of elderly people who live alone by creating a sense of companionship. They may call several times before they actually try to sell something. By then they've established a rapport and they turn up the pressure.

• Don't ever be embarrassed to ask questions. If you are confused by what someone is telling you, just say you want to see something in writing so you can carefully consider it.

• Get the name of the person who called you and ask the National Association of Securities Dealers or your state securities bureau for a copy of their Central Registration Depository file. This should contain information on any lawsuits or complaints that have been filed against the broker. If the person is not even registered, then they are not allowed to sell investments.

• Don't be afraid to report investment fraud. In particular, older people may worry that if they admit they have been victimized, they will be judged incapable of handling their own affairs. Recognize that con artists know about such sensitivities and, in fact, count on these fears preventing or delaying the point at which authorities are notified of a scam, according to a list of 10 self-defense tips for older Americans developed by the NASAA.

After You Choose a Broker

To protect your money, you must be an active client.

• At least every quarter, tell your broker about any changes in your financial condition.

• Read and understand your statements, and keep a copy of all documents you receive from the brokerage firm.

• Keep a log of your conversations with your broker.

SOURCE: *Investor Beware: How to Protect Your Money from Wall Street's Dirty Tricks,* by John Lawrence Allen.

In the end, Roper says, the best advice is simply never buy anything over the phone during a call that you have not initiated. Why take that chance?

But you may be tempted if you hear that someone from your church or community group has a great investment. Alice McInerney, assistant New York attorney general in charge of investor protection, warns that swindlers often target such groups. They get a couple of people from the group involved in some kind of Ponzi scheme. These schemes promise a high rate of return, but pay it from the funds that come in from new investors. So for a while, the investors make a good return. Friends hear about it and want to get in on the deal; their money goes to pay off previous investors. But eventually, and inevitably, the whole deal collapses when new people stop coming. Just remember, if a deal sounds too good to be true, it probably is—even if a friend is telling you about it.

Many people seek out professional advice from brokers at Wall Street firms. They may decide they are willing to pay broker commissions because they don't have the time, the inclination or the expertise to make investment selections. Unfortunately, sometimes investors put their trust in a dishonest broker and end up losing their money.

Even if most brokers are honest, Allen says it is wrong for investors to put total trust in them. "There exists in every relationship with every broker, financial adviser and money manager, a basic conflict of interest," he says. "You must approach every suggestion with 10 pounds of salt."

If you don't carefully monitor your investments, you may not notice that your broker is guilty of churning—excessive trading to generate big commissions. Your broker may be suggesting investments that are inappropriate, considering your goals and risk tolerance. Or your broker may be making unauthorized trades.

These are illegal practices. But before you get embroiled in a court case or an arbitration proceeding with a broker, there are ways to help prevent fraud in the first place. Allen, author of *Investor Beware,* a book about how to protect yourself from investment fraud, gives the following suggestions:

• Before you even consult a broker, decide how much you can afford to invest and for how long. You should assess your goals and how much risk you are willing to take. Then you will be prepared to clearly tell a broker what your needs are.

• Choose a broker carefully. In addition to ordering their enforcement file, and one for the brokerage, meet potential brokers in person and bring along a list of questions to ask them. If you're asking articulate, intelligent questions, you're letting him know who's in control, Allen says. He knows he's in for trouble if he puts you in the wrong investments.

Most brokerage firms require clients to sign a statement agreeing to forgo legal suits and submit to binding arbitration in the case of a dispute or complaint. Roper says this is not necessarily a bad thing because the legal system can be very expensive and time consuming.

If you have a dispute about an investment start by sending a written complaint to the brokerage firm. If you can't resolve the problem, file a complaint with your state securities bureau, the Securities and Exchange Commission and the NASD. If necessary, ask for a hearing before an arbitration board.

Investing in a Cause

"Socially Responsible" Mutual Funds Make Their Mark

Put your money where your mouth is. That's one way to describe socially responsible investing.

You probably have a favorite cause. It could be environmental issues, or the advancement of women and minorities in the workplace. You may even have written letters to the editor of a newspaper, donated money or joined an organization to promote the cause of your choice. You may be so adamantly opposed to abortion that you have picketed an abortion clinic. Or perhaps you're concerned about nuclear power and have demonstrated against a nuclear reactor in your community.

Why not go one step further and make sure your savings are invested in companies that match your values? That's a question an increasing number of people are asking themselves today.

Socially responsible investing, or SRI, sounds great. But because it involves your hard-earned savings, it should not be jumped into like the latest fad. Investing is difficult enough for many people; when you add the social component it becomes much more complicated.

Presumably, you don't want to be a charity. You want to do well—make a profit on your investment—by doing good. So, you not only need to find an investment that matches your social goals, but you also have to find one that matches your financial goals and risk tolerance, and performs well.

Fortunately, as interest in SRI has grown, there are more sources of information on the subject, and more investment advisers who are knowledgeable about it. Today there are also about 40 mutual funds that are classified as social funds, with about $3.1 billion in total assets, according to the Social Investment Forum, a nonprofit trade association.

If you are interested in socially responsible investing, let your head, as well as your heart, be your guide. Spend time learning about SRI.

To get started, here are some answers to basic questions about the subject:

Who decides what is a socially responsible investment?

You do. Although most people associate SRI with a liberal political agenda, it need not be. In recent years, the typical social investor has tended to be a middle-income woman in her 40s, who is concerned about the environment, the military and women's issues, says Peter Kinder, president of Kinder, Lydenberg, Domini & Co., a social research firm. But he says that is changing as the concept is catching on with more men, labor unions and other institutions.

"The idea is simply to vote with your dollars," says Rosemary Brown, an editor at Co-op America, a nonprofit group dedicated to educating people about how to match their consuming and investing habits to their social goals. "We're telling people how to make a difference."

But finding the companies that fit your values is not necessarily simple. The corporate world is not clearly divided into good guys and bad guys. What if a company has a good record on the environment, but poor labor relations? Do you invest in it? You have to set your own priorities.

"When you're dealing with a company that has 15,000 employees, there will be some bad aspects to it," says Kinder. "The world is not black and white. It is comprised of grays. Most social investors are aware that perfection is not something they will find in a company."

How do you get started?

You need to know that there are different types of social investing.

Some people prefer to invest in major corporations and then use their ownership rights to try to force the management to change policies they don't agree with. In the past, for example, many shareholder groups have introduced resolutions to stop banks and other corporations from doing business in South Africa. If this type of activism interests you, you can join a group, such as the Interfaith Center on Corporate Responsibility in New York, and help put shareholder power to work.

But you may not have the time or inclination to go to annual meetings and agitate for change. And you may prefer to avoid investing in any company that violates your principles. Instead, you can direct your investments to companies that share your values.

There are two basic ways to do this. You can invest in a socially responsible mutual fund, or you can have an investment adviser help you select your own portfolio of stocks.

Like all mutual funds, social funds are popular because of their convenience, professional management and because they spread out the risk among many stocks. Many of the social funds do not charge a load, or commission, so you can invest in them without a broker. Ritchie Lowry, president of *Good Money Publications,* says you should select one of these funds much the same way you would select any mutual fund.

Pick several funds that you are interested in, he says. Get the prospectus and annual report for each of them. And see which ones match your financial and social goals.

Each social fund has a particular social agenda as well as an investment goal.

Good Conscience Money

If your conscience is your guide—even for your investments—consider getting a mutual fund that matches your social goals. Here are the top-performing funds that have been around at least three years.

Objec-tive	Fund Name	Sales Charge	Expense Ratio	Cumulative Total Return		
				1-Yr.	3-Yr.	5-Yr.
	Calvert Social Inv.: Bond 800-368-2748	4.75	0.75	11.66%	37.97%	69.72%
	Calvert Social Inv. Eqty 800-368-2748	4.75	1.17	2.14	34.99	63.69
	Calvert Social Inv.: Gro 800-368-2748	4.75	1.28	5.95	34.15	62.20
	Calvert-Ariel: Apprec 800-368-2748	4.75	1.44	7.95	62.83	N/A
	Calvert-Ariel: Growth 800-368-2748	4.75	1.23	8.75	61.60	69.64
	Dreyfus Third Century 800-645-6561	0.00	1.11	5.26	48.21	79.97
	New Alternatives Fund 516-466-0808	4.75	1.04	2.89	35.48	57.76
	Parnassus Fund 800-999-3505	3.50	1.47	17.31	144.83	98.51
	Pax World Fund 800-767-1729	0.00	1.00	−1.06	20.27	65.94
	Righttime: Soc. Awareness 800-242-1421	4.75	2.49	−2.27	35.77	N/A
	Average of All Long-Term Taxable Funds			15.17	56.51	82.74

Objective

 Balanced

 Corporate bond: general

 Growth

 Growth and income

 Small company

 Speciality: alternative energy

Seeks

 Good environmental record

 Good labor relations

 Safe products

 Quality products

 Equal employment opportunity

 Worker safety

 Supports education

Investments in affordable housing

Social Goals

Avoids	*Seeks*

(rows of symbol icons representing the categories below)

Avoids

 Alcoholic beverages and manufacturers

 Tobacco products manufacturers

 Gambling operations

Animal testing

 Labor violations

 South Africa business ties

 Nuclear power

Poor environmental record

 Petroleum companies

 Weapons makers

 Investments in U.S. Treasury securities

SOURCE: Lipper Analytical Services, Good Money Publications

This will determine the criteria, or screens, it uses to eliminate or select companies it will invest in.

Don't be misled by a fund's label, experts say. Some funds call themselves green funds or environmental funds, for example. But look closely at the stocks they hold. You may find they actually invest in trash haulers or other companies that you want to avoid.

And before you invest in a fund be sure to check its track record. Compare it to a benchmark to see how it has performed relative to similar funds. "Social funds are like anything else," says Ted Bernhard, an analyst at the Social Investment Forum. "There are great performers and there are not-so-great performers."

If you would like your money to have a direct impact on your neighborhood, you might consider depositing money in a community development financial institution. These credit unions, banks and loan funds are dedicated to serving the credit and deposit needs of the low- and moderate-income neighborhoods that are often shunned by traditional banks.

"If you don't want your money going to a sultan in the Middle East, you might want to deposit some in an institution that will help create jobs and low- and moderate-income housing in your community," Lowry says.

Can social investing and profitable investing go hand in hand?

"There is no inherent reason you should lose money if you make a social judgment," Lowry says. And he notes you may be better off with a socially responsible company because it is not as likely to have to defend itself from costly lawsuits or to suffer from protracted labor problems.

To better assess the profitability of social investing, Kinder, Lydenberg, Domini has created the Domini 400 Social Index, which is modeled after the benchmark S&P 500 stock index. Kinder says that his index of socially responsible corporations has increased 70.1 percent since May 1990, compared with 58.4 percent for the S&P 500.

And Lowry has created the Good Money Industrial Average and the Good Money Utility Average, which parallel the Dow Jones industrial average. According to Lowry, the GMIA has outpaced the Dow by nearly 3 to 1 since it began in 1977.

What can you accomplish by investing in socially responsible corporations?

That may be hard to measure. At the very least, you will get the satisfaction of investing according to your conscience. But if you think that by withholding your money from tobacco companies you'll bring them to their knees, you're probably mistaken. Still, experts say that socially responsible investing and activism can have an impact. For example they note that in 1994, General Motors Corp. signed the 10-point code of corporate environmental conduct created by the Coalition for Economically Responsible Economies and promoted by investor groups.

Making Stocks Accessible
Investment Clubs Take the Voodoo Out of Investing

CATERINA BARTHA is defying the stereotype of the starving artist. The Manhattan-based choreographer and performance artist recently started an investment club so she can learn to play the stock market and finance her creations with the profits.

"It's like going into unknown territory," she admits. "I have no clue about what it means to be diversified. This is a learning experience. The idea is to take the voodoo out of investing. To make it accessible."

Bartha believes this is an adventure that is best shared with others. Her club started out with about 10 members, including another choreographer, a filmmaker, and a computer programmer. When they were getting organized they didn't know how to go about building a portfolio of stocks.

But Bartha's group was able to learn from the experience of other small investors by joining the National Association of Investors Corp., a nonprofit investor education group that counts 13,300 clubs around the country among its members.

And the numbers are growing. NAIC headquarters in Royal Oaks, Mich., has received as many as 1,200 calls a day from would-be investors. "The interest by the public in stocks is very great now," says Thomas O'Hara, chairman of the board of NAIC. "Also, for 44 years our members have done very well, and we think the word has gotten around."

Of course there are always risks associated with investing in the stock market. Many new investors hope to cash in on it. But it's unclear how they will react when the market trend reverses.

O'Hara, who has been through a number of bear markets in his lifetime, hopes investors have learned not to panic. People who got out of the market after the 1987 crash have seen that those who stayed in made out pretty well, he says.

Most people have chosen to invest in stocks through mutual funds. There are obvious advantages: You don't need a lot of money to invest in a mutual fund; each fund invests in many diverse companies, so you are protected from a dip in one stock or industry; and they are managed by professionals, so you don't have to spend time researching the financial history of companies and monitoring their performance.

Investment clubs offer similar advantages: Members pool their money so they can afford to invest in a diverse portfolio of stocks. In some clubs, members in-

Getting Clubby

OK, so your interest is piqued and you think you'd like to be part of a group determining its own financial future. Here are some tips on organizing an investment club:

Finding Members

• Clubs range in size from three members to more than 35 members, but the optimal size is probably about 15. That way there are enough people to do the work but not too many that some members get bored.

• You don't have to find all the members. Just ask two or three people and let them invite some of their friends to an organizational meeting. Ask people from your church, charity organizations, work place, bridge clubs, condo complex and other groups you may be involved with. A variety of backgrounds brings a variety of experience to your club. You don't need to seek an investment specialist.

• Whatever number of club members you plan to have, invite three or four more prospects. Inevitably, some people that express interest at first will change their minds at the organizational meeting.

• Remember that this is a long-term adventure, and you want people who enjoy each other's company. The members must be committed to learning investment principles and sharing the workload.

Club Philosophy

• Members should agree on the kind of investment philosophy they will follow. The single most frequent cause of early dissolution of investment clubs is conflicting philosophies. A club cannot exist with long-term investors following sound security analysis and short-term traders moving in and out of the market and acting on tips and rumors.

vest as little as $5 a month. It's a great way to learn without putting much money at risk, says O'Hara, a founder of NAIC.

Unlike mutual funds, however, investment clubs don't rely on someone else to manage their portfolios. Members must understand the fundamentals of the stock market. They must take the time to research corporate performance.

That discipline can pay off. "It has been our experience that individuals tend to outperform the professionals if they spend the time to train themselves," O'Hara says. For 23 out of the past 33 years, a sample of clubs surveyed by NAIC has outperformed the S&P 500 stock index.

Although you don't need to join NAIC to start an investment club, many members say the association's investment manuals, seminars and investment philosophy are invaluable. And although it is possible to join an existing club, new members frequently set up their own clubs. That way they start out on equal footing with the other organizers and learn together as they go.

• In addition, members should be willing to commit their time, not just their money. During the first year, when members are learning how to study stocks, a typical monthly meeting lasts two hours, and each member needs to commit about two hours during the month preparing for the meeting. As members become familiar with the process, it takes less time.

Nuts and Bolts

• Set a regular monthly meeting date.
• Decide the monthly amount each member will invest. This should be an amount that is comfortable for every member of the club. Most clubs start at $20 or $25 a month. The amount should be set for the first year, but after that members may wish to vary their contributions and even make withdrawals.
• Choose a club name, elect officers, draft bylaws and agree on operating procedures. The National Association of Investors Corp. offers an investment club manual that will walk you through each step.
• Select a broker. You might want to have one who specializes in handling investment clubs, or you might choose a discount broker.
• Consider joining the NAIC, a nonprofit organization devoted to teaching sound investment principles. Membership includes a stock study program, which teaches you how to make informed judgments about the potential risk and gains of individual stocks. It also includes details on using stock comparison and stock selection worksheets. Membership offers you discounts on computer software, books, magazines and a fidelity bond. An investment club can join for $35 plus $11 per club member per year.
• Start a study program. Whether you join NAIC or not you need to start a program that will teach members basic investment principles and how to evaluate stocks. The goal of the club should be to learn as well as build wealth.

SOURCE: National Association of Investors Corp.

Investment clubs are private groups. Typically they have 12 to 20 members; in some cases, they have been investing together for decades and have developed common bonds. NAIC notes that it can be helpful to enlist an accountant, lawyer or other financial expert as a member. However, many clubs are quite eclectic.

Phyllis Pawlovsky, a director of the New York City Regional NAIC Council, says that her four-and-a-half-year-old club has 12 members, including a teacher, a chemical engineer, an electrical engineer, a legal secretary, a retired stockbroker and a board of education administrator. Four of the members are women and eight are men.

NAIC clubs operate on four basic principles: Invest a set sum every month, regardless of market conditions. Reinvest dividends and capital gains immediately. Invest in companies that seem likely to be worth substantially more five years in the future. And invest in different industries so you spread out the risk.

That sounds fairly simple. But it takes work and discipline to implement these principles. As Pawlovsky puts it: "I never met a stock I didn't like." What NAIC does is give you boundaries and criteria for picking a stock.

In fact, NAIC manuals teach members sophisticated ways to evaluate stocks. The stock selection guide, for example, is a detailed worksheet that clubs use to evaluate a company based on its management performance, price-earnings history, future risk and reward calculations and five-year potential. Once you fill in the worksheets, NAIC provides specific guidelines on when to buy and sell a stock.

The fact that many clubs that have outstanding track records is proof that its approach works, NAIC says. O'Hara's own club has posted a compound annual return of 12.2 percent in the 54 years since it was founded. During that time, members have invested $300,000. He says they have withdrawn $1.5 million and have $2.4 million left.

But membership in NAIC is no guarantee of high returns. It is not unusual for new clubs to show lackluster performance while members learn the ropes, set up their portfolio and pay for broker commissions.

Jack Rodolico, a director of the New York City NAIC Regional Council and treasurer of a club on Long Island, says that broker commissions ate up much of the profits generated by his club in its first three years. "One person dropped out because he was discouraged by a loss of $100," he says. "If you can't afford to lose $100, you shouldn't be in the stock market."

A typical investment club meeting starts out with a review of the minutes of the previous meeting and a report on the performance of the club's portfolio. Then someone usually makes a presentation on a stock that the club is considering buying. The presenter must be prepared to go over the stock selection guide and answer questions about the company's business practices and growth potential.

The discussion of the stock takes up most of the time and it can get heated, Rodolico says. "Then members vote on the stock. If the club agrees to buy shares in the company, then the member who made the pitch is in charge of continuing to monitor the stock. At future meetings, the member is supposed to point out major events, such as acquisitions or management changes, that could affect the stock price."

Individual members and clubs can take advantage of NAIC's low-cost investment plan. This is a way to bypass the broker when purchasing small amounts of stock in certain companies. There is a one-time charge of $5 for each stock you select. NAIC is able to do this because it has joined the dividend reinvestment programs of a number of companies, which allow shareholders to purchase additional stock directly.

If you buy stock through the low-cost plan you are essentially investing under the umbrella account of NAIC. So the first time you invest in a particular company, your check gets routed through NAIC. One drawback of this plan is that the shares don't get purchased immediately. Stock purchases made through a dividend reinvestment program are usually only processed monthly or quarterly.

As with any group, investment clubs are not always harmonious. Sometimes members refuse to do their share of the work. "You always find people who are in it for a quick buck," Rodolico says. "In our club that doesn't work."

Other members may be chronically late making their monthly contribution to the investment pool. In such cases, a club may have to establish late fees. The worst-case scenario is when a member steals from the club. Through NAIC, clubs are eligible to purchase at a discount a bond that insures against fraud.

• For more information about NAIC, write National Association of Investors Corp., P.O. Box 220, Roal Oak, Mich., 48068, or call 810-583-6242.

D-I-V-O-R-C-E

Protecting Your Financial Interests
When Your Love Interest Fades

Happily married couples don't usually plan for divorce. Yet by the time a marriage sours, it can be hard to put aside hurt feelings and calmly sort out complicated financial matters. Sometimes, one spouse is so eager to get out of a relationship that he or she foolishly relinquishes important assets and retirement benefits.

The problem is that while most people have a pretty good idea of how to get into a marriage, they know very little about how to get out of one. And adding injury to insult, the divorce may be more expensive than even the most lavish wedding.

As it turns out, an increasing number of people, especially women, are seeking professional advice before they file for divorce, says Ann Diamond, a financial consultant and author of *Fear of Finance,* a book about women and money.

"Women are coming to me even before they talk to their husband about divorce," Diamond says. This is particularly helpful to wives who have never worked, have no credit history and have been left in the dark about retirement plans, taxes and investments.

Diamond says that many of these women have seen friends go through difficult divorces and want to know more about the system and their rights. They are at a disadvantage because their husbands have a better grasp of finances and have established relationships with lawyers and accountants. They want to start out on a more level playing field.

Divorce is not always a battleground, however. Some couples, especially those who have no children or major assets, manage to split up amicably. But in some states, such as New York, divorce law does not make this easy. Although experts say it is possible to go through a divorce without a lawyer, many couples want some professional advice. The trick is to avoid getting trapped in a costly, time-consuming and adversarial legal struggle.

Before you head to court, you should know something about divorce law in your state. New York, for example, is an equitable distribution state. That means assets acquired during marriage should be equitably divided according to the particular circumstances of the marriage.

In other words, you do not automatically get half of the assets. In determining equitable distribution, the court takes into consideration a number of factors, including how long a couple has been married, disparity in income, and number of children.

Before you even file for divorce, you should start to discreetly document your finances and protect your assets if you anticipate that your spouse will be hostile or vindictive. Ann Peterson, a financial consultant in Georgia and author of *Every Woman's Guide to Financial Security,* suggests the following steps:

• Make copies of your most recent tax return, insurance policies, and most recent bank and brokerage statements.

• Make of list of everything in your home—or, better yet, videotape your possessions.

• Set up a separate mailing address. You can use a post office box. Open a new checking account in your name only and begin applying for your own credit cards, if you don't already have them.

• If your spouse asks you to cosign a loan, refuse to do it. If you sign, you'll be on the hook if your ex later defaults on the loan.

When you finally get ready to file for divorce, consider what will happen to your health insurance coverage. Spouses are entitled to continue to receive benefits through their ex-spouse's employer (if the company has at least 20 employees) for 36 months after the divorce is final. You will receive the group rate, but you will not receive the employer's contribution to your premium. You must request the coverage in writing. After three years, you will be on your own.

Be sure to remove your name from any joint credit card accounts, and notify credit card companies in writing that you will no longer be responsible for charges made on them, Diamond says. Send the letters return receipt requested and then set up a file with all these documents in case if you receive bills for your ex-husband's charges at a later date.

You also may want to withdraw half of the money in your bank accounts or ask the bank to freeze the accounts, Diamond says. At the same time, she says, write to your broker to say that you don't want any transactions to occur without both parties being notified. Send the letter return receipt requested so you have a record of the notification.

It's very important to close any equity lines of credit you and your spouse may have. If you don't do this, you can end up putting your home at risk.

To get a divorce, you may have to submit a settlement agreement to the court. This is a contract that says how your assets will be divided and how debts will be allocated. If alimony or child support are part of the divorce, the agreement should specify the amounts for each.

There are several ways to go about drawing up a settlement agreement. If you and your spouse are on good terms, you can do it yourself, using one of the good books on the market. Make sure the specifics for your state are covered.

If you're too angry and distraught to deal with the settlement agreement yourselves, you may decide to hire a lawyer to represent you. In that case, your

How to Find A Lawyer

You want a lawyer who regularly handles divorce cases and seeks your input for every decision. Here are some places to look:

• Paralegals. Independent paralegals get regular feedback on lawyers' work and can make informed referrals. Paralegals are listed in the yellow pages under "Paralegals" or "Typing or Self-Help Services." You also can call the National Association of Independent Paralegals at (800) 542-0034.

• Personal referrals. If you know someone who was pleased with the services of a lawyer, call that lawyer first. If that lawyer doesn't handle divorces or can't take your case, ask for recommendations.

• Group legal plans. Some unions, employers and consumer action organizations offer group plans that offer comprehensive legal assistance for free or for low rates.

• Prepaid legal insurance. Prepaid legal insurance plans offer some services for a low monthly fee and charge more for additional work. Make sure you're clear on costs and exactly what services you'll receive.

• Lawyer referral panels. Most county bar associations will give out the names of lawyers in your area. But bar associations often fail to provide meaningful screening, which means those who participate may not be the most experienced or competent.

SOURCE: *Divorce: A New Yorker's Guide to Doing It Yourself*

spouse will also hire a lawyer. Just remember that as your legal bills mount, your assets will shrink accordingly.

Marvin Korobow, a matrimonial lawyer, says that if a couple has a simple, uncontested divorce—a short marriage, no children and few assets—the legal bill may total $5,000. But that's just for one spouse. The other spouse's bill may be slightly less, he says, because only one lawyer has to draft the settlement agreement. Complicated, acrimonious divorces will cost considerably more.

If you don't have that kind of money, but still need some help overcoming disputes, you might consider mediation. Barbara Badolato at Divorce Mediation Professionals, says that the mediation approach is more humane than the courts. In the heat of emotion, the average husband and wife can't reach an agreement alone, Bardolato says. Mediation seeks to give them back the power.

Badolato is a social worker. Her partner, a lawyer, can review the settlement agreement and answer other legal questions along the way. The lawyer is not an advocate for either side. The firm charges $250 an hour, and Badolato says couples meet with them once a week, usually for two to four months. Couples who have al-

Breaking Up Is Hard to Do

Here are some points to keep in mind if you're entering the divorce battleground.
• Before the divorce, gather as much financial information as possible. Keep copies of all related papers.
• Establish your own mailing address and checking account, and apply for credit in your own name.
• Insist on keeping your fair share of household items and joint property.
• Negotiate for alimony, if you're unemployed or earn substantially less than your spouse, and child support. Don't be greedy, but don't get taken to the cleaners, either.
• Check into your benefits from your spouse's retirement plans, Social Security, health care, life insurance, Etc.
• Complete a financial inventory and set up a realistic budget.
• Try to live independently, and don't make any long-term commitments right away.
• Keep your children out of the middle. The battle is between you and your spouse; the children need to respect both parents. That's hard to do if the parents are busy berating each other.

Document Check

Here's a checklist of documents and other information you need to have in case your marriage dissolves.

• A complete inventory of your household goods, preferably on video, and notes as to value and purchase date. Check your insurance file for these.
• Personal and business tax returns for the past several years. If you used a tax preparer, the person is required by law to keep copies for three years. Otherwise, call the IRS (800-829-3676) and request Form 4506 (Request for Copy of Tax Form). This form need not be signed by your spouse, assuming the two of you filed a joint return. The IRS charges $4.25 for this service. Processing time is 10 days to two months.
• Financial statements from banks and loan applications. Often things that are overlooked when filing taxes are somehow remembered when proving credit-worthiness.
• Prenuptial agreements, or any other agreements showing how income or assets are to be split.
• Business and home accounting records, including bank statements, ledgers, budget books and check registers.
• Copies of notes payable to you or by you, and outstanding credit card bills.
• Deeds or contracts.
• Personal or business insurance papers.
• Statements from brokerage firms, mutual funds, partnerships or other investment records. This includes appraisals on any collectibles (antiques, jewels, hobby or sports collections).
• A copy of your spouse's pay stub, pension agreement and profit-sharing plan or other retirement program.

SOURCE: Every Woman' Guide to Financial Security

ready drawn up their own settlement agreement, but want a lawyer to go over it with them, also can consult a firm such as Divorce Mediation Professionals.

When you're working out your divorce, Peterson says, you should realize there is a third party to consider: the IRS. So when you're dividing up the house, for example, don't forget to factor in future capital gains taxes. And if you have children, you and your spouse cannot both claim them as dependents. The exemption goes to the parent who provides more than half of the child's support, she says.

The spouse who makes alimony payments receives a tax deduction and the recipient must pay taxes on the income. But child support payments are not considered taxable income, nor are they tax deductible for the parent who makes the payments.

Also, be aware that if you and your spouse filed joint tax returns while you were married, you can subsequently be held liable for back taxes and penalties. Even if your spouse filled out the returns and you merely signed them, the IRS can stick you with the entire bill. There is an innocent spouse defense, but it is difficult to qualify for.

In addition to your home, there is another major asset that is often overlooked during a divorce settlement: a pension plan. Ed Slott, a partner in the accounting firm E. Slott & Co., says that just because you and your spouse have not reached retirement age doesn't mean the wife can't get part of the benefits down the road. The Qualified Domestic Relations Order is a court order that requires the pension plan to set aside a piece of the pension for the ex-spouse. Educate yourself about your pension rights, consumer advocates say, and never sign a waiver of those rights without understanding what you are signing.

Don't forget about life insurance policies. If one spouse retains the policy, he or she will probably want to change the beneficiary. Slott says some people believe they can do this by simply rewriting their will. But that won't hold up in court if the policy has not also been changed, he says. And if the ex-husband agrees to provide child support, the wife may want the settlement to also include a term life insurance policy so that the children will continue to receive some support if he dies.

• To order a copy of *Your Pension Rights at Divorce: What Women Need to Know,* send a check for $16.50 to Pension Rights Center, 918 16th St. NW, Suite 704, Dept. A, Washington, D.C., 20006.

• To order a copy of *Divorce: A New Yorker's Guide to Doing It Yourself,* ($24.95), call Nolo Press at (800) 992-6656.

Betting the Ranch

A Home Equity Loan Could Cost You Your Home, So Know What You're Doing

IT SEEMS TO make perfect sense.

If you take out a home equity line of credit now, you can pay off all your credit card bills and you'll have money left over for the vacation in Bermuda you've been dreaming about all winter. What's more, when your oldest child is ready for college in two years, you can tap into it for tuition bills. And best of all, rates are still low and the interest is tax deductible.

But before you sign on the dotted line, you'd better give it some more thought.

Have you read the loan agreement carefully? Do you know when you'll have to begin repaying the principal? If interest rates suddenly rise, will you be able to make the higher payments? Is there a large balloon payment due at the end of the advance term? Do you even know what that means? And what happens if you lose your job or become disabled?

The bottom line: Are you prepared to lose your home if you fall behind on the payments?

"Home equity loans are dangerous instruments," says Larry Elkin, a financial planner in Hastings-on-Hudson. "You're betting the ranch. It should never be done lightly."

Home equity loans and lines of credits are really just a type of second mortgage. They are very popular because, unlike other types of personal loans, the interest is tax deductible.

For many Americans, their home is their only major asset. They are cash poor, but equity rich. So when they need money for an emergency, they may have nowhere else to turn.

And these days banks are happy to oblige home equity borrowers. That's because many people paid off their home equity loans when they took advantage of low interest rates and refinanced their mortgages, says Keith Gumbinger, an analyst at HSH Associates, a mortgage tracking firm in Butler, N.J. Now, in order to replenish their portfolios, banks are offering low introductory home equity rates.

"It's good news for consumers," Gumbinger says.

But other experts caution that it's only good news for consumers who are smart shoppers and prudent borrowers. Although home equity loans and lines of

You'd Better Shop Around

Don't go with the first lender that offers you a home equity loan or credit line. To get the best deal, pose these questions to at least five, and preferably 10, lenders. Don't rely on the telemarketing department to have all the answers; you may have to speak with a loan officer or customer service representative.

1. What is today's interest rate?

2. What index is that based on?

3. What is the margin over that index?

4. Is there an interest rate ceiling? A floor?

5. Is there a term on the credit line or is it open ended?

6. Is that both the advance and repayment term, or does it balloon?

7. Are there any points charged on the line or loan?

8. What is the maximum percentage of the house value that you'll lend?

9. What, if any, are the closing costs or other fees I'll be required to pay?

10. Is there an annual fee? If so, how much is it?

SOURCE: HSH Associates

credit may be the cheapest loans available, they are also the riskiest. So before you settle on a home equity loan or line of credit, be sure to consider all your other options.

Elkin notes, for example, that many 401(k) plans allow you to borrow against your retirement savings, and the interest is paid back into your own account. You can also borrow from yourself, he says. Many people who have put aside a nest egg are reluctant to dip into it. But it may make more sense to do that than put your home on the line. There is also such a thing as saving money before you spend it, Elkin says.

If you opt in the end for a home equity loan, you need to decide how much you should borrow and what kind of loan or line of credit best suits your needs.

If you're not careful, banks may lend you more money than you can really afford. A few home equity lenders actually prey on credit-starved, low-income and elderly consumers, according to consumer advocates. "Vulnerable consumers are put into loans they can't afford so that they are doomed to lose their home," says Michelle Meier, chief lobbyist at Consumers Union.

Beware, says the group, of unsolicited offers from banks and finance companies who are willing to lend solely on the value of your home without considering your ability to repay. Sometimes these loans seem affordable because the monthly payments are low at first. But after several years, they may require you to pay off the loan all at once.

Frequently these unscrupulous lenders charge high interest rates and high, nonrefundable fees. So always shop around for the best deal. Don't sign anything you don't understand. And have a lawyer review any documents that could put your home in jeopardy.

Even if you're dealing with reputable lenders, you'll find home equity loans can be complicated. But you have to be diligent, Gumbinger says. You really have to read all the paperwork. Yes, it's dry reading. But it's very important.

Don't expect shopping for a home equity loan to be as straightforward as shopping for a first mortgage. Unlike home mortgages, home equity loans are not standardized and will vary from bank to bank. If you are a co-op owner, you will have to look harder to find banks willing to give you a home equity loan and you may have to pay a slightly higher interest rate than homeowners.

The first thing you should decide is whether you want a loan or a line of credit. With a home equity loan, you usually receive the amount you're borrowing in one lump sum and then you make equal monthly payments over the life of the loan. In most cases, they are fixed-rate loans, but they can be adjustable as well.

Gumbinger says you should ask yourself what you need the money for. If you have a specific one-time expense, such as consolidating your credit card bills or adding on a garage, you probably would be better off with a fixed-rate home equity loan. That way you know exactly what your monthly payments will be and you can plan accordingly.

But if you want the loan so you can put your son through college as well as consolidate your debts, you may want a line of credit for its flexibility. Lines of credit work much like a credit card: You are approved for a maximum amount of money, which you can draw upon as you need it. Typically, after you use up the line of credit and repay it, you can start tapping into it again.

There is a major downside to lines of credit. The interest rate is variable, so your payments can suddenly jump if interest rates rise. And some loan agreements allow the bank to reduce or withdraw the line of credit if certain conditions change, such as if you lose your job or if the property value declines.

The amount of money you can borrow depends largely on the amount of equity in your home—the market price minus what you still owe on your mortgage.

Lenders usually will require a new appraisal, and then will lend only a portion of your equity. They may give you a maximum line of credit equal to 80 percent of your equity, but less if the real estate market is weak or if your finances are a bit shaky.

Home equity lines of credit are complicated, so be sure you understand the terms and conditions of any loan you are considering. For example, most have an advance and a repayment term. The advance term is when you are able to draw on the money. During this time, you will be billed each month, but often just for the interest owed.

After five or 10 years, the repayment term starts. At that point, you are unable to borrow more money and you have to make interest and principal payments. But there are many variations. Some lines of credit have no terms, and operate much like a credit card. Others have a balloon—a single large payment—due at the end of the advance period. If you don't have the money, the balloon goes bust—and probably so do you.

When it comes to pricing, you especially need to do your homework. The rate you pay on a line of credit is linked to a specified index of loan rates. Many banks use the prime rate and add a point or so to determine the rate you'll pay. The rate may be adjusted every month or every quarter. Gail Liberman, editor of *Bank Rate Monitor,* an industry newsletter, says that banks are now trying to attract more home equity business by offering special low teaser rates, usually good for a year. To get some idea of what you'll really be up against, ask what the maximum rate could be a year from now, and whether there's a lifetime cap.

Be sure to ask about points and fees. You may be required to pay points based on the maximum amount available on a line of credit, even though you never intend to draw on the full amount. You may have to pay for an appraisal, credit check and recording. And banks usually charge an annual fee for a line of credit. If you're not careful you can get stuck paying $100 a month or more for the annual fee, Liberman says.

Some lenders will give you the option of a home equity loan with no closing costs, but a higher interest rate. Others will waive the annual fee for a year. Because banks are competing for your business, it pays to shop around.

• Get more details on home equity loans and lines of credit. HSH Associates offers a 12-page booklet, *Home Equity: A Consumer's Guide to Loans and Lines,* for $3. To order, call (800) 873-2837.

Knowledge Is Power

Here's a Pop Quiz on Your Financial Education, and It's OK to Peek at the Answers

AMERICANS ARE NOT very optimistic about their financial future.

The majority of Americans say they often worry about money. Nearly half of them say that an unexpected bill of $1,000 would be a big problem. And fully 47 percent say they think more often about money than sex (although they enjoy sex more). These findings, all from the ninth national survey of Americans and their money by *Money* magazine, underscore the problems many people have making ends meet and planning for the future.

Knowledge, however, is your weapon against worry, which presumably is why you're reading *Fiscal Fitness*. Let's see how much you remember:

True/False

1. To protect yourself from unscrupulous brokers you should keep a log of all your conversations, or better yet, tape-record your calls and tell the broker you're taping them.

2. Financial products are so complicated these days that parents should let the schools teach their children about money and finances.

3. Tear up your credit card receipts and bank statements before throwing them out.

4. If your checkbook is stolen, don't worry; you won't be held liable for the losses.

5. It's a good idea to check your credit reports periodically, even if you're not planning on taking a loan.

6. Child support payments are tax deductible for the parent who makes them.

7. Only financial experts with a lot of money to invest can join investment clubs.

8. Making a profit and being a socially responsible investor are not mutually exclusive.

9. If you believe you will be eligible for financial aid by the time your child is ready to go to college, you should start putting your college savings in your child's name.

10. Home equity loans and lines of credit are among the riskiest types of loans you can take out.

How Do You Slice It?

If you're in a 401(k) plan, you decide how to split up your investments. Use this pie chart to illustrate your own 401(k) allocations and then check yourself against the professionals, whose results can be found in the answer key.

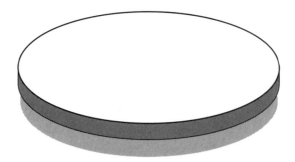

Professionally Speaking

When it comes to their 401(k)s, most individuals play it too safe, risking their investments not to the markets, but to the all-more-certain damage of inflation. If your 401(k) isn't outpacing inflation, maybe you should take a hint from the professionals. Here's how pension fund managers allocate assets:

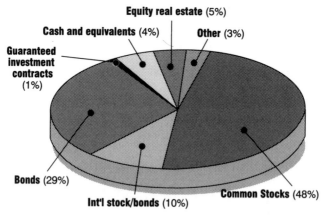

Equity real estate (5%)

Cash and equivalents (4%)   **Other** (3%)

Guaranteed investment contracts (1%)

Bonds (29%)

Int'l stock/bonds (10%)   **Common Stocks** (48%)

SOURCE: Greenwich Associates 1993 study

Multiple Choice:

1. If you are in the process of getting divorced, which of the following should you do?

A) Make a list of household items and joint property.

B) If you don't already have your own credit card, begin applying for one, and remove your name from any joint accounts.

C) Make copies of bank and brokerage account statements and tell your broker not to make any transactions without informing both you and your spouse.

D) Close any lines of credit.

E) All of the above.

2. The definition of socially responsible investing is:

A) Investing only in companies that have signed the code of conduct created by the Coalition for Economically Responsible Economies.

B) Avoiding companies that conduct animal research, pollute the environment or produce tobacco products.

C) Investing in companies that share your values.

D) Investing in green funds.

E) None of the above.

3. Which of the following investment pitches should make you wary?

A) If you don't invest today, you will have missed the opportunity of a lifetime.

B) There's no time to send you more information.

C) I know plenty of other people who want in on this deal but I'm offering it to you first.

D) All of the above.

E) A and B.

4. What is a good age to start teaching children about money?

A) Four or 5 years old.

B) Fourteen years old.

C) Eighteen years old.

D) It's never too soon.

5. Which of the following are good ways to get children in the habit of saving money?

A) Tell them you will match every dollar they put into a savings account.

B) Give them a piggy bank and encourage them to save for a goal, such as a toy they've been wanting.

C) Tell them they'll never get to go to college unless they start saving when they're little.

D) A and B.

E) All of the above.

6. Can you borrow against your 401(k) plan?

A) Yes, as long as the amount does not exceed 75 percent of the amount in the fund.

B) It depends on your plan. Some allow you to borrow, and some do not.

C) Only if you have reached age $59^{1/2}$.

D) None of the above.

7. If you have a dispute with your broker, which of the following steps should you take?

A) Send a written complaint to the brokerage firm.

B) File a complaint with your state securities bureau.

C) File a complaint with the Federal Trade Commission.

D) File a complaint with the Securities and Exchange Commission.

E) All of the above.

F) A, B and D.

8. What is an environmental mutual fund?

A) A fund that invests in companies that do not pollute the environment or engage in mining.

B) A fund that invests in companies in the waste disposal business.

C) A fund that will not invest in nuclear power plants, companies that pollute the environment or conduct animal testing.

D) All of the above.

E) The term environmental fund is used in many different ways and by itself is meaningless.

9. How soon can you receive a lump sum payment from your 401(k) plan after you leave your company?

A) Ten days to two weeks.

B) One month.

C) Two months.

D) It can take many months.

E) None of the above.

ANSWER KEY

True/False

1. True. Such records can be helpful in resolving disputes or if you take the broker to arbitration.

2. False. There is no guarantee that your school system has a consumer or financial education curriculum, or that it reflects your own attitudes toward saving and spending money.

3. True. Be careful what you throw into the garbage because some con men go "dumpster diving" in search of credit card numbers, and other financial identification they can use to defraud you.

4. False. You may be held liable if your checkbook was stolen because you were careless and left it in a public place.

5. True. Mistakes take time to fix, so you don't want to wait till you need a loan. Also, you can make sure there are no fraudulent charges or accounts on them.

6. False. Although alimony payments are tax deductible for the spouse who makes them, child support payments are not. The recipient of the alimony must pay taxes on the money, but child support payments are not taxable income.

7. False. These clubs are for ordinary people who want to exchange ideas and pick stocks together.

8. True. An entire industry that includes several mutual funds has grown up around this idea.

9. False. The financial aid available to you will be reduced by a larger amount if the college fund is in your child's name than if the same amount of money is your name.

10. True. If you can't make the payments, you lose your home.

Multiple Choice

1. E	**3.** D	**5.** D	**7.** F	**9.** D
2. C	**4.** A	**6.** B	**8.** E	

Putting Gold in the Golden Years

Start Saving While You're Young, and If It's Too Late for That, Start Saving Now

"**E**VERY TIME I GO on vacation and sit under a palm tree, I think, 'Wouldn't it be great to do this forever?'" says Lee Rosenberg, cofounder of ARS Financial Services. "Then I get depressed because in a week, I'm back in the rat race."

Sound familiar?

Unfortunately, if you're not setting aside enough money now, you may never be able to afford to retire to a tropical island. Nearly half of the Americans recently surveyed by *Money* magazine said they will have either just enough money to meet their living expenses in their retirement years, or they will fall short of what they need.

Rosenberg, who is the author of *Retirement Ready or Not,* concurs: You almost cannot find a person who is on target.

Many people don't even have a clue of how much they will need when they retire, experts say. And the fact that people are living longer than ever means that your retirement savings may have to support you for 20 to 25 years.

Maybe it's time to take stock of your retirement needs and find out whether you're on track to achieving financial independence. If you've never calculated how much you'll need to live on after you retire, you should be prepared for a shock.

In his book, Rosenberg estimates that a 45-year-old person who is earning $60,000 a year would need an annual income of $144,321 to maintain the same standard of living at retirement 20 years from now. John Blankinship Jr., a financial planner in Del Mar, Calif., and president of the Certified Financial Planner Board of Standards, says he doesn't like to go through this exercise with people just starting their careers because he doesn't want them to become discouraged by what may seem to be an unattainable goal.

Of course, young people have a powerful weapon on their side: the power of compounding. If you start saving even small amounts for retirement when you are young, you will be ahead of the people who put it off because they have so many other pressing financial obligations. Rosenberg notes that for every 10 years you delay saving for retirement, you have to save three times as much to catch up.

One of the biggest mistakes people make when it comes to saving for retirement is thinking they don't have to do it on their own, says Howard Schneider, vice president of the American Association of Retired Persons' Investment Program from Scudder. Many companies are phasing out pension plans in favor of 401(k) plans, in which the employees make most, if not all, of the contribution.

And as for Social Security, I think people should not expect to rely on it as anything more than a supplement to their private pension and private savings, Schneider says.

So you're basically on your own. That's especially true for the baby boom generation, which is at a disadvantage compared to the generation that's retiring now, Rosenberg says. Baby boomers are less likely to have a company-funded pension plan. Unlike their parents, they generally aren't in the habit of saving money. And they are not likely to see their homes grow in value the way their parents' homes have appreciated. All the more reason to start planning for retirement now.

Begin by estimating your retirement living expenses. Some experts say that, as a rule of thumb, you will need 75 percent to 80 percent of your current income. That's not true for everyone, however. In fact, Rosenberg believes the greatest myth is that you'll spend less during retirement.

There is no doubt that some expenses will be less. You won't have the same transportation costs because you won't be commuting back and forth to work. Your clothing expenses will probably be less, especially if you now work in an office where you have to dress formally.

Even if you remain in the same tax bracket, your tax bite will be somewhat less because you won't be paying into Social Security. And after you retire, perhaps you will have paid off your mortgage and be out of debt.

But these savings may be depleted by new expenses; for example, you may spend more on travel, eating out and medical bills. And you need to consider whether you want to have money left over to leave to your heirs.

Finally, you should be sure to factor in the cost of living of the area where you plan to retire. For example, you may need more money if you will be retiring in the Northeast.

Now you should have an estimate of what you'll need to live on when you retire. But remember, the total is in today's dollars. Depending on how many years until you retire, that figure will balloon—and it will continue to balloon during the years of your retirement.

Consider this example, from *Planning for Retirement,* a guide produced by the AARP Investment Program from Scudder: Ben and Thelma estimate they will need $30,000 a year in today's dollars to maintain their current standard of living when they retire seven years from now. So, assuming 4 percent inflation per year, they will actually need $39,478 during the first year of retirement.

But if they live for another 27 years, by the 27th year of their retirement they will need $113,829 to maintain an income equivalent to $30,000 today. Most ex-

Sharpen Your Pencil and Boost Your Savings Now

Use this worksheet, adapted from Seattle accounting firm Moss Adams' retirement education program, "How to Retire Rich," to set an annual retirement savings goal. The worksheet assumes that you will live 10 years beyond today's 17-year life expectancy for a 65-year-old. It also assumes that your retirement kitty will grow 8 percent a year, the historical average for a conservative mix of stocks and bonds, and that inflation will run at 5 percent a year. While that's higher than the current 3 percent, it's in line with the average for the past 30 years. Recalculate your savings goals every year or two to take into account shifts in your retirement plans, the performance of your investments, and changes in Social Security and your company pension. Our example is a 37-year-old earning $41,675 annually, planning to retire at age 67 and employed by a company that contributes 2 percent of annual salary to a retirement plan.

	Example	Your Figures
1. Annual income needed at retirement Use 80 percent of your current income.	$33,340	
2. Estimated annual Social Security and pension benefits	11,724	
Call the Social Security Administration at (800) 772-1213 for a projection of your annual benefit. Ask your company's employee-benefits office to estimate the annual pension you will receive in today's dollars. Enter the total of both.		
3. Annual retirement income needed from savings and investments	21,616	
(Line 1 minus line 2) Multiplied by factor A below	18.2	
4. What you must save by retirement	393,411	
5. What you've already saved:		
A. IRAs, SEPs and Keoghs	11,000	
B. Vested amounts in employer plans such as 401(k)s, 403(b)s and profit-sharing accounts	37,000	
C. All other investments, including savings accounts, CDs, mutual funds, stocks and bonds	14,500	
Total of A, B and C	62,500	
Multiplied by factor B below	2.33	

6. Projected value of your current savings at retirement	145,625	
7. Total retirement capital you need to accumulate (Line 4 minus Line 6)	247,786	
Multiplied by factor C below	0.022	
8. Annual savings needed to reach your goal	5,451	
9. Minus what you expect your employer to contribute annually to your company savings plan	833	
10. What you must save each year until retirement (Line 8 minus line 9)	4,618	

Age at retirement	55	56	57	58	59	60	61	62	63	64	65	66	67
Factor A	23.3	22.9	22.6	22.2	21.8	21.4	21.0	20.5	20.1	19.6	19.2	18.7	18.2

Years to retirement	1	3	6	9	12	15	20	25	30
Factor B	1.03	1.09	1.18	1.29	1.40	1.53	1.76	2.02	2.33
Factor C	1.000	0.324	0.155	0.099	0.071	0.054	0.038	0.028	0.022

SOURCE: *Money* magazine's *Money Guide on Retirement,* 1994 edition

perts say that if you are in good health you should plan on supporting yourself until you are 85 to 90 years old.

Once you've estimated how much money you'll need for retirement, it's time to see what resources you will have to meet those expenses. There are three main areas to consider: Social Security, private pension plans and your own retirement savings, including 401(k) plans and IRAs.

Ask your employer and the Social Security Administration for help figuring out how much you will receive in annual income from them after you retire. The difference between that total and the amount you need to live on when you retire is the amount you must generate from your own savings.

So now add up what you have already saved toward retirement, and estimate what it will be worth by the time you are ready to tap into it. You want this amount to fill in the gap between your expenses and the amount you'll receive from Social Security and your company pension plan, if any. And you want it to last for all the years of your retirement.

If all this has you confused, Rosenberg has some simple advice: People in their 20s and 30s should try to save 5 percent of their income toward retirement.

When they reach their 40s, he says, they should increase that amount to 10 percent.

A final piece of advice: Don't count on an inheritance from your parents or other family members for the income you will need in retirement. You never know when unexpected medical bills or other expenses—or even a change of heart—may cause it to fall through.

For more help with retirement planning:

• You can order a free copy of *Planning for Retirement, a Guide for Investors Aged 50 and Over,* from the American Association of Retired Persons' Investment Program from Scudder. Telephone (800) 322-2282 and ask for extension 6286.

• To order a copy of *Retirement, Ready or Not,* call Career Press at (800) 955-7373. The book sells for $14.95, plus shipping and handling.

Budget, and Budget Again

The Leaner Your Spending is Today, the Fatter Your Cushion Will be Tomorrow

Do you know any of these people? Maybe one of them is someone like you.

• Dan is 60 years old. He wants to work at least five more years, but his company is retrenching and he's worried that he could be forced to take an early retirement. He's not ready for that yet—financially or emotionally.

• Maria and Rick have been so busy juggling mortgage payments and college tuition for their kids, they haven't really thought much about retirement. But after Rick recently celebrated his 45th birthday, they began to take stock of their future, and now they're not sure they'll be able to afford to retire at 65.

• Ron and Sandy are in their early 40s, and they're expecting their first child. It's fantastic. But Ron just realized that by the time the baby is grown and ready for college, they'll almost be ready for retirement. How will they pay for both?

• Laura knows she's got something called a 401(k) plan at work, but why should she worry about retirement when she's not even 30 yet? Besides, she has enough trouble finding money to pay off her credit card bills every month, let alone save for retirement.

No matter what your age, you're probably not saving enough for your retirement, financial planners say. This is not a fact that should discourage you; it should make you stop and consider what you can do about it.

Everyone has options. Consider this: Wouldn't you rather sacrifice a few restaurant meals now if it means that when you retire you can afford to travel and enjoy life more fully?

Economizing on meals can help, but it's probably not going to solve all your retirement problems. The first step, as simple as it sounds, is to make retirement part of your financial goals. "If you don't have a goal for your money, it's too easy to dip into your savings," says Ginita Wall, a financial planner and accountant in San Diego.

Almost everyone agrees that the most important thing you can do to secure your financial future is to put as much money as you can into tax-deferred retirement accounts. "Put more money into a 401(k), 403(b), IRA, SEP, or any combination of letters and numbers that leads to a stash of cash for your retirement," says Wall, the author of *The Way to Save*.

Some people may think they can't afford to put another $200 a month into their retirement account, she notes. But they don't realize that because it comes out of their pretax income, it may only reduce their take-home pay by $130. Put another way: It lowers your overall tax bill.

The money you put into these accounts grows rapidly because the tax on the interest is deferred. If it is automatically deducted from your paycheck, you don't have to think about it and you don't have a chance to spend the money.

And if your employer matches a portion of the money you put into a 401(k) account, then you get an added bonus that typically can be 50 cents on the dollar. Think of it as an investment that pays you 50 percent with no risk. If you're not taking full advantage of the matching funds, it's like throwing money away.

Don Underwood, a vice president at Merrill Lynch & Co., says that many people make the mistake of just investing the amount necessary to get matching funds. "Say my company matches 50 percent up to $3,000 a year. So I put in $3,000 and my company puts in $1,500. I've got $4,500, and that's great. But why stop there? I may be able to contribute more than that before I reach the limit. Ask yourself if you're contributing all you can to your retirement account."

If you have fully funded your 401(k) account, then you should consider an IRA, financial planners say. Even if you don't qualify for the tax deduction, it can make sense to invest in a nondeductible IRA. The benefit is this: Although your IRA contribution will not reduce your taxable income, the interest in the account will grow more rapidly than a regular investment because you won't pay taxes on it. Be aware, however, that you must keep records of these accounts forever so that you won't overpay on taxes when you begin to withdraw the funds.

And don't assume that you have to invest your IRA money in stodgy bank certificates of deposit. You can choose among a wide array of mutual funds as well as bank products for your retirement account.

Of course, it would be hard to find someone who doesn't think it's a good idea to put money into a retirement account. The problem is finding a way to save more money. "Then it comes down to the dreaded B word—budget," says Underwood, who is the coauthor of *Grow Rich Slowly.*

Take a good hard look at where all your money is going. Look at places in your life that are a cash drain but that you aren't getting that much pleasure from, says Wall. Maybe you're paying for premium channels on cable that you never use. Maybe when you're depressed you go out and buy new clothes that end up sitting in the back of your closet; it would be less expensive to cheer yourself up by going to a movie or having espresso with a friend. Or maybe you should consider putting off that expensive vacation for a year or two, and instead saving the $3,000 or $5,000 you would have spent.

"It's always tough to cough up $2,000 to put in an IRA on April 15th," Underwood says. But when you think about it, he notes, that's $5.47 a day. "It always comes down to budgeting. You've got to cut down on something. Unfortunately too many people want instant gratification."

Save Yourself

You can't depend on raises to increase your savings; for one thing, they're hard to get, and second, a $1,000 raise doesn't mean you put $1,000 more into your savings because you have to pay income taxes. But you can find ways to divert money from spending into savings, and 100 percent of that money can go right to work. Some ways to get it:

• If you receive a big annual bonus, live on your regular paycheck and bank the bonus for retirement.

• When you pay off your car loan, keep making the payments—to your savings account. In a few years, you'll have enough to buy your next. What's the point? You won't have to pay interest on another loan, and that money goes toward retirement.

• When you redeem coupons or shop sales, don't spend the savings. Find the line on the receipt showing how much the coupons came to, and write a check to your retirements account.

• Ask your employer to withhold more money for taxes than you need; then bank the refund for retirement. This isn't the best way, since you lose some interest payments, but the money is out of reach, which is the only way some people can manage to save.

• Ask a mutual fund to make automatic withdrawals from your checking account each month. It's less tempting to raid mutual funds for spending money, and it treats your savings like other bills that must be paid. (It's also a good way to buy mutual funds—gradually and steadily.)

SOURCE: *The Way to Save,* by Ginita Wall

Sometimes it's possible to increase your retirement fund by simply reconsidering how the money is allocated. The biggest mistake people make is to invest too conservatively, financial planners say. Although stocks are riskier and more volatile than bonds or insured bank accounts, they will outperform other investments in the long run. So the younger you are, experts say, the more retirement money you should have in stocks, lowering the proportion as you get older.

Another way to increase your savings is to reduce your debt burden. If you have credit card debt, check the interest rate you're paying. Then find out if you can switch to a lower rate card. And be sure you're making more than the minimum payment each month, so you can pay off the balance.

And if interest rates are low, you should consider refinancing your mortgage. Then, if you can reduce your monthly loan payment, take the savings and put it into your retirement account.

Some people are faced with tough decisions. How do they pay for the mortgage, save for their children's college education and fund their retirement? Never forgo one goal for the others. Even though the college tuition bills are looming, you should still put something into your retirement accounts, he says.

After college is paid for, take the amount you were spending on education and redirect it to your IRA or 401(k) account. And when you finally own your home free and clear, take the money you've been spending on your mortgage and switch it to your retirement accounts. This extra infusion will help you catch up if you've fallen behind in saving for retirement.

If you still find you're coming up short, experts say, you may have to consider ways to reduce your retirement needs. For example, maybe you'll decide to sell your home and move into a smaller, less expensive apartment. Taxes will be less and it will be easier to maintain. Maybe you'll also want to consider moving to a less expensive part of the country.

But what about the couple that waits to have children until they're in their 40s? They'll be paying for college at the same time they're approaching retirement. And they may also find themselves caring for elderly parents. If you get hit with the triple squeeze, you will probably have to put off retirement, Underwood says.

But that's not necessarily so bad. People live longer than they used to, and so they'll still have many years to enjoy retirement. And many people don't know what to do with themselves after they retire, anyway. They may want to continue working after they're 65—perhaps just at a slower pace.

"Many people are switching to less strenuous, more interesting careers later on in life," Wall says. "My father is 77 and is teaching half time. And this is a second career for him."

Rule of Thumb: It's one thing to say you should adjust the amount of stock you own as you get older; it's another thing to actually figure it out. One rule of thumb that can still serve as a good starting point: The percentage of your money that should be in stocks should be equal to 100 minus your age. Under this formula, if you're 45 years old, you should have 55 percent of your money in stocks.

Saving for Retirement

A weekly investment of $35 invested at 9 percent interest would provide these totals at age 65:

At Age	Total at Age 65
22	$1,000,000
30	$450,000
35	$300,000
40	$175,000
45	$100,000
50	$60,000
55	$30,000
60	$11,500

SOURCE: *Your Ten-Step Blueprint*

Tax Deferral Isn't Everything

Annuities Are Complicated and Costly, and Investors Often Can Do Better Elsewhere

If YOU'RE LIKE most people, you'd jump at a chance to put some of your savings into a tax-deferred investment. After all, who doesn't want to put off paying taxes on the earnings and give their money a chance to grow more quickly?

Unfortunately, as with many good things, there's a catch. In this case, it's not always true that you're better off with a tax-deferred investment. "It's a myth," says Glenn Daily, a Manhattan-based insurance consultant. "You can actually end up losing money if you jump headlong into a tax-deferred investment without realizing that the costs may outweigh the benefits."

And the most costly and complicated tax-deferred investments are annuities. Although sales of annuities, especially variable annuities, are skyrocketing, many financial experts say you should be careful about investing in them. It's not that annuities are inherently bad, they say. They are just inappropriate for many people.

Think of it this way: You wouldn't spend hundreds of dollars to fly to another city just because a store there has a sale on a VCR you want. So, too, financial planners say, you shouldn't put money into an annuity if you won't hold it long enough for the interest earnings to offset the costs. And you shouldn't put money into an annuity if you have a better investment option.

Unfortunately, it's not easy to evaluate the merits of an annuity because they are complex financial products. When you're shopping for a VCR, it's not that critical for you to understand digital tracking. But if you're considering an annuity, you need to know something about its features because your retirement savings are at stake.

So if someone comes to your door to make a sales pitch for an annuity, here's some help sorting out the pros and cons:

Annuities are basically contracts with insurance companies. They are designed to provide you with income to live on during your retirement years. With the most common type of annuity, prior to retirement you agree to invest money in a lump sum or periodically, and after a certain number of years you withdraw the money, without penalty, as you need it. Although you don't get to deduct the principal you invest in an annuity from your taxable income, the tax on the earnings is deferred until you withdraw the money.

The theory is that by the time you retire and withdraw your money, you will be in a lower tax bracket. In the meantime, your earnings will compound more quickly because of the tax deferral. But tax laws change, and there is no assurance that your tax bracket will be any lower when you reach retirement age, Daily notes.

The most standard type of an annuity is a deferred fixed annuity. It pays you a guaranteed minimum rate of return for a set amount of time, such as a year, three years or five years. At the end of the period, the rate is adjusted. Think of it as a certificate of deposit, except for one important difference: Unlike a bank CD, a fixed annuity is not insured by the government. And the security of your investment is based on the stability of the insurance company. So you need to research the insurance company just as thoroughly as the products it is offering.

A deferred variable annuity allows you to choose among a number of mutual funds, or some combination of guaranteed accounts and mutual funds. There is more risk than with the fixed annuity because the rate of return on the mutual funds is not guaranteed. But the potential for reward is higher. You usually have several funds to choose from and can switch your funds among them without having to pay capital gains tax.

A deferred annuity refers to the fact that you invest in it over a period of time and the payout is delayed until after you retire. There are some advantages to fixed and variable annuities. Unlike IRAs, they don't require you to begin withdrawing the funds at age $70^1/2$, and there is no ceiling on how much you can invest each year. In addition, an annuity may offer a guaranteed death benefit for your heirs.

With deferred annuities you can elect to receive the funds in a lump-sum payment, or the funds can be annuitized so you receive income from the fund each year.

There is another, lesser known type of annuity called an immediate annuity. It is designed for people who have already retired and want to continue to shelter their money while they live on a portion of the savings. For example, a retiree who receives a lump-sum payment from a pension plan can invest some or all of it in an immediate annuity. The payouts begin right away and can be structured to continue for life.

Like deferred annuities, they can be either fixed or variable. In an immediate variable annuity, your monthly payout fluctuates according to the performance of your investment choices.

One drawback to immediate annuities is that if you die, your heirs get nothing. "Those who die early subsidize other annuity holders," Daily says. "This gives the insurance company the ability to make payments for life." However, there are ways to structure the contract so your heirs get some of the benefits. For example, you can choose a 10- or 20-year guarantee period. If you die during the period you have chosen, your heirs will continue to receive your payouts until the end of the guarantee period.

To provide for a larger inheritance, retirees may want to invest a portion of their savings in an immediate annuity and a portion in a low-load variable universal life insurance policy, Daily says.

Before you invest in an annuity, here are some things to consider:

Be sure you have taken full advantage of any retirement plans available to you, such as a 401(k) plan. These are always preferable to an annuity because the money you invest reduces your taxable income. In addition, many companies will match a portion of the money you invest in them. And annuities usually have much higher fees and expenses, which can eat away at your earnings.

After you've put the maximum in your qualified retirement accounts, you may want to consider a nondeductible IRA before an annuity. The reason, experts say, is that nondeductible IRAs have the same tax advantages as an annuity but usually have lower annual fees. And you can elect to invest them in low-load or no-load mutual funds. The downside is that you have to keep meticulous records for nondeductible IRAs so that when you finally withdraw the money, you can make sure the government doesn't tax you again on the principal.

If you are in a high tax bracket, you also should consider municipal bonds. The pretax return on the bonds may not be as high as you could get investing in a variable annuity. But as Lewis Altfest, a Manhattan financial planner, points out, municipal bonds are permanently tax free, so you can frequently do better with them.

If you have taken advantage of all your other options and have additional savings that you won't need to touch until you're 59$^{1}/_{2}$, you may be a good candidate for an annuity. "The bottom line is that they are ideal for people who have money but don't need it now and have a long time horizon," says Joe Jordan, vice president in charge of Metropolitan Life Insurance Co.'s Pension and Savings Center in New York.

Before investing in an annuity, you need to shop around. Pick several annuities and compare the costs and early withdrawal penalties. The average annual expense of a variable annuity contract that's open to the public was 2.12 percent in 1992, according to Variable Annuity Research & Data Service, based in Roswell, Ga. That is nearly a point higher than many no-load mutual funds. Although annuities usually are sold without an upfront commission, be aware that they usually impose hefty surrender charges if you withdraw a substantial portion of your investment in the early years of the contract.

But don't just look at cost, says Ben Baldwin, author of *The New Life Insurance Investment Advisor.* Consider the diversity of the investment options offered by the annuity as well as the financial condition of the insurance company. Also consider the track records of any mutual funds that you must choose among. You can monitor their performance in financial publications such as *Barron's* or through specialized newsletters published by Morningstar, the *Annuity and Life Insurance Shopper,* and the *Variable Annuity Research & Data Service.*

Some experts say that the higher cost of an annuity may be worth it if you consider the convenience and flexibility of the products. For example, Baldwin says, many annuities allow you to put your principal into a guaranteed account and have the interest invested in mutual funds.

But remember, before you invest in a deferred annuity, be sure you will be holding it long enough to offset the costs. Many people don't invest in annuities until they are in their 50s, but it can take 10 years or even 25 years before the gains begin to outweigh the contract expenses.

How to Survive the Loss of a Job

Save Up Beforehand, Negotiate with Creditors and Lay Off Charge Cards

THEY CALL IT DOWNSIZING, as if we were talking about shifting the buttons on a suit. Or it's called reduction in force. Either way it looms like a dark gray headline rolling off the front page. One day NYNEX announces it is laying off 16,800 employees over three years. And another day AT&T says it is eliminating 15,000 jobs over two years. The list goes on and on. Public sector, education, manufacturing, high-tech. The next challenge may be yours.

If you fall victim to the next wave of layoffs, how will you pay your bills until you find a new job?

Few people are prepared for such an event. In addition to the financial strain, getting laid off is demoralizing and disorienting. Some people compound the problem by refusing to face up to the seriousness of the situation.

The best thing to do, experts say, is to go on the offensive. Find out what you can do to take control of your finances. Above all, don't wait for the bill collectors to come pounding on your door.

Keep in mind that it is often possible to anticipate getting laid off. Rumors of corporate downsizing often precede the actual announcement. You can also assume that if your company is losing money, it might have to downsize at some point. When you see warning signs, don't wait to get a pink slip to begin developing a survival plan.

Everyone should have an emergency fund. If you have time to prepare for getting laid off, make sure that your contingency fund equals three to six months of living expenses and that you keep it in a safe, easily accessible account. Then you can use the fund to supplement any severance package or unemployment benefits.

If you and your spouse or companion both work, it's a good idea to arrange your budget so that you can afford to live on one income if the other person is out of work for a long time, says Larry Elkin, a financial planner in Hastings-on-Hudson. "I call this jobless insurance," he says.

Losing a job always hurts, but it really becomes a crisis for people who have been living beyond their means. "When the money stops coming in, you have to be prepared to cut back on your spending," says Paul Richard, vice president of the National Center for Financial Education, a nonprofit organization. "The

How to Survive a Credit Crunch

When the bills are due and money is tight, there are some strategies that can help with problem. As with all debt, it is important to contact your creditor if you believe you will soon fall behind on your payment schedule. Creditors may be willing to work out an extended payment schedule.

Mortgage: Your mortgage is an important bill—try to pay it first. Your mortgage may or may not appear on your credit report each month, but payment information will, in most cases, be reported to the bureaus if you become 90 days or more overdue on your payments.

Bankcards: Visa and MasterCard are the most valuable references on your credit report, so pay them on time, even if it is only the minimum monthly payment.

American Express: American Express cards must be paid in full each month. If you don't pay, you are considered late and that information will likely be reported to all the major credit bureaus.

Car Loans: You don't want to get behind on a car loan because in some states your car can be repossessed after you've missed only one payment. If your car is worth more than you currently owe on it, you may be able to refinance your loan with lower monthly payments. If not, your lender may agree to a temporary schedule of reduced payments.

Child Support: Delinquent child support can reflect very negatively on your creditworthiness. All child support payments $1,000 or more in arrears must be reported to credit bureaus if the credit bureau requests that type of information.

Taxes: The IRS can be extremely tough if you don't pay your taxes on time. If you are notified by the IRS that you owe past-due taxes, make every effort to pay them as quickly as possible. If you can't pay, contact the IRS to try to arrange a repayment schedule.

Medical Bills: Most medical bills are not reported to credit bureaus until they are sent to collections. It's likely that you can work out a modified payment schedule with the doctor or hospital. Be sure to confirm any agreements in writing and ask for confirmation that smaller payments will not harm your credit rating.

Student Loans: Federal student loans may be deferred if you are having financial difficulties. If your loan is deferred, you will not be required to make any payments during the deferment period and no interest will accrue during this period. Remember, though, that you cannot qualify for deferment if your student loan is in default.

Small Bills: Set aside small bills, such as those for magazine subscriptions, book clubs, or local accounts, but be sure to contact the creditor if you think the account will be turned over to collections.

SOURCE: "Guidelines for Juggling Your Bills" from *The Ultimate Credit Handbook,* by Gerri Detweiler biggest mistake people make when their income is interrupted is instead of reducing their standard of living, they try to maintain it on credit cards," he says.

Some basic strategies for coping with a job loss:

• Start by listing any income you'll still have coming in. Then make a list of your normal monthly expenses. Next, figure out how you can reduce those expenses. Richard suggests cutting back on entertainment. "Do more things that are free and home-oriented," he says. "And do things yourself that you would normally pay others to do, such as lawn service or laundry or cleaning."

Other stopgap measures include holding a garage sale and selling your second car. Consider selling other assets, such as a boat, and using the proceeds to reduce your debt burden.

• Don't go overboard in eliminating everything that helps you relax and give you pleasure, however. For example, it's probably a good idea to maintain your health club membership if you're not going into debt to do so. Exercise can help you feel better about yourself. "Emotional wellness is very important when you're job hunting," Richard says.

• Don't do anything to dig yourself deeper into debt. "Do not charge anything," says Gail Liberman, coauthor of *Improving Your Credit and Reducing Your Debt.* "Pay for everything with cash." This is not the time to try to pay off your credit card bills. "I usually don't recommend making [only] the minimum payments, but this is one case in which you may need to, just to keep afloat," says Gerri Detweiler, author of *The Ultimate Credit Handbook.*

• Prioritize your debts. Some bills are essential, such as rent and mortgage payments, utility bills, car payments and unpaid taxes, says Robin Leonard, author of *Money Troubles: Legal Strategies to Cope with Your Debt.* Others, such as the hardware store bill, are nonessential.

Even if you consider a bill nonessential, don't stop paying altogether. Always try to make a small payment toward the bill so that you can avoid hurting your credit record.

• Let your creditors know if you are having trouble paying the bills. Believe it or not, most lenders will appreciate it if you disclose your financial problems so that they don't have to chase you down for the money later on. If you have a good record with them and show them you're making every effort to pay them back, they may be lenient with you. They may allow you to temporarily suspend your payments, or allow you to pay only the interest for a while. They even may cut your interest rate if it is higher than the going rate.

• Arrange to meet with a loan officer to discuss your mortgage payments. Come prepared to show how you are reducing your spending, Elkin says. And come with a specific idea of what they can do to help you get through this period. "Walk in and say, 'We have a problem and here is how I think I can solve it,'" he says. And if the bank official is unbending, don't give up. Go to a higher level. Start with a loan officer and after that, if necessary, contact a vice president.

Many loans are secured. That means if you are delinquent on your payments, the creditor can seize the property that is designated as the collateral, including your house or your car. But remember, lenders don't always want to seize your property. Banks are in the business of making loans; most don't want the headaches of managing real estate, and too much of it looks bad on the balance sheets they give to regulators and investors. So they may prefer to help you work things out.

If you owe money on a consumer product you bought, the creditor also may prefer to make a deal, Elkin says. That's because if you end up filing for bankruptcy protection, they may get stuck with the entire bill.

• After you negotiate a repayment plan with a creditor, remember to ask them not to report you to a credit bureau, Detweiler says. The goal is to work out a plan to pay back your creditors and keep your credit record intact.

While you are looking for a new job, find ways to increase your cash flow. An obvious suggestion, Richard says, is to get a part-time job to help make up for the shortfall.

Consider borrowing from a family member. Unless it is an outright gift, however, think of it like any other debt obligation and draw up a schedule for repaying the money.

If you're the one making the loan, make sure you're really helping your relative through a tough period and not just subsidizing a lifestyle that the person can't afford.

Another option is to borrow from your 401(k) plan at work, assuming you have one and that it allows loans. True, you have to pay the loan back with interest, but it's not so bad because the money goes to you.

Under certain circumstances, you may want to tap into your home equity. One advantage of a home equity loan is that the interest is tax deductible. But these loans and lines of credit are inherently dangerous because you can lose your home if you can't make the payments. Many experts say you should only resort to one if you truly have a temporary cash-flow problem.

• Don't cash in your retirement plan unless you have exhausted all other options and are totally out of money. For one thing, you will have to pay taxes and stiff penalties if you are withdrawing the money before age $59^1/2$. Remember, if you cash in your retirement accounts to help you get through a temporary problem, you are jeopardizing your long-term future.

• If you're having trouble finding a new job, be sure to consider all the possibilities. Elkin believes that too many people in this situation are reluctant to follow the jobs to other cities. "I wonder how many unemployed construction workers sat out the construction boom in South Florida after the hurricane," he says.

Even though you are out of work and are experiencing financial difficulties, remember that you have rights. Many times a creditor will pass an overdue bill to a collection agency. If that agency then begins to call you and constantly badger you for the money, you have the legal right to tell them to leave you alone, Leonard says.

Tell them orally to stop bothering you and then get their address and the name of a contact person and send them a letter to that effect. After that, they can tell you only that their collection efforts have ended or that they are going to sue you for the money.

Leonard also suggests that if you are contacted by a collection agency, try to get the original creditor to take back the bill and negotiate a repayment schedule with you. "Usually they will give you more room to maneuver than a collection agency," she says. And if you work things out directly with the original lender, there is a greater chance that they will extend credit to you in the future.

If you lack discipline or become depressed and overwhelmed by the burden of looking for a job and trying to pay the bills, you may need professional help. Consider contacting one of the more than 850 nonprofit Consumer Credit Counseling Service offices around the country.

These services will help you develop a budget and a repayment plan. You can also take advantage of a plan they offer in which they will negotiate the repayment plan with your creditors. Then you make one monthly payment to the counseling service and they pay your bills and deal with creditors.

There is an initial consultation fee and a monthly fee for the payment service. You also should know that if you use a counseling service's repayment plan, it is likely to show up on your credit report. So be sure to ask the counseling service how that will affect your ability to get credit in the future.

But it might be worth it if it means no more calls in the middle of night from bill collectors. "The peace of mind alone may be well worth going to a counseling service," Detweiler says.

For more information on how to deal with a financial crisis:

• *Money Troubles: Legal Strategies to Cope with Your Debts* by Robin Leonard. Published by Nolo Press for $16.95. Call 800-992-6656.

• *Improving Your Credit and Reducing Your Debt* by Gail Liberman and Alan Lavine. Published by John Wiley & Sons for $14.95. Call 800-225-5945.

EXERCISE 40

When the Worst Hits

*Personal Bankruptcy Gives
You a Shot at Another Chance*

YOU MAY THINK you could never end up in bankruptcy. After all, you're no deadbeat.

But few people are immune to a financial crisis. Imagine that you're suddenly laid off and you can't find a new job for more than a year. Or you have a major medical emergency and your insurance won't cover the experimental treatment your doctor recommends.

The bills pile up. Before you know it, the bank is threatening to foreclose on your home, and collection agencies are at your door. You owe money to the IRS, and some creditors are suing you. You feel like you're being swallowed up by quicksand.

It's a depressing scenario. But in such extreme cases, personal bankruptcy can provide you with a fresh start. And fortunately, it's so common today that it doesn't carry much of a stigma. Although it will hurt your credit record, if you're at the point of considering bankruptcy, your credit record may already be marred by unpaid bills and creditor lawsuits.

Even if your financial problems are not yet severe enough to file for bankruptcy protection, you should know something about how the law works. Used to its full advantage, bankruptcy requires some preplanning and some knowledge of your different options. And it's important to know that just the threat of bankruptcy can give you leverage to negotiate repayment schedules with some creditors.

There are two main types of personal bankruptcy, Chapter 7 and Chapter 13. In both cases, when you file your bankruptcy petition you receive an automatic stay, which puts a stop, at least temporarily, to all lawsuits, foreclosures and collection activity.

By far, the most common type of personal bankruptcy is Chapter 7. When you file for Chapter 7, your assets—except for certain property that you are allowed to keep—are liquidated to pay off your creditors; in return, many debts are discharged, or erased.

This sounds like a convenient way to get rid of pesky creditors. But before you rush out to file for Chapter 7, you should know that bankruptcy law will not absolve you of all debts. Taxes and alimony payments, among other things, are not covered. And you can only file for Chapter 7 every six years.

Lingo of the Courts

Some of the terms you'll need to know if you file for bankruptcy.

Automatic stay: An injunction that stops lawsuits, foreclosure, garnishments, and all collection activity. The automatic stay takes effect the moment a bankruptcy petition is filed.

Bankruptcy petition: A formal request for protection of the bankruptcy laws.

Chapter 7: The portion of the federal Bankruptcy Code providing for liquidation and distribution of a debtor's nonexempt property to his creditors.

Chapter 11: A business reorganization under protection of bankruptcy codes. A Chapter 11 debtor forms a plan of reorganization to keep its business alive and pay creditors over time. People in business or people who have assets greater than the debt limits set for Chapter 13 cases can seek relief in Chapter 11.

Chapter 12: Bankruptcy protection for family farmers.

Chapter 13: Bankruptcy protection for wage earners which allows debtors to keep property and pay debts over time.

Cure: To pay money that is past due under a contract or lease.

Discharge: A discharge releases a debtor from personal liability for discharged debts and prevents the creditors owed those debts from taking any action against the debtor or his property to collect the debts. Creditors are prohibited from making any communication regarding the debt with the debtor, his relatives, employees or friends.

Exemption: Certain property the Bankruptcy Code or applicable state law permits a debtor to keep from creditors.

Fraudulent transfer: A transfer of a debtor's property for which he receives nothing or receives something worth less than transferred property's value.

Liquidation: Disposal of a debtor's property for the benefit of his creditors.

Plan: Under Chapter 13, a debtor's detailed description of how creditors' claims will be paid over a period of time, usually three years.

Secured claim: A debt for which property has been pledged to a creditor to insure payment. A home mortgage is one example.

341 meeting: A meeting at which the debtor appears before creditors to be questioned about his financial affairs.

Unsecured claim: A claim for which none of a debtor's property has been pledged.

SOURCE: *Personal Bankruptcy: What You Should Know,* by Alice Griffin

If you own your home, you're probably a better candidate for Chapter 13 bankruptcy. "The purpose of Chapter 13 is to prevent foreclosure and to pay the arrears over time," says Sheldon Barasch, a bankruptcy lawyer. It is considered a reorganization of your debts, as opposed to a liquidation of assets in Chapter 7.

Even if you qualify for a Chapter 7 or a Chapter 13 bankruptcy proceeding, you may want to consider trying to reach an out-of-court settlement with your creditors. Unsecured creditors have an incentive to avoid bankruptcy because they may only receive partial payment or nothing at all. It's in your interest to try to maintain the best possible credit record. So, you or your lawyer can try to negotiate a repayment plan with them in which they grant you some leniency and agree not to report your financial problems to the credit reporting agencies.

A bankruptcy filing will stay on your credit reports for 10 years after the fact. And if you apply for a job that pays more than $20,000 a year or for more than $50,000 in credit or insurance, a credit bureau can report the bankruptcy indefinitely. In fact, however, they frequently delete all mention of the bankruptcy after 10 years, notes Robin Leonard, coauthor of *How to File for Bankruptcy,* a book about Chapter 7.

Despite the seriousness of bankruptcy, it is possible to rebuild your credit with lenders afterward. Chances are, some of the same companies you owe money to have recently filed for bankruptcy themselves.

"Ironically, some companies consider you a better credit risk after you've emerged from bankruptcy because you have no debts and can't file for Chapter 7 for another six years," says Alice Griffin, author of *Personal Bankruptcy: What You Should Know.*

If you're turned down for a credit card, you can always get a secured card. These are credit cards that are backed by money you have on deposit in the bank. After you use the card for a period of time, making prompt payments, you can apply for a regular credit card.

But bankruptcy is not without its consequences: You should realize that during the 10 years after bankruptcy you may find it very difficult to get a mortgage unless you put down a large down payment. You may have trouble renting an apartment because you're considered a bad credit risk. And if you want a credit card or loan, you won't get the best rates. They're reserved for the most creditworthy customers.

And the whole process will be of little help if you're one of those who end up filing for bankruptcy because you've never learned to live within your means. Many compulsive spenders return to bankruptcy court time and again. Experts say the only way for them to break this cycle is to learn to budget and save money. In extreme cases, Leonard says, habitual spenders should seek help from groups like Debtors Anonymous.

More likely, though, you'd end up in bankruptcy court because of an unexpected financial crisis. That's what bankruptcy was invented for—to give you a much-needed opportunity to start over.

For more information on filing for bankruptcy, consider the following:

• *Filing for Individual Bankruptcy: What's It All About,* a booklet published by the Association of the Bar of the City of New York. Cost: $5. To order a copy, call 212-382-6695, or write to The Association of the Bar of the City of New York, 42 W. 44th St., New York, N.Y. 10036-6690.

• *Personal Bankruptcy: What You Should Know,* by Alice Griffin, Esq., published by Cakewalk Press. Cost: $13.95. To order a copy, call 800-507-2665.

Bankruptcy: Chapter and Verse

Chapter 7 Keeps Creditors at Bay, but Chapter 13 Can Save Your House

IF YOU'RE BEING sued by creditors and harassed by collection agencies, bankruptcy may seem like a life raft in a sea of sharks. As soon as you file a petition with the bankruptcy court, all the lawsuits and attempts to foreclose on your home and seize your wages must stop. And the court steps in to mediate with your creditors.

But some of the relief may be temporary at best. And as a result of filing for bankruptcy, you must surrender control of your finances to the court. So, before you take that step, you need to know which type of personal bankruptcy is best for you. And you need to find out how the law works. Will you be able to keep valued possessions? Will bankruptcy erase all your debts? Do you need a lawyer?

Most people opt for Chapter 7. In this kind of personal bankruptcy, your assets—except for a certain amount of property that you are allowed to keep—are liquidated and divided among your creditors; the remaining debt, if it is covered by the law, is discharged, or wiped out.

Exactly what you are allowed to keep in Chapter 7 is determined by each state. In New York, for example, property that is safe from creditors includes such things as furniture, apparel and either $2,500 in cash or $10,000 in equity on property you own.

One way to determine if this type of bankruptcy is appropriate for you is to take the light at the end of the tunnel test, says Robin Leonard, coauthor of *How to File for Bankruptcy,* a book about Chapter 7. The idea, she says, is to deduct your basic living expenses from your take-home pay. Then add up all your debts. If it's clear that there is no way you could pay off these debts over a two- or three-year period, then you're a candidate for Chapter 7 bankruptcy.

Next, you should consider the kind of debts you have. Some won't be discharged by a Chapter 7 proceeding. For example, you can't get out of paying alimony, child support, recent tax bills, student loans that are less than seven years old or any debt obtained by fraud.

Ideally, a person who files for Chapter 7 bankruptcy should have no major assets that they want to protect, such as a home, and should have debts that can be discharged, such as credit card debts and medical bills.

Assessing Your Assets

You must list every item of property that you own or have an interest in as of the date you file a bankruptcy petition. Such items may include:

• Real estate, including houses, cooperative apartments, condominiums, time-shares, cemetery plots and investment property.

• Cash at home, in savings accounts, checking accounts, credit unions and safe deposit boxes.

• Household goods and furnishings, including appliances, television sets, radios, stereo systems and components, computers, VCRs and furniture.

• Books, art objects and collectibles.

• Apparel, jewelry, sports equipment and other personal possessions.

• Motor vehicles, including cars, trucks, mobile homes, motorcycles and snowmobiles.

• Boats and equipment.

• Business assets, such as office equipment, inventories, receivables, farm animals and equipment, patents and copyrights.

• Investments in stocks, bonds and government securities (savings bonds and Treasury bills, notes and bonds).

• Any interest in insurance policies. If you are the beneficiary of a life insurance policy and the insured dies within six months after you file for bankruptcy, the proceeds will be included as your asset.

• Pensions, profit-sharing plans, annuities, individual retirement accounts, 401(k), Keogh and other types of retirement plans.

• Personal injury or other legal actions you may have against others.

• Any interest as a beneficiary of the will of another person who has died or as the beneficiary of a trust. If someone dies within six months after you file for bankruptcy, your inheritance will be included as your asset.

• Tax refunds.

• Security deposits.

SOURCE: *Filing for Individual Bankruptcy: What's It All About?* published by the Association of the Bar of the City of New York

You don't have to wait until you're broke to file for Chapter 7 bankruptcy. But timing is important, and you'll want to do some planning before you file. You should realize that you can only file for Chapter 7 bankruptcy once every six years. That means you need to be able to pay for bills once you emerge from bankruptcy.

And you can't charge up luxury items, such as jewelry and trips, and then file for bankruptcy. Nonessential bills like that won't be erased by bankruptcy.

Know Your Debts

If you fail to list a debt on your bankruptcy petition, it might not be discharged and you may be obligated to pay it. Even if you question the validity or amount of a particular debt, list it anyway since it probably will be discharged. You may note on the petition that the claim is disputed. Below are types of debts that you should include:

Priority: Debts that are paid first to creditors. For individuals, the most common type of priority debt is federal or state income tax. Taxes due for fewer than three years will not be discharged and must be paid.

Secured: Debts associated with specific items of property. If the debt is not paid, the lender may repossess the property. Even though a bankruptcy has been filed, a secured debt must be paid in full if you wish to keep the secured asset. Examples: houses, cars, furs, appliances, jewelry, cooperative apartments and condominiums.

Unsecured Debts: The vast majority of debts listed on bankruptcy petitions are unsecured debts. These include:

Credit card debts
Rent
Utility bills
Hospital and doctor bills
Taxes (other than those entitled to priority)
Student loans
Personal injury actions against the debtor
Parking tickets and moving violations
Arrears in child support, alimony and equitable distribution awards
Personal loans
Auto loans
Loans from relatives and friends
Debts as a cosigner
Restitution debts
Debts arising from driving under the influence of alcohol or drugs

SOURCE: *Filing for Individual Bankruptcy: What's It All About?* published by the Association of the Bar of the City of New York

What's more, you can't show preferential treatment to one creditor over another before filing. For example, if you owe money to your mother, you can't pay her back and then file for Chapter 7. If you try that, the court can order you to get the money back and distribute it among all your creditors.

You might think twice about filing for Chapter 7 if you have a loan that was cosigned by a family member or friend, because they will be held liable for the full amount. If you settle a family debt or a debt with a business associate, you can't file for Chapter 7 until a year after that, says Alice Griffin, author of *Per-*

sonal Bankruptcy: What You Should Know. If you pay off a bill owed to someone besides a relative or business associate, you have to wait 90 days after that to file for bankruptcy.

Griffin gives this example: Say you have $10,000 in savings and $30,000 in debts, including a $10,000 student loan, $10,000 in credit card bills and $10,000 in medical bills. You should use your savings to pay off the student loan, then wait 90 days and file for Chapter 7 bankruptcy. That way you won't have any debts when you emerge from bankruptcy, she says.

Chapter 7 bankruptcy is a fairly simple proceeding, and many people handle the paperwork themselves. You can purchase the forms from most legal stationers for about $10. The cost of filing a bankruptcy petition is $150.

If you want a lawyer to represent you, make sure you know what the fee includes. You want the lawyer to prepare your petition, file the petition, attend the meeting in which your creditors can question you about your debts, and handle any creditors who object to having their debt discharged, Griffin says.

Be aware that while Chapter 7 can delay an eviction, it usually cannot prevent you from being evicted by your landlord if you are a renter. And finding a new apartment can be difficult after you've filed for bankruptcy because many landlords check credit records before giving prospective tenants a lease. So, no matter what your financial problems, make your rent payment one of your top priorities.

If you own your home and want to protect it from your creditors, then Chapter 13 bankruptcy may be more appropriate for you. To qualify for Chapter 13, you must have a regular income. This type of bankruptcy allows you to stave off creditors while you come up with a repayment plan. It usually takes about three years to complete the reorganization and emerge from Chapter 13.

Under a Chapter 13 reorganization plan, you will have to pay your tax bill first. Then you will fully pay your secured debts, such as a mortgage or auto loan. At the time you file for Chapter 13, interest stops accruing on unsecured debts, such as department store bills and credit card bills. They get paid last, and, typically, you don't have to pay them in full.

Chapter 13 will stop a bank from foreclosing on your home. However, in New York State, if you wait until the bank has auctioned off your home to file a bankruptcy petition, it will be too late to reverse the process and reinstate your mortgage.

Because Chapter 13 is a complicated procedure, most people hire a lawyer to advise them. It is not something you ever do on your own, Griffin says. After the reorganization plan is approved, you pay an agreed-upon amount to a court-appointed trustee each month, who distributes it to your creditors.

Your lawyer's fee will be added into the amount you must pay the court. And the trustee, who administers the case, will take 10 percent of the money paid into the plan.

Chapter 13 proceedings have a high failure rate, but if the reorganization plan becomes unworkable, you can ask the trustee to modify the plan. There is no restriction on how often you can file for Chapter 13. You can file for Chapter 13 even if you just emerged from Chapter 7 or Chapter 13.

But if you have more than $100,000 in unsecured debts or more than $750,000 in secured debts, you are not eligible for Chapter 13. In that case, you can file a Chapter 11 bankruptcy petition. However, Chapter 11 is designed for business bankruptcies and can be costly and time-consuming for an individual. If your debts exclude you from a Chapter 13 proceeding, you may be better off avoiding a complicated Chapter 11 court proceeding and hiring a lawyer to negotiate directly with your creditors, some experts say.

Don't forget that many creditors, especially unsecured creditors, would prefer to avoid bankruptcy court because they may get back only a portion of the money owed them, or none of it at all. So, they may be very willing to arrange an out-of-court repayment plan. Says Griffin: Just about anything you can do in bankruptcy, you can do out of bankruptcy.

Further Reading

• For more information on filing Chapter 7, pick up a copy of *How to File for Bankruptcy,* by Stephen Elias, Albin Renauer and Robin Leonard. It's published by Nolo Press and costs $25.95. To order a copy, call (800) 992-6656.

You Can't Take It with You

But with a Will, You Can Decide Who Gets What After You're Gone

WAKE UP, baby boomers. It's not the 1960s anymore. In case you haven't noticed, you're middle-aged. And many of you haven't prepared a will.

Some legal experts say that 70 percent of all people die without a will, says Lisa Berger, author of *Feathering Your Nest*. The figures are stunning.

As Berger explains it: "There's a certain amount of denial, especially among the baby boom generation. And there's also a misconception. People think: 'I only need a will if I have a sizable estate or want to make an unusual bequest.' But that's not true."

If you die without a will—called dying intestate—the state in which you reside will decide how to divide up your estate. And if you have no relatives with a legal right to inherit, the state gets everything. What's more, without a will, the court will appoint a guardian for your children, if they are minors.

Most people would prefer to decide these things for themselves. That's what a will is for. And with so many nontraditional families today, wills are all the more important. If you have been married more than once and have children by both marriages, if you have stepchildren, or if you are unmarried but are living with a companion, you need a will to be sure you have provided for all of your loved ones.

Preparing a will doesn't have to be an expensive, complicated proposition. However, there are specific steps you must take so that your will holds up in court. You can't simply write down your wishes on a piece of paper, date it, and put it in a safe place.

You can hire a lawyer to execute your will, or you can buy a book, kit or computer program that tells you how do it yourself. Erica Bell, a partner in the Manhattan law firm of Weiss Buell & Bell, says that the fee for having a lawyer draw up a will varies considerably, depending on the size and complexity of the estate. The legal bill for a simple will generally ranges from $350 to $500, she says, but a more complex will can cost several thousand dollars in legal fees.

One of the most common mistakes people make when they draw up their own will is not following the letter of the law when they sign it, Bell says. In New York, for example, you must sign your will in the presence of two witnesses. Your witnesses cannot be anyone who stands to benefit from your will. They also cannot be the same persons named as executor, trustee or guardian in your will.

Once your will is executed, if you scribble on it or cross out something and write over it, it becomes invalid. If you decide you want to make changes, you

Taking Inventory

A personal record will help your survivors organize your affairs after your death. You should include the fact about your finances and information about the location of all of your important papers. Keep a copy in your desk drawer and another copy clipped to your will.

1. Social Security Number
Husband _____ Wife _____

2. Life insurance
Policy number _____ Company _____
Face Value _____ Beneficiary _____
Name, address and phone number of agent: _____
_____

3. Savings and Checking Accounts
Account number _____ Name of financial institution _____
Location of passbook or statements _____

4. Certificates of Deposit
Account number _____ Name of financial institution _____
Location of Documents _____

5. U.S. Government Bonds
Serial numbers and denominations _____
Location of bonds _____

6. Securities
List of stocks and/or bonds _____ List of mutual funds _____
Name, address and phone number of broker _____
_____

7. Safe Deposit Box
Box location _____ Key location _____ List of contents _____

8. Pension and Profit-Sharing Plan
Company and account number _____
Name and address of employer _____ Beneficiary _____
_____

9. Retirement Plans
Individual retirement plans, Keoghs and 401(k)s _____
Location of accounts _____ Account numbers _____
Beneficiary _____

10. Motor vehicles
Make, type and year _____
Location of ownership papers _____

11. Real Estate
Location of properties _____
Location of mortgage or ownership documents_____

12. Description and Location of Personal Property (jewelry, furs, collections, etc.)_____
_____

13. Health, Home and Personal Insurance
Policy number _____ Company_____
Policy type _____ Policy location _____

14. Location of Tax Records _____

15. Credit cards
Company _____ Account number _____
Name on card _____
Location of card _____

16. Major Creditors
Name _____ Address _____ Phone number _____
Location of notes, contracts or receipts _____

17. Will
Location of original and copy _____

18. Personal Information
Names and Addresses of:

Parents_____

Siblings_____

Descendants _____

Former spouse_____

Date of divorce and location of divorce decree_____

Attorney_____

Accountant _____

Financial planner_____

(continued next page)

Location of Other Documents:

Marriage and birth certificates _____

Military records _____

Citizenship papers _____

Adoption papers_____

Alimony agreement _____

Important warranties and receipts _____

SOURCE: *The Lifetime Book of Money Management*

must either execute a new will or draw up an amendment to your will, called a codicil. A codicil also must be signed, dated, and witnessed.

And don't try to be cute and videotape your will. Experts say it won't hold up in court.

Logic may tell you to store your will in your safe deposit box. But resist the temptation to do this. In many states, safe deposit boxes are sealed upon death. So it can take a court order to get into it. It's much more convenient to keep your will in a safe place at home and inform a family member where it is filed. If a lawyer draws up your will, the firm may be able to keep it on file. If so, ask for a receipt and a copy for your records. If your spouse or partner has a safe deposit box in their name only, you may choose to store your will there.

In addition to the will, it's a wise idea to make a list of all your bank accounts, investment accounts, safe deposit boxes, insurance policies, pensions, etc., to help your executor administer your estate. Attach this to your will. This list will also be invaluable to your family members in the event that you are ever incapacitated by an illness or accident.

When you're drafting your will, keep in mind that there are several basic elements to consider:

• It should name an executor of your estate. This is the person who will administer the terms of the will. The duties include locating and making an inventory of your assets, having them appraised and paying your debts and any taxes due. The executor also notifies your insurance company of your death and divides up your estate according to your instructions.

It can be a time-consuming job, so check with the person you want to name executor to be sure they are willing to accept the responsibility. Executors are paid a percent of the estate's value; the amount is usually set by state law.

• If you have children, you should name a guardian in your will. Almost invariably, this is the issue that people anguish over most, Bell says. As with the executor, you should check with the person you want to name guardian.

You should name your beneficiaries in your will. Experts say that it's often unwise to specify dollar amounts for your beneficiaries because the size of your estate may change considerably between the time you make out your will and the time you die.

Instead, it's better to designate the proportion of your estate that your beneficiaries are to receive. So, for example, you may want to give half of it to your spouse and have the rest equally divided among your children.

It is common for people to make donations to charity in their wills. Or they may want to leave a nominal gift to each grandchild. In these cases, you would probably want to specify an amount of money.

Some people leave detailed instructions in their wills on how their tangible property should be divided up. Even if your possessions aren't valuable, you may have sentimental reasons for wanting to designate who will get them after you die. And it will make the executor's job easier if you are specific.

It's often a good idea to talk to your immediate family members about how you intend to divide up your property. Berger says her father has asked each of his children for a list of household items they'd like to have. "Wills can be a contentious issue," she says. "And some children don't want to bring up the issue with their parents because they don't want to appear to be gold-diggers or to invade their privacy. But you should talk about it."

People frequently put the instructions for their burial in their will. It can be important for unmarried couples to have this in writing so that a funeral home will feel comfortable taking instructions from a nonfamily member, Bell says. However, you should also be sure to separately communicate these wishes to a family member or companion because your will may not be read immediately after your death.

Pets are considered part of your tangible property. If you want to provide for them after your death, you should set aside a certain amount of money for their care. But don't try leaving money to your pets. "They have no capacity to receive money," Bell says.

If you are drawing up your own will, be sure you don't make the mistake of trying to leave your life insurance to one person if another family member is named on the policy as the beneficiary. Similarly, if you have a joint bank account or investment account, you cannot leave it to someone else in your will.

And if you decide to disinherit a family member, it is still a good idea to leave them a nominal amount, such as $100, experts say. That way the person will have a hard time contesting the will on the basis that he or she was inadvertently left out.

Finally, don't confuse a living will with a will. Bell prefers to call a living will a health-care decision declaration. It is designed to state what kind of medical care or medical intervention you want if you are incapacitated or are unable to communicate. Living wills are simple to complete and are binding. Once you complete a living will, be sure to give copies to your family members so they are aware of your wishes.

If You're Court-Wary

A Living Trust Lets Your Heirs
Escape Complex Probate Systems

TRUSTS HAVE BECOME the superheroes of estate planning.

They can slice away at taxes, avoid the probate system and give you more control over your estate.

Sounds great, if only trusts could save the day for everyone. But all trusts are not alike. So let's start with the basics.

Although trusts traditionally have been a tax-saving device for the wealthy (more about this later), living trusts are being marketed to middle-income families for other purposes. Those are the ones you've probably heard the most about.

The reason: Living trusts allow you to avoid the often time-consuming and costly court process called probate. Ever since Charles Dickens wrote *Bleak House,* probate has been viewed as a painful system in which bickering relatives, lawyers and appraisers gradually pick apart an estate until nothing is left.

A living trust is so named because it is created during your lifetime. In a standard living trust, you put your major assets—your home, any other real estate, your bank accounts and other investments—into the trust. You name yourself as the trustee and you select someone to succeed you as trustee when you die or become incapacitated. This type of trust is revocable, which means that you can cancel or change it at any time.

"A living trust is very useful in the right circumstances," says Charles Groppe, a partner in the Manhattan law firm of Putney Twombly Hall & Hirson. But make no mistake, he adds, "It is not a tax-saving device."

Lisa Berger, author of *Feathering Your Nest,* a book about retirement planning, says that a living trust is "like a safe deposit box where you put your assets to keep them out of probate court."

Upon your death, the trust becomes irrevocable. The trustee you named will then distribute the assets according to your instructions. The advantage is that this can be done immediately, without going to court.

This is especially helpful if you have property in more than one state; otherwise, it will have to go through probate in all of the states where your property is located. And if you have a family-owned business, a living trust allows your beneficiaries to continue running it without a hitch after you die.

A trust is not the only way to provide your beneficiaries with immediate access to your assets. Joint ownership of property, investments and bank accounts

Trusty Terms

Here are some words to know as you plan your estate.

Asset: Something owned by an individual or company that has monetary value.

Beneficiary: The person named to receive property under a will or trust.

Estate: All assets, including but not limited to personal property, real estate, and investments left by a person at death.

Estate tax: The tax levied on the estate of a deceased as opposed to a tax levied on the person inheriting all or part of the estate.

Grantor: The person who establishes a trust, sometimes also called a trustor.

Inheritance tax: A tax levied by some states on the value of property inherited by a person.

Inter vivos trust: A trust created during a person's lifetime, also called a living trust.

Irrevocable trust: A type of trust that cannot be changed or canceled after it is created.

Joint tenancy with the right of survivorship: A type of ownership in which two or more people own the same property. When one owner dies the property automatically passes to the other joint owner or owners, bypassing probate.

Pour-over will: A supplement to a living trust that collects any unaccounted-for assets and directs them into the trust at the time of death.

Power of attorney: A written document in which a mentally competent person appoints a person or institution to make decisions if he or she becomes incapacitated.

Probate: The state court process that a will must go through before the assets can be distributed to the beneficiaries.

Revocable living trust: A type of trust created during the holder's lifetime that allows assets in the trust to pass to the beneficiaries without going through probate. It can be changed or canceled.

Testamentary trust: A trust that is created after a person dies, according to the terms of his or her will.

Trustee: The person named to manage and distribute a trust's assets to the beneficiaries according to the instructions in the trust agreement.

SOURCES: *Feathering Your Nest: The Retirement Planner* by Lisa Berger; *Estate Planning Made Easy* by David T. Phillips and Bill S. Wolfkiel.

can also circumvent probate. However, with joint ownership you no longer have total control over the assets.

A living trust has other benefits. Berger notes that if your family has a history of Alzheimer's disease, you might want to set up a living trust so that the person you appointed to succeed you as trustee can step in and manage your affairs when you are no longer able to do so. Note, however, that you can do the same thing without a trust—you can legally designate someone to manage your affairs if you become disabled by giving the person durable power of attorney.

Unlike a will, a living trust is not a matter of public record. So you may want to consider one if privacy is important to you.

And a living trust tends to be more difficult to challenge than a will. There is no automatic opportunity to lodge objections to a trust, says Erica Bell, a partner in the Manhattan law firm of Weiss Buell & Bell. But with a will, it is built into the system. In addition, there is a theory that if you have had a living trust for many years, it is evidence of the validity of the instructions.

A living trust may be a good choice for you, but don't make that decision without doing your homework.

First of all, you still need a will, experts say. For one thing, if you have minor children you need a will to designate a guardian for them. And some lawyers recommend supplementing a living trust with what is called a pour-over will. This is designed to catch any assets that you forgot to include in your trust, and to direct them into the trust at the time of your death.

Next, find out about the cost and time involved in your state's probate process. Compare that to the cost of drawing up a living trust and transferring property into it. Then consider the size and complexity of your estate and your goals.

Despite the bad public image, the probate process varies considerably depending on where you live, and can be a lot easier than it was in *Bleak House*. Some states have an expedited probate for simple estates.

Too often people decide to set up a living trust without analyzing whether it makes sense for them and is cost effective, Bell says. "I'm worried that people don't realize that a trust requires good record keeping, and that after they set up a trust they must transfer their assets into it. And that can be expensive."

If you hire attorneys to draw up a living trust, you also will have their fees to pay. Before you decide to forgo a lawyer and do it yourself with a living trust kit, you should know that they are not usually geared to the laws of a particular state, Bell says. So if you use a kit, you may still need to double-check your work with an trust expert in your state.

If you have doubts about what to do, consult a reputable adviser—not a stranger who happens to knock on your door. As living trusts have gained popularity, they have become fodder for scam artists. In 1994, the American Association of Retired Persons and the National Association of Attorneys General issued a special alert about door-to-door salespeople who use high-pressure tactics to get people to buy overpriced living trusts.

Trusty Tax Shelters

Protect Your Estate and Your Heirs by Setting Up a Trust

You DIDN'T WORK HARD all your life just for the IRS to claim a big chunk of your savings after you die.

Instead, you want to make sure your estate will be distributed to your heirs according to your wishes. That's where trusts can help.

But creating the right trust requires considerable planning and some tough decision-making. Put bluntly, trust planning requires you to mentally kill off every generation of your family, says Charles Groppe, a partner at the law firm of Putney, Twombly, Hall & Hirson in Manhattan. The idea is to imagine who would be the beneficiary of your estate in different scenarios, depending on who dies first.

This macabre mental exercise can become especially complicated if you have been married more than once and have children from one or more of the marriages. Imagine that a husband wants to provide for his new wife after he dies, but he also wants to be sure his children from a first marriage receive some inheritance after she dies. If he bequeaths his estate to his second wife, he has no assurance she will include his children in her will.

The solution, says Lisa Berger, author of a book about retirement planning called *Feathering Your Nest,* is a Qualified Terminable Interest Property Trust, or QTIP.

The husband sets up a trust so that after he dies, his wife will receive the income from the trust. He may even structure the trust so she has access to some of the assets at the discretion of the trustee who runs it. But she has no direct control over the trust assets. After she dies, the remaining estate goes to the trust's beneficiaries—in this case, the man's children by a first marriage.

A word of warning: Depending on where you reside, you may not be able to use a trust to prevent your surviving spouse from taking part of your estate outright. The rule is aimed at protecting a widow's right to a portion of her husband's estate. The only way around this, Groppe says, is if a couple voluntarily signs an agreement in which they waive the right to the survivor's share of the estate. You'll need to consult a lawyer to be sure such an agreement is properly executed.

Trusts also can be useful if a father is worried that his children will squander their inheritance, or if he wants to specify how the inheritance can be used, such as for a college education. In that case, the father can set up a trust that will pro-

Death and Taxes

You may escape taxes when you die, but your heirs won't. Use this worksheet to help them survive the tax maze.

	Your Estate	Example A	Example B
Add up the value of your assets, based on current market value. Include the following: home, vacation home, IRAs, 401(K)s, pensions, life insurance policies, stocks, bonds and other investments, collectibles and other personal property, business equity. **This is your GROSS ESTATE**		$800,000	$1,670,000
Deduct from your estate the following: funeral expenses, estate administration expenses debts, mortgages, charitable deductions.	−	−50,000	−120,000
This balance may pass in whole or in part to your spouse tax-free.		750,000	1,550,000
This is the MARITAL DEDUCTION	−	−400,000	−550,000
What remains is your **TAXABLE ESTATE**		350,000	1,000,000
Now compute your **TENTATIVE TAX** on your taxable estate from the tax tables on following page. (An estate of $600,000 or less is exempt from federal taxes.)		0	345,800
Subtract the **UNIFIED CREDIT.** You can subtract a maximum of $192,800 from your tax bill.	−		−192,800
			153,000
Subtract your **STATE TAX CREDIT.** This is any allowable credit for death taxes you pay to the state.	−		−33,200
What remains is the estate tax owed to the federal government. **AMOUNT OF FEDERAL ESTATE TAX**		0	$119,800

Estate Tax Tables

If your estate is:

More than . . .	. . . But less than	Your tax is	
$500,000	$750,000	$155,800 + 37% of the amount over $500,000	
$750,000	$1,000,000	$248,300 + 39%	$750,000
$1,000,000	$1,250,000	$345,800 + 41%	$1,000,000
$1,250,000	$1,500,000	$448,300 + 43%	$1,250,000
$1,500,000	$2,000,000	$555,800 + 45%	$1,500,000
$2,000,000	$2,500,000	$780,000 + 49%	$2,000,000
$2,500,000	$3,000,000	$1,025,800 + 53%	$2,500,000
$3,000,000		$1,290,800 + 55%	$3,000,000

SOURCES: *The Ernst & Young Tax-Saving Strategies Guide 1994; Estate Planning: Clear Answers to Your Most Important Questions* by Alex J. Soled.

vide income for his children, but will be managed by a trustee according to his wishes.

Parents of a disabled child may want to create a trust to be sure the child is adequately cared for after they die. If a trust is drawn up correctly, it can help shelter assets so that the child can continue to receive government aid. Karen Greenberg, a financial planner who specializes in financial advice for parents of disabled children, says that a special needs trust, or Escher trust, is a means of ensuring the disabled person will qualify for government benefits, while still receiving income and principal from the trust for other quality of life items.

Trusts are also commonly used to reduce estate taxes. This is not usually an important consideration unless you have an estate worth more than $600,000—the threshold for federal estate taxes. That may sound like a lot of money. But by the time you add together the current value of your home, your pension plan, 401(k) plan, life insurance policy and other savings, you may have a much larger estate than you think.

You are allowed to deduct certain expenses from this total before you arrive at the amount used for calculating federal estate tax. They include such things as funeral expenses, income taxes owed, and other bills that must be paid from the estate.

Don't forget that in addition to federal estate taxes you may have to pay state estate taxes or inheritance taxes, or both. Five states, including New York, have no inheritance tax on the recipient but instead levy taxes on the entire estate, Berger says. The state's threshold may be lower than for federal tax.

The good news is that the IRS and most states allow an unlimited marital deduction. That means no matter how large your estate, if you bequeath it to your spouse, there will be no estate tax.

However, the tax bite comes after your spouse dies. Say for example, your estate is worth $1.2 million. You leave it all to your wife so there is no estate tax. When she dies, however, half of it will be tax exempt and the other half will be subject to estate tax. And that can add up to quite a bite.

In this scenario, there is a way to avoid getting hit with any taxes. It's often referred to as a bypass trust or a credit shelter trust. And it basically works this way: When the husband dies, he leaves his wife $600,000 outright. And he puts $600,000 into a family trust that will provide income for his wife as long as she lives. When she dies, she bequeaths $600,000 tax-free to her heirs. And because the trust is a separate entity, it can be passed on tax free to the designated beneficiaries.

Be careful if you are considering bypassing your children and giving your estate to your grandchildren, Groppe says. This may trigger an additional generation-skipping tax. The government imposes this tax because, in effect, you have deprived it of a generation's worth of taxes. There is a $1 million exemption. But this is a complicated area of the tax law, requiring professional advice.

There are also a variety of irrevocable trusts that can effectively shelter assets from estate taxes. For example, there are irrevocable life insurance trusts. Some parents who don't want their children to have to sell property or the family business to pay for estate taxes set up insurance trusts. That way the policy can be passed tax-free to the heirs, who then can use the cash to pay the estate tax bill. And there are charitable remainder trusts, which are one of the few tax shelters left because they can reduce your income tax while you're alive.

The hitch with an irrevocable trust is that once you create one, you can't change it.

Before you consult an lawyer or other professional about setting up a trust, it's a good idea to educate yourself. Learn more about the different kinds of trusts and carefully consider how they may fit your goals. Martin Censor, a lawyer and senior editor at Warren Gorham Lamont, a Manhattan publishing company, says that most people could cut the amount of time spent with a lawyer and save up to 50 percent in professional fees if they prepare themselves first.

Finally, shop around for a good lawyer or financial adviser. Don't be shy about interviewing several experts about their fees and services. And, as Berger notes in her book, be suspicious of an attorney, financial planner or bank trust department that urges you to completely turn over the reins to your estate by giving total power of attorney.

For Further Reading

• The American Association of Retired Persons has a guide for $12.95 called *Organizing Your Future,* which describes legal tools available to you if you become incapacitated. Send a check, made payable to Legal Counsel for the Elderly, to: AARP's Legal Counsel for the Elderly, P.O. Box 96474, Washington, D.C., 20090-6474.

• *Feathering Your Nest: The Retirement Planner,* by Lisa Berger, published by Workman Publishing, $12.95.

• *Estate Planning: Clear Answers to Your Most Important Questions,* by Alex J. Soled, published by Consumer Reports Books, $22.95.

Whom Do You Trust?

A trust doesn't run itself; you need to pick someone to do that, and it's not a task to be done lightly. Your choice will determine whether your carefully laid plans succeed or fail after your death.

You need to appoint a trustee who is able to make sound investment decisions, handle tax matters, administer the trust according to its instructions, and who will be around for the life of the trust, says Larry Elkin, a financial planner.

If you have a large and complicated trust it may not be realistic to expect a family member or friend to be willing or able to take on these responsibilities. So you may want to consider a professional trustee. Keep in mind that most banks and trust companies will not handle small trusts.

Some banks only accept trusts of more than $1 million. Other smaller banks set the threshold at $200,000. Chemical Bank, the nation's third largest manager of trusts, accepts personal trusts of $500,000 or more.

Although fees vary, there is usually a flat annual fee, as well as an annual fee that is based on the size of the trust. For example, Chemical charges a flat fee of $1,250. It also charges a percentage of the trust, which starts at a little more than 1 percent for the first $500,000, and decreases as the size of the trust increases. That means the total annual fee for a $500,000 trust would be about $7,190. There also can be additional charges if a trust is complicated.

Ask your lawyer or accountant for recommendations on finding a trustee. Before you make a decision, interview several trustees and ask about their fees and management style. In the past, some banks and trust companies have been criticized for being too costly and too conservative in their investment decisions. To prevent potential problems have the trust drawn up with a provision allowing the family to change the trustee, Elkin says.

Scrambling the Nest Egg

*Withdraw that Retirement Money
as Carefully as You Saved It*

As YOU BEGIN the countdown to retirement, do you dream of buying a luxury condominium in Florida, going on an African safari, or spending endless hours restoring antique cars?

Before your fantasies run wild, you'd better be sure you can afford these plans. The fact is, Americans are retiring earlier and living longer. And that means you'll have to carefully manage your retirement income just to maintain your standard of living for all the years ahead.

"Many people don't understand what they will need in retirement," says David Certner, a senior coordinator at the American Association of Retired Persons. "Although they may be reasonably well off at 65, that may not be the case 15 years later."

The other thing to consider is that you're going to be receiving several dizzying sums of money at once—probably more than you've ever had or will ever have again. But don't let the potential riches make you careless; your golden years will be quickly tarnished if you withdraw the money the wrong way or don't have a plan on how to reinvest it.

"We spend our whole lives putting money into retirement plans, and very little time thinking about taking it out," says Joel Isaacson, a Manhattan financial planner.

So before you say good-bye to the daily grind, you need to draw up a financial plan. First, consider the types of retirement income that may be available to you:

• The traditional company pension plan, also called a defined benefit plan. The amount of the pension benefit is based on salary and years of service. The pension often is not available to the retiree in a lump-sum payment. Instead, it is doled out in fixed payments for as long as you live.

• A defined contribution plan offered by your employer, such as a 401(k) plan. You elect to contribute part of your salary into a tax-deferred account. In many cases the employer matches a certain amount of your contribution. When you are ready to retire you either take out the money in a lump sum, roll it over into an IRA, or withdraw a portion of it annually based on your life expectancy.

• Individually funded pensions, such as individual retirement accounts. You can begin withdrawing these IRA funds, as well as defined contribution plan

Warning: IRA Rollovers Can Be Hazardous To Your Financial Health!

New rules require you to be extremely careful about how you roll over your 401(k) funds into an IRA, or you could suddenly find that a chunk of the money is missing.

In the past, you could simply ask your employer for a check for the amount in the retirement fund and you then had 60 days to decide what to do with it.

Now you must arrange for your employer to transfer your funds directly into an IRA account—called a trustee to trustee transfer—or else your company is required to withhold 20 percent of your money for taxes.

This may not sound so serious, but it's harder than you may think to extricate yourself from this mess.

Say you have $100,000 in your 401(k) plan. Your employer withholds 20 percent and gives you a check for $80,000. If you want to keep the tax deferral, you now have 60 days to deposit $100,000 into an IRA. Unfortunately, you'll never get the $20,000 back from Uncle Sam that quickly. So in order to avoid paying taxes, you have to come up with $20,000 and wait until the following April for the IRS to refund your money.

What happens if you don't happen to have an extra $20,000? Tough luck. You suffer the tax consequences.

To add insult to injury, your tax-deferred account will be permanently smaller; the rules don't allow you to redeposit your refund when you finally get it back from the IRS.

funds, without penalty once you turn 59$^{1}/_{2}$. And you can postpone making any withdrawals until you reach age 70$^{1}/_{2}$; at that point, you will pay a penalty if you don't start tapping into the funds.

• Social Security benefits. If you have worked for a minimum of 10 years and paid FICA (Federal Insurance Contributions Act) tax, you are eligible to receive Social Security. You can choose to begin receiving reduced benefits at age 62. You can postpone payments until age 70. The longer you wait, the larger your benefits. Nonworking spouses are also eligible for some benefits.

Like most Americans, you will probably receive retirement income from more than one of the sources mentioned above. In addition, you may have some money in nonretirement savings, such as bank accounts and mutual funds. Once you have made an inventory of your retirement funds, you need to develop a plan for withdrawing them.

Each of the two types of company retirement plans has drawbacks that could lower your standard of living. If you have a traditional defined benefit pension that provides lifetime benefits, the hitch is that the income won't keep pace with inflation. If you have a defined contribution plan, the disadvantage is that the funds may run out before you die.

If you've got both, you ideally want to come up with a strategy that gives you the security of an annuity, as well as a hedge against inflation. Isaacson gives the example of a client who had a defined benefit plan that could have been taken as a lifetime pension or as a lump sum, plus a profit-sharing plan. He told her to take the pension as a guaranteed income for life, and then roll most of the profit-sharing plan into an IRA where it could be invested for growth. The rest was set aside as an emergency fund. (If you don't have a defined benefit plan from your employer, and you're worried that you won't be able to manage your investments well enough to make your income last for life, you can take a portion of your IRA or 401(k) funds and buy an annuity contract from a life insurance company.)

Next, you have to choose how you want to get paid from your defined benefit plan. Assuming you aren't allowed to take it as a lump sum, you'll be getting a monthly check as long as you live. Unless you say otherwise, it must be paid to you as a joint-and-survivor annuity. This means that your spouse will continue to receive all or a portion of your benefits after your death. Your spouse can waive this right, which means a bigger check for you while you're alive—but your spouse gets nothing after you're gone.

Which option should you choose? Many insurers encourage couples to waive the joint-and-survivor annuity, and use the additional pension income to buy a life insurance policy with the spouse as beneficiary.

You'll have to do the math to see whether it works for you, but one advantage is that the insurance policy is better for your heirs. That's because a joint-and-survivor pension annuity ends with the death of you and your spouse. But with an insurance policy, if your spouse dies first, for example, you can designate your children as beneficiaries.

Although this strategy sounds good in theory, it often is shortsighted, many financial planners say. The extra money you make by choosing the single-life annuity is taxable, so you won't pocket as much as you think. You may find you can't afford to replace the annuity benefit with a comparable insurance policy, or you may not be insurable, says Martin Nissenbaum, a partner at Ernst & Young. "Generally the negative factors outweigh the positive factors," he says.

In addition, your spouse has given up a valuable right to pension benefits in return for an insurance policy. If the marriage subsequently breaks up, you can name a new beneficiary on the insurance policy, leaving your ex-spouse with nothing.

As for the rest of your assets, experts say you should first consider how to protect yourself from taxes so that your nest egg will last longer. Don't ever forget that the government is waiting in the wings to get its hands on all the money that has been growing in tax-sheltered retirement accounts.

The rule of thumb is that you always use after-tax money first, so that your retirement income will continue to grow tax deferred, Nissenbaum says.

If you have a 401(k) plan, one option is to withdraw the money all at once. If you are 59^1/$_2$, you can do so without penalty, but you will have to pay income tax.

However, the IRS gives you a one-time break called forward tax averaging. There are two types, five-year and 10-year, the latter available only to people born before 1936.

Forward tax averaging calculates taxes at a special rate as if the money is being withdrawn evenly over a number of years. It results in a much reduced tax bill, which you pay all at once. Then the money is yours.

But if you want to avoid paying all the taxes up-front on a 401(k) account, you can roll it into an IRA and keep deferring taxes that way. You can always make a partial withdrawal if you need to, paying income taxes at your normal rate. However, you can't avoid the taxes forever; when you reach age 70^1/$_2$, the rules say you must begin making a minimum level of withdrawal based on a calculation dictated by the IRS.

Sounds complicated? Well, the reality is that you must take an active role in ensuring your financial security in retirement. Employers are already shifting the responsibility to you by eliminating the traditional company pension in favor of 401(k) plans. And although Social Security provides a source of income that is indexed to inflation, you should never count on government funding for your support.

So before you call the travel agent about that cruise around the world, or the real estate agent about a second home in Arizona, educate yourself about tax law and retirement plans. Then consult a financial planner or an accountant about your options. This is one of those times in life when it is difficult to go it alone.

Just remember to choose an adviser carefully. Some unscrupulous financial experts are only too happy to make big commissions by putting your nest egg into investments more suited to their futures than to yours.

**For more information on pension plans and retirement,
consider the following:**

• To request an estimate of your future Social Security benefits, call 800-772-1213.

• *Receiving A Lump Sum Distribution: A Guide For Investors Aged 50 And Over,* a free booklet published by AARP Investment Program from Scudder. To order a copy, call 800-322-2282, ext. 4536.

• *A Guide to Understanding Your Pension Plan,* a free pension handbook from AARP, Stock No. D13533. To order a copy send a post card to AARP (Promotion E0670), 601 E. St. NW, Washington D.C. 20049. Be sure to specify the title and stock number.

• The Pension Rights Center has a list of publications on pension topics that are available for small fees. To obtain the list, call 202-296-3776 or send a stamped self-addressed envelope to Pension Rights Center, 918 16th St. N.W., Suite 704, Washington, D.C. 20006.

Sun Belt or Snow Belt?

*Deciding How, Where, or Whether
to Make that Big Retirement Move*

YOUR KIDS ARE GROWN and you retired several years ago. But you're still rattling around a four-bedroom house, spending too much time cleaning and too much money on utility bills and real estate taxes. Is that your idea of how to spend your golden years?

Perhaps there's a better way. Why not sell your home and move to a smaller, more affordable house or apartment? And while you're at it, why not move to a state with a better climate and lower taxes? Plenty of other people have done it. What's stopping you?

The question of where to live after retirement is not a simple one. There are many factors to consider, not the least of which is your sentimental attachment to your home and its proximity to your children. Whatever your final decision, it will affect your finances and quality of life for years to come.

If you bought your house 25 or 35 years ago, chances are that it is much more valuable; it may be your biggest asset.

If you stand to make a big gain on the sale of your home, then consider your alternatives.

Lee Rosenberg, cofounder of ARS Financial Services in Valley Stream and author of *Retirement Ready or Not,* says trading down to a less expensive home can be a very smart financial move because you can use what's left over to improve your standard of living.

There's another plus: You may be eligible for a special, one-time capital gains exclusion. The IRS says that once you reach age 55, you can exclude from taxes up to $125,000 in capital gains on the sale of your primary residence.

That means if your capital gain is $125,000, you don't have to put the money into another home in order to avoid taxes. If you want, you could invest the money in stocks and rent a condominium.

If your capital gain is $275,000, you could take the exclusion on $125,000 of the gain, and defer taxes on the rest by rolling it over into a new home.

Before you rush to sell your home, be sure to check the eligibility rules for the exclusion. You must have owned and lived in the home for three of the five years preceding the sale. There is only one $125,000 exclusion per couple. For example, say that a man is considering remarrying and both he and his fiancée are over

Hot Spots

Here's a sampling of popular retirement cities and how New York City/Long Island compares.

COST OF LIVING INDEXES
100 = U.S. Average

	Avg. Housing Price	Food at Home	Health Care	Transportation
Austin, Texas	96	101	104	104
Greenville, S.C.	80	92	101	89
Las Vegas	113	97	111	107
New York City	249	142	204	129
Long Island	231	120	135	119
Phoenix	107	100	111	116
San Diego	235	107	125	116
San Francisco	372	110	118	120
Seattle	172	118	133	111
Tampa	93	98	92	99
Tuscon, Ariz.	97	103	115	102
Washington, D.C.	179	115	116	112
W. Palm Beach, Fla.	144	95	94	111

TAXES

	Personal Income Tax				Property	
	Highest Marginal Rate	Social Security Exemption	Elderly Tax Pref- ferences	Sales Tax Rate	Tax Rate % of Home Value***	State Estate Tax
Austin, Texas	0			8.00	2.29	
Greenville, S.C.	7	•	•	5.00	0.85	
Las Vegas	0			7.00	0.98	
New York City	7.5*	•		8.25	1.29	•
Long Island	7.5*	•		8.50	2.49	•
Phoenix	6.9	•	•	6.70**	0.75	
San Diego	11.0	•	•	7.75	1.09	
San Francisco	11.0*	•	•	8.50	1.03	
Seattle	0			8.20	0.89	
Tampa	0			6.50	1.82	
Tucson, Ariz.	6.9	•	•	7.00	1.12	
Washington, D.C.	9.5	•	•	6.00	1.08	
W. Palm Beach, Fla.	0			6.00	1.87	

WEATHER

	Annual Avg. Temp.	No. of Days of Precipitation****
Austin, Texas	68.1	84.2
Greenville, S.C.	60.1	117.6
Las Vegas	79.6	25.9
New York City	54.5	120.6
Long Island	51.0	117.0
Phoenix	85.1	35.6
San Diego	70.5	42.1
San Francisco	64.9	67.2
Seattle	51.4	155.6
Tampa	81.4	106.7
Tucson, Ariz.	81.7	52.7
Washington, D.C.	66.5	111.7
W. Palm Beach, Fla.	82.6	128.8

*New York City residents pay an additional maximum rate of 3.4 percent on personal income; San Francisco residents pay an additional 1.5 percent on earnings.
**Tax varies according to item purchased. Range is 6 percent to 8.7 percent with the average being 6.7 percent.
***Taxes paid in 1992 on four-bedroom, 2,600-square-foot house in neighborhoods with family income of $75,000.
****More than 1/100th inch of precipitation.

SOURCES: Places Rated Almanac; National Conference of State Legislatures; *Money* Magazine; *The Weather Almanac;* National Climatic Data Center.

55 and own homes. If they sell the homes before the wedding, they each get an exclusion of $125,000. If they wait until the honeymoon is over, they get only one exclusion.

The capital gains exclusion is a one-time offer, but you can choose when to take it. That means if you sell your home now at a capital gain of just $70,000, you may decide to save the exclusion for the next time you sell your home, when you anticipate a bigger gain.

When you get ready to calculate the capital gain, don't overlook the value of any capital improvements you made in your home over the years. If you added a new roof, put in a swimming pool, or renovated the bathroom, these things increased the value of the home. But you need good records to document what you paid for these improvements, says Ann Diamond, a financial consultant.

Take the total value of these capital improvements and add it to the original price you paid for the home. This is your cost basis. Then subtract the cost basis from the sale price. The result is your capital gain.

So imagine that you have taken the big step and put your home on the market. You've already found a buyer. Soon you'll have a windfall in the bank.

Now what? Where should you move? Perhaps you have friends in Boca

Raton, Fla., who've been telling you how great it is there. They could show you around, help you find a place to buy, and introduce you to people. How about it?

It may be that Florida is the perfect place to spend your retirement years. But before you put money down on a beachfront condo, you should be sure. "One of the biggest mistakes I see people making is buying a home too fast," Diamond says. "I think it's a better idea to rent for a period of time. Most people have been to Florida in the winter, but they often don't realize what the summer can be like there."

Do some research before you select a retirement destination. You may want to compare several places. Visit them. Find out about the taxes and cost of living. Consider the climate, public transportation, quality of health care, and the amenities available.

"Be clear about your expectations, resources and needs," Diamond says. For example, if you think you'll want to work part-time because you'll be bored or you'll need the extra income, be sure to take that into account. It can be hard to find a part-time job, except for volunteer work, if you live in an area with many other retirees.

"And remember that it can take time to make friends and develop a support system in a new place. Some people choose to retire in places like Florida because they know so many people who have already moved there."

Many people also choose Florida because of the tax benefits of living there. It has no state income tax, no gift levy and the estate tax is a dollar for dollar deduction from the federal estate tax. And if you live in Florida, the first $25,000 of the assessed value of your principal residence is exempt from property tax. In his book, *Fifty Fabulous Places to Retire in America,* Rosenberg says that Florida ranks first among 10 popular retirement states for smallest tax bite.

In order to realize these benefits, however, you must establish legal residence in Florida. And that means you also must prove that you no longer owe taxes in your former home state. Even if you can prove you've changed your residency, the state where you once earned your living may continue to lay claim to the taxes on your pension income.

Some states try to raise tax revenues by aggressively pursuing people who claim to have moved out of state. In New York, the Tax Department conducts about 4,000 audits a year of such people, says Paul R. Comeau, a Buffalo lawyer and coauthor of *The New York Residency Audit Handbook.* The audits have resulted in additional tax assessments of $125 million a year, he adds.

To escape your original state's jurisdiction there is a two-step process: you must prove you are no longer a resident and are no longer domiciled in the state.

Many states define a resident as someone who maintains a permanent residence and spends more than 183 days a year in the state. That sounds pretty straightforward. But in fact, it may not be easy to prove where you have been every day of the year. You should keep a diary, and retain all other documents, such as phone bills, credit card receipts and airline tickets, says Lawrence A. Greenberg, a senior trust officer at Chemical Bank's Palm Beach office.

Comeau has one client, a former New Yorker who now lives in Florida, who goes so far as to stop by his local police station every day to ask an officer to sign a paper attesting to his presence there.

Domicile is more subjective than residency. It refers to the place you intend to be your permanent home. You may vote in Florida, file tax returns there, open your bank accounts there and think of yourself as a Floridian. But if you come back to New York for five months in the summer, continue to play golf and keep a home in New York, you may be deemed a New Yorker for tax purposes. Among the criteria:

• You retain your family home.

• You continue to own a home-state business or are actively involved in running it, even if you do so by phone and fax.

• You spend most of your time in your old state. For example, you may spend five months there, four months in Florida and three months in Europe.

• You keep your most valued possessions in the home state even though you have a primary residence in Florida. If your wedding album, stamp collection, and antiques are still in your old home, the state may say your heart's still here.

• Your visit your family frequently. Comeau says that if the state decides that your family is the most important factor in your life, then it may rule that you are still domiciled there.

• You retain active membership in clubs.

Florida is not the only state without a personal income tax. Alaska, Nevada, South Dakota, Texas, Washington and Wyoming share that distinction.

In addition, you will want to check the sales tax and property tax rates before you select a retirement destination. If you take the right steps to establish residency, you can save money by moving to a state with low taxes.

But financial experts say that taxes shouldn't be your primary consideration. Why move to Florida if you will miss the change of seasons, or if you want to live somewhere you won't need a car? Says Greenberg: "In the end, you should never let the tax tail wag the dog."

Retirement Resources

For more information about retirement destinations, you can pick up the following:

• *Issues to Consider Before You Move to Florida,* a free brochure from Chemical Bank. To request a copy, call 800-835-8710.

• *50 Fabulous Places to Retire in America,* by Lee Rosenberg and Saralee H. Rosenberg, published by Career Press. Cost: $14.95. To order, call 800-955-7373.

• *Places Rated Almanac: Your Guide to Finding the Best Places to Live in North America,* by David Savageau and Richard Boyer. The book rates 343 metropolitan areas and compares living costs, housing, job outlook, transportation, education, health care, crime, the arts, recreation and climate. Published by Prentice Hall Travel. Available in bookstores for $20.00.

• For tips on selling your home and other considerations, *Retirement Ready or Not: How to Get Financially Prepared—in a Hurry,* by Lee Rosenberg, published by Career Press. Cost: $14.95. To order, call 800-955-7373.

A Healthy Retirement

You Need to Know About Insurance
Options Before You Buy

IF YOU ARE ABOUT to retire, or if you are already 65 or older, you cannot afford to be uninformed about your health care options.

For one thing, an increasing number of retirees must provide their own health insurance to fill in the gaps not covered by Medicare. In 1993, less than half of all large employers provided retiree health benefits, according to a recent survey by Foster Higgins, a consulting firm. And only one in 10 small employers extended health coverage to retirees that year.

Now, consider the sobering fact that about 1.5 million people over age 65 live full-time in some type of residential care facility at a cost of between $30,000 and $100,000 per year, says Joseph Matthews in his book *Beat the Nursing Home Trap*. Matthews also notes that more than five million older Americans receive some form of in-home health care or assistance.

Senior citizens must have a financial plan for coping with these costs. Unfortunately, it's hard to understand the maze of government health programs and the various types of supplemental private insurance policies. And laws governing them often change. What's more, this is an area that is prone to abuse. Senior citizens are easy targets for unscrupulous agents who sell them more insurance than they need or policies that don't fit their needs.

There is a lot of bias in insurance sales pitches, says Ann Krull, who oversees the Health Insurance Information, Counseling and Assistance Program— HIICAP for short—for New York's Office for the Aging.

Since 1993, the federal government has allocated funds for all states to provide free insurance counseling services to older Americans. HIICAP is one of them. It is designed to provide unbiased and up-to-date answers to questions about health insurance for senior citizens.

"In an average month, we get about 350 phone calls and maybe 80 visits at our sites," says Amy Bernstein, the HIICAP coordinator for New York City. A vast majority of the callers want help figuring out how Medicare works or picking out a supplemental insurance policy, she says.

Here are some of the basic facts you need to know about Medicare and the supplemental policies, called Medigap:

Medicare is the federal health insurance program for people 65 and older. The coverage is divided into two parts: Medicare Part A, for hospital insurance, and

Medicare Part B, for medical insurance. If you are eligible for Part A, there is no charge. However, there is a monthly premium for Part B, which changes every January. In 1994, the monthly premium was $41.

You can enroll in Medicare three months before or three months after you turn 65. There is also a general enrollment period every year, between January and March. Your Part B premium is 10 percent higher for each year you delay enrolling.

If you continue to work after age 65 and are covered by your employer's health plan, you should apply for Part A because it is free. But the United Seniors Health Cooperative, a nonprofit group in Washington D.C., suggests not applying for Part B until just before your employer's coverage expires.

Why? Because after you apply for Medicare Part B, there is a six-month period when you are eligible for open enrollment in Medigap insurance. This means that insurers selling Medigap policies cannot turn you down for any reason.

Many people are confused about what Medicare covers. One of the biggest misconceptions is that it covers long-term nursing home care, Matthews says. In fact, Medicare only covers a limited amount of such care and only under limited circumstances.

Medicare also doesn't pay for all your medical and hospital bills. That's why you need a Medigap policy. In 1965, when Medicare was formed, it was expected to pay for 80 percent of the average health care bill of senior citizens. Today, as health care costs have exploded, Medicare pays for less than half of these bills, according to the United Seniors Health Cooperative.

For example, Medicare requires you to pay a $696 deductible before Part A hospital coverage begins. Medicare Part B pays only 80 percent of medical services after a $100 annual deductible. In addition, Medicare does not pay for most prescription drugs. If you're retiring from a company that only required a small copayment for prescription drugs, you could be in for a real shock when you have to start footing the entire bill yourself.

Fortunately, changes in federal law have made it easier to shop for a policy to fill in the gaps.

Federal regulations now limit Medigap to 10 standard policies. The core benefits offered by all 10 policies include the following: Payment of the copayment for hospitalization up to 150 days and an additional 365 days per lifetime, the 20 percent copayment for medical care, and payment for the first three units of blood.

The Medigap policies are referred to as Plans A through J. Plan A offers the basic benefits only. The other nine plans will have various additional benefits.

Getting good Medigap insurance is something you have to be very careful about, Matthews says. People have a habit of buying a policy with more benefits than they need.

The United Seniors Health Cooperative gives the following advice for shopping for Medigap insurance:

• Learn about Medicare's basic coverage and gaps.

• Study the 10 standard Medigap plans and benefits. Decide what coverage would best meet your needs and circumstances.

• Compare only policies that meet your needs. Although benefits are identical for all Medigap plans of the same type, premiums can vary widely from one company to another and so does the potential for premium increases.

• Consider other options. Check to see if you are covered by your employer. If you have limited income and assets, you may be eligible for free government coverage. Compare Medigap coverage and costs to other services from health maintenance organizations.

The least expensive Medigap policy is Plan A. However, even the price of these plans will vary depending on such things as the method used to calculate the premium and the sales commission. Some premiums are set according to your age at the time you buy the policy. That means if you were 65 when the policy was issued, you will pay the same rate the company charges people who are 65 from then on, no matter what your age. This doesn't mean, however, that the rate will stay the same forever.

Other methods adjust the premium as you grow older. These policies may seem very affordable when you are 65, but 15 or 20 years later, the rate will have increased substantially.

Some states, such as New York, have community ratings, which means the premium attached to a plan is not linked to the age, gender or medical condition of the person who buys the insurance. In other words, everyone who buys a Medigap Plan A from a certain insurer will pay the same premium in New York.

But don't expect any combination of Medicare and Medigap to pay all your health costs. Total coverage is unrealistic, some experts say, because the premium could be higher than your potential expenses. Even with the most complete Medigap insurance, you will still have to pay for such things as routine physicals, dental care and cosmetic surgery, as well as a $250 deductible for prescriptions—and 50 percent of the prescription bills after that, up to $3,000 a year. You pay for prescriptions above $3,000.

An alternative is a health maintenance organization that has a contract with Medicare. For a monthly fee, it will provide seniors coverage that includes preventive care, and sometimes dental care and prescriptions. One downside, however, is that you are limited to the doctors and hospitals that participate in the plan.

When buying Medigap insurance, you should be aware of your rights. Federal regulations prohibit insurers from selling you duplicate coverage, using high-pressure tactics, and making fraudulent or misleading comparisons of coverage. And once you are enrolled in a Medigap policy you have the right to renew the policy as long as it is still offered by the insurer.

Finally, remember that there is no need to go it alone when selecting a Medigap policy. Call your area office on aging for free counseling.

For more information on Medicare and Medigap:

• A health maintenance organization limits your choice of health care providers to plan participants, but usually reduces your health care costs and offers services that aren't available under Medicare. The New York State Office for the Aging offers a free booklet, *Choosing an HMO: a Guide for Medicare Beneficiaries.* To request a copy, call 800-342-9871.

• The United Seniors Health Cooperative publishes *Managing Your Health Care Finances: Getting the Most Out of Medicare & Medigap Insurance, Revised.* The cost is $8.50, plus $1.50 for postage and handling. Also offered is *1994 Medicare & Medigap Update,* an eight-page guide that is free with any order from the organization. If ordered separately, it costs $2.50, plus $1.50 for postage and handling. Send a check to United Seniors Health Cooperative, Publication Sales Department, 1331 H St. N.W., Suite 500, Washington, D.C. 20005-4706. Or you can charge it to your credit card by calling 202-393-6222.

Keeping Your Money Out of the Home

Nursing Homes Aren't Your Only Option for Long-Term Care

THE DODGERS ARE MOVING back to Brooklyn. Johnny Carson is coming back to late-night TV. And you don't have to worry about the cost of nursing home care.

Dream on!

You probably don't delude yourself about sports franchises or television lineups. Nor should you deny the frightening possibility of long-term nursing home care.

The fact is, at age 65 you have a 43 percent chance of ending up in a nursing home at least once in your life, according to the *New England Journal of Medicine.* In many cases, these nursing home stays are short—three months or less.

But for those who end up needing nursing home care for a year or more, the cost can be catastrophic. Nationally, the average price of such care ranges from about $30,000 to $60,000 a year, depending on where you live. In expensive areas, such as New York, the cost can easily reach $200 a day, says Bruce Birnbaum, director of advanced planning at Comprehensive Financial Services. At that rate, most people would quickly deplete their assets to pay for nursing home care.

If the prospect of being reduced to poverty scares you, or the idea of having no estate for your children upsets you, you're going to have to do some advance planning.

Basically, these are your options:

• You can pay the nursing home bills yourself for as long as your money lasts, and then Medicaid will step in and pay the bills.

• You can give away your assets so you're eventually eligible for Medicaid.

• You can avoid going to a nursing home and, instead, receive less-expensive in-home care.

• You can take out long-term care insurance and hope it will cover most of whatever needs eventually arise.

The first option is the one that raises the specter of poverty and no inheritance. The second option might let you avoid that if you give your money to your heirs before you die. So one of the most crucial decisions to make is this: Should you shift your assets so you will immediately qualify for Medicaid?

Caution for the Long Term

Long-term care insurance isn't for everyone. It is still a relatively new product, with many bugs to be worked out, warns Consumers Union. Only those who can afford to pay high premiums for many years and who have substantial assets to protect should even consider a policy. If you want to take a chance on coverage, consider the following:

Cover All Bases. Buy a comprehensive policy that pays for nursing home stays and home care. Be sure to choose home care benefits that cover a wide range of services.

Cheap Seats. Beware of buying the lowest-priced policy just because it's cheap. It may offer inferior coverage and its premiums may increase when you can least afford to pay more.

Going Up. Inflation protection is a must. Choose a company that charges a level premium for the inflation rider. Compounded inflation protection is best. Look for inflation protection that continues throughout your lifetime.

Age Guard. Beware of the potential for unaffordable price hikes. No one should buy an attained-age policy, a policy that starts out low but rises with the policyholder's age.

Changing Employers. If you buy through your employer, be sure you can continue your coverage if you change employers, or if the employer terminates the plan.

Wellness Rider. Avoid policies that require a hospital stay of at least three days before the company will pay nursing home benefits. That requirement is illegal in 38 states. Also be wary of policies that require care be medically necessary for sickness or injury. Many nursing home patients are not sick or injured and may not be covered under such a policy.

Help at Home. If you buy a home care policy, try to buy one that covers home-health aides, who primarily help patients with personal or custodial care, rather than one that pays only for skilled personnel. Better yet, look for a policy that pays for homemaker services.

Second Opinion. Ask your agent for the shoppers' guide on long-term care written by the National Association of Insurance Commissioners before you buy. Take some time to read it.

Highlights. Insist on receiving the outlines of coverage that highlight the major aspects of the policy. Make sure the form numbers on the brochures and the policy match.

SOURCE: Consumers Union

"Some people say it's a violation of the spirit of the law to hide or give away assets in order to have your needs paid for by programs intended for the poor," says Joseph Matthews, author of *Beating the Nursing Home Trap.*

"The other side is that this is one of the only countries in the industrial world that doesn't provide long-term care for its citizens," he says. "The fact that a program is available if you know how to use it justifies taking advantage of it."

Carole Lamson, an elder law attorney, says that shielding assets to become eligible for Medicaid is not illegal and is no different than trying to find ways to reduce taxes. "No one says you have a moral obligation to pay the maximum amount of taxes," she says.

Some policymakers apparently disagree; the government has recently made it more difficult to pull off this strategy, so you need to thoroughly understand the law.

The rules say that you have to spend down your assets to a certain level to qualify for Medicaid. You also can usually keep your home, although the state may put a lien on the property while you are still alive as a condition for receiving Medicaid benefits. When you die, if your spouse is no longer living, the state can force the sale of the house to recover some of the benefits you received. Upon your death, the state also can recover Medicaid payments from other assets in your estate, from revocable trusts, and from property held in joint tenancy.

If you decide to give away your assets, you must do so 36 months before you apply for Medicaid or enter a nursing home; otherwise it is not considered a valid transfer. This look-back period was recently expanded from 30 months.

If you make an invalid transfer, your eligibility for Medicaid will be delayed for a period determined by the value of the asset transferred, divided by the average monthly nursing home cost in your state.

Say, for example, you transfer a home worth $200,000 to your children during the 36-month period before you apply for Medicaid. If the average monthly nursing home cost in your state is $5,000, then you divide $200,000 by $5,000. The result is 40. That is the number of months before you would be eligible to receive Medicaid.

In addition to giving away your assets now, you can set up a Medicaid trust, which shields your assets from Medicaid claims and passes to your heirs when you die. But you can't get any income or touch the assets, and it's irrevocable. Beware if someone tells you to set up an income-only Medicaid trust. In the past, these trusts were popular because they allowed people to draw on the income from the assets and still qualify for Medicaid. Recent changes in the law have put their viability in doubt, so make sure you get solid professional advice.

A final word about shifting assets to qualify for Medicaid: The nursing home you prefer may not accept Medicaid. In fact, when you're reduced to government benefits, you may have little choice about which facility you end up in.

If you decide not to transfer your assets, you may want to consider a long-term care insurance policy as an alternative.

MediLanguage

Here are some terms that will help you work your way through the maze of Medicare and Medicaid.

Carrier: A private insurance organization that contracts with the federal government to handle claims from doctors and suppliers of services covered by Medicare Part B Medical Insurance.

Continuing-Care Retirement Communities: Residential communities that provide apartments, common areas and dining rooms, as well as medical and nursing facilities.

Copayment: The portion or percentage of covered medical costs that you pay.

Custodial Care: Nonmedical personal care, such as assistance with activities of daily living, including eating, walking and dressing. It is provided by people without professional skills.

Death Benefits: A provision in some long-term care insurance policies that says if you die, it will refund to your estate any premiums you paid minus any benefits the company paid on your behalf. To receive these benefits you must have paid premiums for a certain number of years.

Deductible: A fixed amount of money you are often required to pay toward health care bills before insurance payments begin.

Explanation of Medicare Benefits: Official notice from Medicare Part B that shows the approved charges, the amount paid for services, and the deductible amount owed.

Health Maintenance Organization: A network that offers Medicare beneficiaries all services covered by Medicare and supplemental insurance for one, prepaid price. The HMO manages all care.

Home Care: A variety of medical and personal services provided at home to a partially or fully dependent elder.

Home-Health Agency: A public or private organization that specializes in giving skilled nursing services and other therapeutic services such as physical therapy at home.

Hospice: A program operated by a public agency or private organization that engages primarily in providing pain relief, symptom management and supportive services for terminally ill people and their families.

Life-Care Communities: Senior housing facilities that offer independent living, assisted living and nursing home care.

Long-Term Care Insurance: Private insurance policies that pay a certain amount each day for nursing-home care and/or home care.

Medicaid: State-run health care programs for the poor or disabled, jointly financed by federal and state governments. For low-income elderly people who qualify, Medicaid covers many long-term care costs, including home care and nursing facility care.

Medicare: The federal health insurance program for individuals 65 and older and for those who qualify under disability rules. Part A helps pay for hospital care, a limited amount of care in a skilled nursing facility and home health care. Part B helps pay for doctor's services and outpatient hospital services, among others.

Medigap: Private health insurance designed to pay some of the costs not covered by Medicare.

Non forfeiture Benefits: A provision in some long-term care insurance policies that returns to policyholders some of their investment in the policy if they drop their coverage.

Nursing Homes: Long-term care facilities for people who need regular nursing and medical care and assistance with daily tasks.

Senior Communities: Apartment complexes or neighborhoods, complete with social and recreational activities designed for active, independent older Americans.

Skilled Nursing Facility: A specially qualified facility that has the staff and equipment to provide skilled nursing care or rehabilitation services and other related health services.

Skilled Nursing Care: Care that can be provided only by or under the supervision of licensed nursing personnel.

Reverse Mortgage: If you own your home free and clear, a reverse mortgage makes it possible to convert some of the equity in your home into spendable cash while you retain ownership of your home.

Waiver of Premium: A provision that allows you to stop paying premiums once you begin receiving benefits from your long-term care insurance.

SOURCES: *Beat the Nursing Home Trap: A Consumer Guide to Choosing & Financing Long-Term Care,* by Joseph Matthews; United Seniors Health Cooperative; National Association of Insurance Commissioners.

Many consumer advocates warn that these policies are relatively new and are not standardized, making it difficult to shop for one. Matthews says they are a gamble because they are costly, and you don't know if you'll ever need one. "With life insurance, you know that you'll die," he says. "But you could pay a lot of money for long-term care premiums and it may be wasted."

What's more, you might pay premiums for many years, and then find you can't afford them anymore. Unless you have a special provision in your policy, you're out that money. And unless you have built-in inflation protection, your policy may be almost worthless by the time you need it.

And before you sign up for a long-term care policy, don't forget to check on the financial health of the insurer who's receiving your money. A number of rating firms analyze insurance companies and give them a letter grade to reflect their financial condition. For example, ask for A.M. Best's guide to insurers at your public library.

Some states are trying to come up with new options for long-term care. New York State has joined forces with private insurers in a program called the Partnership for Long-Term Care. The result is a special long-term care policy that allows you to retain all your assets and still qualify for Medicaid benefits in New York after you have exhausted the policy's benefits.

"It's expensive and not portable," Lamson says of the partnership policy. In other words, if you leave New York, you'll get the insurance, but not the Medicaid asset waiver.

The partnership policy is expensive, in part, because it provides for three years of nursing care at a minimum of $100 a day, and it has inflation protection equal to 5 percent compounded annually. Birnbaum says that the annual premium for a partnership policy for a 65-year-old person would range from about $1,500 for minimum benefits, to $2,500 for higher levels of coverage.

By comparison, a nonpartnership policy for three years of nursing home care at $150 a day would cost a 65-year-old person about $1,355 a year, he says. It would not include an automatic inflation protection, however.

To really bring costs down, consider in-home care. Medicaid pays for that, too, and there's no look-back period in most cases. For many millions of people, this is a viable alternative, Matthews says.

Long-term care is one of the most complicated issues facing Americans today. Be sure to take advantage of free insurance counseling for senior citizens offered by area offices on aging. And, if necessary, talk to a reputable lawyer or financial planner.

Helpful Publications

• *A Shopper's Guide to Long-Term Care Insurance,* published by the National Association of Insurance Commissioners. Send a postcard with your name, address and the name of the publication to NAIC, Publications Dept., 120 W. 12th St., Kansas City, MO 64105-1925.

• *Guide to Choosing a Nursing Home,* published by the U.S. Department of Health and Human Services. Send your name, address and the name of the publication to Consumer Information Center, Dept. 87, Pueblo, CO 81009.

• *Beat the Nursing Home Trap: A Consumer's Guide to Choosing & Financing Long-Term Care,* by Joseph Matthews, published by Nolo Press ($18.95). Call 800-992-6656.

• To order one of the following publications from the United Seniors Health Cooperative, call (202) 393-6222.

Home Care for Older People: A Consumer's Guide, a 120-page booklet, $10.50 plus $1.50 for postage and handling.

Long-Term Care: A Dollar & Sense Guide, Revised, a 90-page booklet, $8.50 plus $1.50 for postage and handling.

• For a reprint of "Gotcha! The Traps in Long-term Care Insurance," (Code: RO107), which appeared in the June 1991 issue of *Consumer Reports,* send a check for $3 made out to Consumer Reports, to: Bulk Reprints, Consumer Reports, P.O. Box 53016, Boulder, CO 80322.

You Wanted to Know
Answers to Frequently Asked Financial Questions

Q: I would like to transfer my Series E savings bonds to my grandchildren. Would I have to pay taxes on them?

A: If the savings bonds are now in your name only, they must be reissued in order to change the ownership to your grandchildren. And when you do that, it becomes a taxable event, says Portia Redfield, the New York District Director of the Treasury Department's U.S. Savings Bond Division.

That means if you have been deferring taxes on the bonds, as most people do, you will have to pay the federal tax that has accrued so far on them. The process is much like cashing in the bonds and buying new ones for your grandchildren, except for one thing: If you have older bonds with a guaranteed minimum interest rate of 6 percent, the reissued bonds would retain that rate for the period of time left on them. New bonds have a minimum guaranteed rate of 4 percent.

Q: How can I minimize the tax consequences of removing funds from an IRA or 401(k)?

A: IRAs and 401(k) retirement programs allow you to defer taxes on your savings so that the interest compounds more rapidly and so that by the time you start to withdraw the money, you should be in a lower tax bracket. But ultimately, you will have to pay the piper, says Lewis Altfest, a Manhattan financial planner. He says that the main thing you can do to minimize taxes on these savings is to postpone withdrawing the money as long as possible and take out only the minimum amount. Other than that, you can try to find more deductions, or if you have losses on securities, try to use them to offset the taxes on the retirement withdrawals.

Q: Are money market funds offered by banks insured?

A: This is an important question, and one that many people are confused about. A recent survey by the Securities and Exchange Commission found that 66 percent of those who bought mutual funds through a bank thought that money market funds had federal deposit insurance. That is not true.

There are two kinds of money market accounts: Money market bank accounts, which are insured by the Federal Deposit Insurance Corp., and money market mutual funds, which are sold through many banks, and are not insured. Before you open an account, ask whether it is insured, and then get it in writing.

Q: Are 401(k) funds only for retirement savings, or can they be used for other reasons?

A: Many companies allow employees to borrow money from their 401(k) plans. If so, you would be able to borrow 50 percent of your money, up to $50,000, and you would have five years to repay the loan. If you are using the money to buy a home, you can have more time to pay it back. Although you would have to pay interest on the loan, the interest is paid into your account.

If your company has no loan provision, you would be able to withdraw money from your account only in the event of extreme hardship, such as a sudden medical emergency. Even then, you would have to show that you have no other means to pay for the emergency. And you would be hit with taxes and an early withdrawal penalty. If you leave your job, you can withdraw your funds, but again you will face a stiff penalty and taxes.

Q: Are zero-coupon bonds tax-free?

A: It depends. There are several types of zero-coupon bonds. They all have one thing in common: They do not make interest payments. Instead, you buy the bond at a fraction of the face value. By the time it matures, the interest has built up within the bond and you receive the face value.

Joel Isaacson, a financial planner, points out that there are zero-coupon municipal bonds, which are tax-free if issued by the state in which you reside; there are Treasury zeroes, which are free of state and local taxes (a savings bond, incidentally, is a zero-coupon bond); and then there are corporate zeroes, which are taxable unless they are held in a retirement account. If you hold zero-coupon corporate bonds, you must pay taxes each year even though you aren't receiving any interest payments.

Q: What does a consultation with a financial planner usually cost?

A: That depends on how they charge for their services. Some receive only a commission on the investments they sell you; some charge a fee for their advice, as well as commissions on the investments they sell you; and others only charge a fee, and don't have a financial stake in the investments they recommend.

Fee-only financial planners often will not charge for an initial consultation. During that session they will find out what kind of advice you need and give you an estimate of the cost. Many fee-only planners charge by the hour. Some charge a flat fee for certain services, such as developing a long-term financial plan. If you are asking a planner to manage your money on an ongoing basis, some charge a percent of your assets. The hourly rates generally range from $125 to $280. Ron Rogé, a New York financial planner, says that it typically takes about 25 hours to do a comprehensive plan for a two-income couple with children; the plan would address retirement and education needs, estate planning, tax projections, etc.

Q: Can you invest IRA money in any mutual fund? Or does it have to be put into annuities run by insurance companies?

A: You have a wide variety of choices of where to invest your IRA money, from bank certificate of deposits to most mutual funds. You can establish an IRA account at a discount brokerage firm and invest in individual stocks, mutual funds, or foreign currency futures contracts, if that's your idea of investing. Or you can avoid paying commissions by investing your retirement funds in a no-load mutual fund. The only thing you don't want to put your IRA money into is an investment that is already tax-free, such as a municipal bond, since the yield is so much lower.

Q: How do I contact a mutual fund if I don't have a broker?

A: No-load mutual fund companies generally have toll-free numbers so that you can call them directly and order a prospectus. Some magazines, such as Business Week and Kiplinger's, publish annual rankings of mutual funds, which are usually accompanied by a list of the phone numbers for mutual fund companies. In addition, many mutual funds advertise their phone numbers in newspapers and financial publications. You also can find some phone numbers by dialing directory assistance at 800-555-1212, or checking a mutual fund directory at your library. Once you have received the prospectus, you can buy shares in the fund directly.

Q: How do you find a reputable financial planner and how do you check on his or her track record?

A: Ann Diamond, a Manhattan financial consultant, suggests asking your friends if they know a planner they can recommend. You also may want to call one of the industry trade associations and ask for the names of some planners in your area.

"Don't just interview them by phone," Diamond says. "Meet them in person, and be prepared to discuss what you want to accomplish. Be sure to ask if they charge a commission, fee or some combination."

If the planner sells stocks and bonds, they should be registered with the Securities and Exchange Commission. You can call the SEC to ask if there is a disciplinary history on file. You also can check with your local Better Business Bureau.

To check on a broker, call the SEC at 202-272-7440.

To get names of financial planners in your area, you can contact any of the following associations:

The National Association of Personal Financial Advisors (fee-only financial planners) at 800-366-2732.

The International Association of Financial Planners at 800-945-4237.

The Institute of Certified Financial Planners at 800-282-7526.

Q: How good is the guarantee on an annuity?

A: Glenn Daily, an insurance consultant, says that the guarantee is only somewhat better than the financial strength of the company behind the annuity. In other words, you need to know something about the financial health of the insurance company you are dealing with. Although there is a guarantee association in each state that is supposed to protect consumers if an insurance company becomes insolvent, Daily says that the insurance fund does not kick in automatically. Indeed, some so-called funds have no money in them, but instead consist of a dubious commitment by major insurers to bail out a failing firm.

"There is no iron-clad guarantee," Daily says. "It's not like the Federal Deposit Insurance Corp. With the FDIC, the fund is triggered when a bank becomes insolvent and depositors usually have immediate access to their money. When an insurance company goes under, you may eventually get all of your money back, but it could take years. And some people may only get a portion of their money back, depending on the situation and their particular contract."

Q: What is the difference between a global fund and international fund?

A: A global funds buys securities around the world, including in the United States. But an international fund buys securities in all countries except the United States. If you've got money invested in other domestic mutual funds and you're trying to diversify overseas, you probably want an international fund.

Q: Is there any reason to shift a child's assets to the parent during the fiscal year that the child will be applying to colleges for financial aid?

A: Probably not. In fact, it may be illegal. Before you switch any money around, there are two things to remember: One, when you will apply for financial aid, you will have to submit at least one year's tax return. If it shows that your child had, say, $1,000 in interest income last year, but you now say the child has no assets, they will ask what happened to the money. Second, you should consult a lawyer before you switch money from your child's account because it is generally illegal.

One way around this may be to reduce your child's account by using that money to pay for any big-ticket items needed for college, such as a computer or car, suggests financial consultant Ann Diamond.

Raymond Loewe, president of Educational Planning Inc., in Marlton, New Jersey, says that if you are unlikely to qualify for financial aid, it probably makes sense to keep assets in your child's name because it is taxed at a lower rate. But if you are a financial aid candidate, Loewe says, you should know that a child's money is always deemed more available to pay for college than is the parents' money. That means if a child has $10,000 in savings, his or her financial aid will be reduced by $3,500; but if the same $10,000 is in the parent's name, the financial aid will be reduced by $600.

Q: I'm confused about federal insurance on my various retirement accounts. Recently I read that the government is insuring less in terms of total accounts. Is this true?

A: There has been a change in Federal Deposit Insurance Corp. rules on retirement accounts. Until now, you could have different retirement accounts at one bank (such as an IRA and a Keogh plan), and each account was separately insured up to $100,000. So you could have had a maximum of $400,000 coverage on these accounts at one bank. Now, retirement accounts will be added together for insurance purposes. That means if you have more than one retirement account at one bank, only a total of $100,000 will be protected by FDIC insurance. If you have any questions about your accounts, check with your bank, or call the FDIC consumer hotline at 800-934-3342.

You Should Be in Shape By Now

See How Your Mental Muscle on Money Matters Has Been Toned Up

FIFTY short chapters ago, *Fiscal Fitness* set out to help you firm up your financial plans and build up your wealth. We have the basics of money management—everything from budgeting, saving and investing to buying a home, saving for college and retiring. We hope *Fiscal Fitness* has informed and motivated you. Now let's see how much you remember.

True/False

1. As a rule of thumb, when you retire you will need about 50 percent of your current income.

2. One of the biggest mistakes people make when saving for retirement is investing too conservatively.

3. You should have an emergency fund equal to six weeks of living expenses that is deposited in a safe, easily accessible account.

4. Mutual funds sold by banks are federally insured.

5. In general, the higher the return on an investment, the greater the risk that you could lose money.

6. If you're having trouble paying your bills, let your creditors know.

7. If you are considering buying a home, one of the first things you should do is send for copies of your credit reports to make sure there are no mistakes on them that would prohibit you from qualifying for a mortgage.

8. Filing for Chapter 7 bankruptcy is a great way to get out from under all your debts.

9. If you file for Chapter 7 bankruptcy, your landlord can't evict you from your apartment.

10. One of the biggest disadvantages of an annuity is that they are often very expensive.

11. One advantage of an annuity is that there is no ceiling on how much you can contribute each year.

12. Home equity loans and lines of credit are among the riskiest types of loans you can take out.

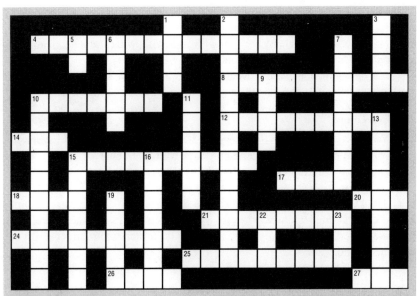

ACROSS

4. Should only be a supplement to retirement savings.
8. If you name your grandchildren as beneficiaries, you may be subject to a _____-skipping tax.
10. A couple will likely pay higher taxes when _____.
12. Before you invest you need to know your risk _____.
14. Your liability can exceed $50 if you lose your _____ card. (abbr.)
15. The legal document governing a mutual fund.
17. Mutual fund sales commission.
18. Before the wedding a couple should agree on a financial _____.
20. The measurement of inflation. (abbr.)
21. The day a bond expires and all principal is returned to the investor.
24. A tax-exempt bond.
25. Credit card debts, rent and doctor bills are _____ debts.
26. You can begin teaching your _____ about investing.
27. The IRS allows forward tax averaging _____ time(s).

DOWN

1. Cutting up your credit cards is one way to get your _____ under control.
2. Companies that keep a record of your personal financial history.
3. Insurance rating guide.
5. A safe investment but not a good inflation hedge. (abbr.)
6. The IRS has six years to call an _____.
7. A mutual fund that mixes stocks and bonds.
9. When choosing long-term health care, there's no need to go _____.
10. A good saving tool is automatic payments from your checking account to a _____.
11. Best long-term investment.
13. A piece of property that the Bankruptcy Code permits a debtor to keep from creditors or something you declare on your taxes is called an _____.
15. A major asset often overlooked in a divorce settlement.
16. Living trusts allow your heirs to avoid _____.
19. A prepaid finance charge to the mortgage lender.
22. Uniform Commercial Code. (abbr.)
23. Year-to-date. (abbr.)

13. If you invest in a stock mutual fund right before it makes its capital gains distribution, you stand to make an immediate windfall.

14. If you have a joint bank account with your wife, you cannot bequeath your half of the account to your best friend in your will.

15. When you shop for a Medigap insurance plan to supplement your Medicare coverage, you have 10 standardized policies to choose from.

Multiple Choice

1. You have two children in college. In 10 years you'll turn 65. How can you pay for tuition bills and at the same time save for retirement?

A) Tell your children to get a job and forget about college.

B) Forget retiring at 65 and work as long as you can.

C) Help your children with tuition and at the same time continue to put something—even a small amount—toward your retirement fund. Then, after they graduate, take the amount you were spending on tuition and redirect it to your retirement fund.

D) None of the above.

2. You just got a raise. You want to be fiscally fit, so what's the best thing to do with the extra money?

A) Give it to charity.

B) Treat yourself to something you've been wanting, such as new furniture or a vacation to Paris.

C) Put the extra money in your retirement account.

C) If you have credit card bills, pay them first and then put the extra money into your retirement account.

E) C or D.

3. Dollar cost averaging is . . .

A) A new way to calculate the return on your mutual fund investment.

B) A plan for making regular investments so that if you are investing in both good times and bad, any losses you incur will average out.

C) A way to calculate whether, on average, your investment is beating inflation.

D) None of the above.

4. Which of the following best describes an annuity?

A) It's a federally insured retirement account.

B) It's a contract with an insurance company that is designed to provide income during your retirement years.

C) It's a life insurance policy that you can tap into if you need to.

D) None of the above.

5. What are some of the risks associated with annuities?

A) If you have a fixed annuity, the security of your investment is only as good as the financial strength of the insurance company behind it.

B) If you have a variable annuity, there is no guaranteed rate of return if you choose to invest in stock and bond mutual funds. And there is the risk that you can lose principal.

C) If you withdraw a substantial portion of your annuity in the early years of the contract you may be stuck paying hefty surrender charges.

D) All of the above.

6. Which of the following investment pitches should make you wary?

A) If you don't invest today, you will have missed the opportunity of a lifetime.

B) There's no time to send you more information.

C) I know plenty of other people who want in on this deal, but I'm offering it to you first.

D) A and B.

E) All of the above.

7. Which of the following are good ways to get children in the habit of saving money?

A) Tell them you'll match every dollar they put into a savings account.

B) Give them a piggy bank and encourage them to save for a goal, such as a toy they've been wanting.

C) Tell them they'll never get to college unless they start saving when they're little.

D) A and B.

E) All of the above.

8. Why would a department store be willing to negotiate a special repayment schedule if you're in a financial bind?

A) It's a common courtesy given to good customers.

B) They need business, and even deadbeats are better than no customers at all.

C) They know that if you file for bankruptcy there's a chance they won't get any of the money you owe them.

D) None of the above.

9. What requirements must be met before people can call themselves financial planners?

A) They must register with the Securities and Exchange Commission.

B) They must be certified by the Institute of Certified Financial Planners.

C) They must hold a two-year degree in financial planning.

D) All of the above.

E) There are no requirements.

10. Which of the following apply to living trusts?

A) They allow you to bypass the court probate process.

B) Unlike a will, they are private.

C) They are more difficult to contest than a will.

D) A and B.

E) All of the above.

11. When will Medicare pay for nursing home care?

A) Never.

B) Any time you need nursing care and assistance with daily living chores.

C) Only when you enter a facility that accepts Medicare.

D) Only under certain circumstances following a hospital stay and then only for limited period.

12. If you want to give away your assets so that you qualify for Medicare coverage when you enter a nursing home, how many months before you apply for Medicare must you shift the assets?

A) 24

B) 30

C) 36

D) 60

13. After you retire, you move to a low-tax state. Which of the following can your former state use as a basis for claiming you still owe it taxes?

A) You retain your family home and you keep many of your valued possessions there.

B) You spend much of your time visiting family members in your old state.

C) You retain active membership in clubs in your old state.

D) You continue to operate a business that is based in your old state.

E) All of the above.

14. If you don't have much money, why should you have a will?

A) So that you, and not the court, can decide who gets your money and other assets.

B) So you can avoid taxes.

C) So that you get to choose a guardian for your minor children in the event of your death.

D) A and C.

E) All of the above.

ANSWER KEY

Crossword Puzzle

Across

4. Social Security
8. Generation
10. Married
12. Tolerance
14. ATM
15. Prospectus
17. Fraud

18. Plan
20. CPI
21. Maturity
22. Municipal
23. Unsecured
24. Teen
25. One

Down

1. Debt
2. Credit Bureaus
3. Best
5. CD
6. Audit
7. Balanced
9. Solo
10. Mutual Fund

11. Stocks
13. Exemption
15. Pension
16. Probate
19. Point
22. UCC
23. YTD

True/False

1. False. You are more likely to need 75 to 80 percent. And it could be more if you intend to travel frequently or maintain two homes after you retire.

2. True. Although you will protect your principal by choosing safe investments, the danger is that your savings won't keep pace with inflation. If that happens, when you retire, you might have to lower your standard of living.

3. False. You should have three to six months of living expenses in an emergency fund.

4. False. Mutual funds are never insured by the FDIC. Banks are increasingly getting into the investment business, so when in doubt about a product they are pitching, ask if it is FDIC insured. If they say it is, get it in writing.

5. True. In other words, if it seems too good to be true, it probably is. You usually don't get a fantastic return on an investment without taking some added risk.

6. True. Creditors will usually be more lenient if you are upfront about your problems and demonstrate you're making an effort to pay them back.

7. True.

8. False. Although Chapter 7 bankruptcy will erase many debts, it will not absolve you of many obligations, such as alimony payments and most tax bills.

9. False. A bankruptcy filing may delay an eviction, it cannot prevent it altogether.

10. True

11. True

12. True. If you can't make the payments, you lose your home.

13. False. The opposite is true. If you invest right before a fund makes a capital gains distribution, you will receive a payment. That sounds good, but it cuts the value of your original investment—and even if you choose to reinvest the capital gains payment, you pay taxes on it.

14. True. When you die, any property, securities, or bank accounts held jointly with another person automatically go to the surviving joint owner.

15. True. This makes it easier to compare prices when shopping for a plan.

Multiple Choice

1. C   2. E   3. B   4. B   5. D   6. E   7. D   8. C
9. E   10. E   11. D   12. C   13. E   14. D

Newsday chart by Richard Cornett

About the Author

CHRISTINE DUGAS has been a business reporter for the past 12 years. She joined *Newsday* in 1987, and has been writing the "Fiscal Fitness" column since June 1993. Prior to coming to *Newsday,* Dugas was a staff editor at *Business Week* and the managing editor of *Ad Forum Magazine.*

Her awards include the Saatchi & Saatchi Advertising Journalism Award in 1985, Atrium Award for a fashion/retailing writing in 1989, New York Newswomen's Front Page Award for deadline writing in 1989, Newspaper Guild of New York Page One Award for business reporting in 1989, Lincoln University Unity Award for economic coverage in 1991, New York State Associated Press Association award for business writing in 1992.

Dugas has a master's degree from the University of Wisconsin and is a graduate of Bowling Green State University in Ohio. She began her journalism career as a free-lance writer in Latin America and the Middle East, and worked as a reporter at the *Las Vegas Sun.* Prior to becoming a reporter, Dugas taught high school English in South America and Central America. She is married and lives in Manhattan.